"Sometimes in the Wrong, but Never in Doubt"

"Sometimes in the Wrong, but Never in Doubt"

*George S. Benson
and the Education
of the New Religious Right*

L. EDWARD HICKS

The University of Tennessee Press / Knoxville

The paper in this book meets the minimum requirements of the
American National Standard for Permanence of Paper for Printed
Library Materials. ∞   The binding materials have been chosen
for strength and durability.

Library of Congress Cataloging in Publication Data

Hicks, L. Edward, 1946–
    "Sometimes in the wrong, but never in doubt" : George S. Benson and the
education of the new religious right / L. Edward Hicks.—1st ed.
        p.   cm.
    Includes bibliographical references and index.
    ISBN 0–87049–865–7 (cloth: alk. paper)
    1. Conservatism—United States. 2. Christianity and politics—United States.
3. Evangelicalism—United States. 4. Fundamentalism—United States.
5. Benson, George S. (George Stuart), 1898–1991. 6. National Education
Program (U.S.).   I. Title
JC573.2.U6H43   1994
320.5'2'0973—dc20   94-20275
                                                        CIP

Contents

Preface

Recent history textbooks are filled with photographic images of influential men and women at pivotal moments in history. There are usually pictures of British Prime Minister Neville Chamberlain on his return from the fateful meeting with Adolph Hitler, promising "peace in our time"; General Douglas MacArthur wading through the Philippine surf to make good his promise, "I shall return"; or that familiar picture of a smiling President Harry S. Truman holding a copy of the *Chicago Tribune* issue that had incorrectly reported his 1948 election defeat. In some future political biography of Ronald Reagan, historians may well recall two pictures depicting equally crucial moments in his political career. Until years later, few people realized the importance of the minor footnote to the 1964 presidential campaign, in which the semi-retired actor Ronald Reagan delivered a nationally televised pro-Goldwater speech. Reagan, who had once been a liberal Democrat, had emerged as an earnest spokesman for the conservative cause before 1964, but in the years to come, as the Reagan legend grew, this "would be remembered as The Speech, the transcendent moment when Reagan made the leap from concerned private citizen to active politician. It was The Speech, along with the avalanche that buried Goldwater, that put Reagan on the road toward replacing the Arizona senator in the hearts of the stricken conservatives, who now desperately needed a new spokesman."[1] Reagan went on to become governor of California, but his 1964 speech had captured the imagination of a determined band of conservative politicians who remembered his message that night and later called upon him as the savior of conservative ideology in the United States in the 1980s. That speech placed Reagan squarely on the national political stage and created the first indelible image that might be used in our hypothetical political biography. Although Reagan's emergence as a viable national conservative spokesman was tremendously important to his political career, probably his most important step into the national limelight might be another transcendent moment in Dallas, Texas. At this time, the New Religious Right, searching for sympathetic leadership, abandoned Jimmy Carter and instead turned to the Republican party, whose substantial reorganization and conservative redirection was being orchestrated by Ronald Reagan.

Reagan's speech supporting Goldwater, the first image in our hypothetical biography, represents the actor's emergence as a viable alternative candidate for millions of conservatives recoiling from their bitter defeat in 1964. The second picture, however, captures that moment when Reagan emerged as the political hope of millions of newly mobilized conservative Christians who now were demanding from American politics a morally based conservatism. Some analysts of the 1980 election indicate that it was the voting strength of the "New Religious Right" that helped propel Reagan to the presidency in 1980. A few days after the election, when some estimates indicated that Moral Majority preachers had stimulated the registration of one to two million new white southern fundamentalist voters, pollster Lou Harris suggested that "Moral Majority–influenced voters were responsible for some two-thirds of Ronald Reagan's ten-point majority."[2]

The 1976 candidacy of Jimmy Carter, a self-professed "born-again Southern Baptist," had aroused hope within some religiously conservative circles, where it was felt that he might make a significant impact morally on the presidency. Consequently, Carter garnered significant support from Southern Baptists, as well as from other conservative denominations. However, as far as his religious supporters were concerned, Carter's four years in office produced too few favorable resolutions of religiously significant issues to warrant further support from his own Southern Baptists. As a result, Carter rather quickly alienated much of his denominational support. However, for what soon would be labeled the Religious Right, Jimmy Carter proved to be a blessing in disguise.[3] Ironically, as Clyde Wilcox has argued, by failing to live up to the sociocultural expectations generated by his campaign, Carter helped to mobilize those fundamentalists who eventually contributed to his 1980 defeat. In convincing many such Christians of their obligation to participate in politics, Carter's candidacy "helped to break down the long-standing feeling among evangelicals and fundamentalists that electoral politics was not the proper realm for Christian activity."[4]

The apparent failure of Carter's administration in important areas convinced many of the Religious Right's leaders, including those he had helped mobilize in the 1976 campaign, that more must be done. In their opinion, Carter had appointed too few evangelicals or fundamentalists to policy-making positions.[5] Even though Carter personally opposed abortion, the Religious Right believed that he had intentionally avoided a legislative fight on the issue. It also appeared to them that the Carter administration intended to support court-ordered busing as a means of achieving racial balance in public schools. They were dismayed, too, when the Internal Revenue Service removed the tax-exempt status of some southern private academies which many in the government felt had been created in an obvious attempt to maintain racial segregation. Despite pro-segregationist arguments from within their own denominations, the vast majority of conservative Protestant school founders denied any racist intent and instead asserted that it was the "generally liberal socio-moral climate of the public school which they found offensive."[6] Many of these schools had been started and supported by conservative religious organizations as bastions against what the latter viewed as a dangerous incursion of "secular humanist" ideology into the public school curriculum. As the Religious Right saw it, this constellation of ideas, which included "a disbelief in God, belief in evolution, rejection of moral absolutes, belief in the innate goodness of men to govern the world equitably, and emphasis upon internationalism and world government,"[7] had become the dominant ideology of public schools and the federal bureaucracy.

According to conservative religious groups who supported tax exemption for church-related schools, the evidence was overwhelming that "secular humanists" were determined to rid public education of any religious overtones, including moral values derived from religious philosophy. In their private schools, the New Religious Right activists were "working to create social institutions which would permit them to reproduce their own culture sheltered from modernizing influences."[8] The arguments of such thinkers as James Dunphy convinced the Religious Right of the seriousness of the battle being waged for control of public education. Dunphy, a popular contributor to journals characterized by the right as "secular humanist," was generally ignored by the more scholarly conservatives but produced heated reaction within much of the Religious Right. He strengthened its resolve when, for example, he announced that

> the battle for humankind's future must be waged and won in the public school classroom by teachers who correctly perceive their role as the proselytizers of a new faith: a religion of humanity that recognizes and respects what theologians call divinity in every human being. These teachers must embody the same selfless dedication as the most rabid fundamentalist preachers, for they will be ministers of another sort, utilizing a classroom instead of a pulpit to convey humanist values in whatever subject they teach, regardless of the educational level—preschool day care center or large state university. The classroom must and will become an arena of conflict between the old and the new—the rotting corpse of Christianity, together with all its adjacent evils and misery, and the new faith of humanism.[9]

Despite mounting antireligious rhetoric of this sort, President Carter disappointed many supporters from the Religious Right who had assumed that the conservative cultural and religious values associated with Carter's Baptist background would spark legislation to stop the spread of "secular humanist" ideals in government and the public schools. At the very least, they had expected the Carter administration to make some public effort to support their position. However, Carter's apparent lack of concern about the ban against prayer in public schools, as well as his failure to oppose abortion, alienated many religious conservatives. As Kevin Phillips observes, Carter's stock dropped rather quickly "among Southerners generally and among fundamentalists in particular." In consequence, "three key national secular New Right strategists, Richard Viguerie, Paul Weyrich and Howard Phillips, took bolder measures"[10] after they determined, early in 1978, that the "millions of fundamentalists in America were a political army waiting to be mobilized."[11]

In one of their meetings, the trio formulated the concept of a nondenominational religious coalition, later known as the Moral Majority, to be launched into partisan politics as the New Religious Right.[12] Although initially limited to supporters of the Reverend Jerry Falwell of Lynchburg, Virginia, very quickly the name "Moral Majority" was applied to all the various member groups of the New Religious Right coalition.[13] By 1980, all that remained was for the coalition to endorse a suitable presidential candidate. However, an event crucial in American political history occurred in Dallas, Texas, which offered the fledgling Moral Majority the opportunity to elevate a new champion of its political agenda.

During the weekend of August 21, 1980, in the midst of the presidential campaign, the Religious Roundtable sponsored a National Affairs Briefing. The roundtable's founder and chairman, Ed McAteer, invited several prominent speakers, such as noted television evangelists Jerry Falwell, M. G. (Pat) Robertson, James Kennedy, and James Robison, thereby offering them the opportunity to voice Moral Majority concerns in a political rally. President Jimmy Carter had declined McAteer's invitation to appear, but Ronald Reagan accepted, eagerly addressing this audience of fifteen thousand gathered in Reunion Arena. Reagan spoke pointedly: "When I hear the First Amendment used as a reason to keep traditional moral values away from policy making, I am shocked. . . . The First Amendment was written not to protect the people and their laws from religious values, but to protect those values from government tyranny."

To the cheering throng, whose outright endorsement he eagerly sought, Reagan offered a disingenuous salute: "I want you to know I endorse you and what you are doing."[14] In response, fifteen thousand fundamentalists rose to cheer Reagan, who unwittingly had propelled himself into the imagination of the New Religious Right and, in so doing, had acquired support that would be crucial in the coming election.[15]

George Benson was a featured speaker at the same meeting. This man, too, failed to realize the historical significance of this political rally. However, Benson's participation in the meeting represented a fitting culmination of a forty-year career promoting Americanism. Early in the 1960s, Ronald Reagan had worked closely with Benson to produce the film, *The Truth about Communism*. Twenty years later, Benson appeared on a program with Reagan, now the presidential candidate who best represented the political views of the New Religious Right, for which George Benson had helped lay the foundations and of which he still was an integral part. In forty years of campaigning for the Old Religious Right, Benson never had committed his own National Education Program (NEP) exclusively to any political party.[16] Instead, his support had been "for the cause Reagan represented."[17] As a later newspaper editorial put it:

George Benson was a member of the Moral Majority years before there was one. In an era when most fundamentalist clergymen would as soon be seen hoisting a highball with the local madam as become involved in something as worldly and tawdry as politics, Benson already was laying the foundation for what would become known as the Religious Right.[18]

Acknowledgments

This project began in 1986 as an analysis of Church of Christ missionaries and the methodology they developed. Since that time, the work has changed direction considerably. In its various forms, the project has required the assistance and cooperation of many people. Dr. Major L. Wilson, a superb scholar at Memphis State University, whom I had the foresight to select as my dissertation director, devoted considerable time and effort to the realization of this book. The other members of my dissertation committee, Dr. Charles W. Crawford, Dr. Joseph M. Hawes, Dr. F. Jack Hurley, and Dr. William R. Marty, contributed substantially to its scholarly merit by pointing me toward pertinent information in their various areas of expertise. Their suggestions broadened the scope of the study and forced me to keep a certain historical distance from my subject.

Several other noted scholars were patient and kind in helping a struggling scholar turn a dissertation into a finished manuscript. Dr. Ed Harrell, Auburn University, has been involved with this project since a meeting of the American Society of Church History in 1986. He has offered advice, contributed primary source materials, and edited several versions of the manuscript. Dr. Richard Pierard, Indiana State University, is an expert in this field who on several occasions provided valuable criticism. Dr. James B. McSwain, Tuskegee University, provided invaluable editorial help; much of the credit for a readable final product must go to him. Professor Mark Dawson of the English Department, Faulkner University, Montgomery, Alabama, contributed critical insight from his disciplinary perspective. Another biographer of Benson, Dr. John Stevens, chancellor emeritus of Abilene Christian University, Abilene, Texas, provided invaluable assistance and contributed much primary source material. In addition, his sermon at Dr. Benson's funeral in 1991 provided the very appropriate title for this book. Indeed, George Benson was "never in doubt" about fulfilling his duty to God and country.

Each of these scholars has contributed mightily to this project. Their analyses of style and content were offered without attempting strongly to influence my interpretation. As a result, all errors in content or faulty historical interpretation are my own.

I would like to thank the editorial staff at the University of Tennessee Press, especially Meredith Morris-Babb, Kimberly Scarbrough, and Stan Ivester, for their confidence and assistance.

There are several others who contributed many hours to this project. Although she may not be in total agreement with my interpretation, I wish especially to thank Marguerite O'Bannon Benson, who was a gracious hostess during the many hours I consumed interviewing her late husband. Ed McAteer, of the Religious Roundtable, also opened his home for an extensive interview. Robert H. Rowland and his staff at the American Citizenship Center, Oklahoma Christian University, Oklahoma City, deserve special thanks for allowing me access to their files and for allowing me to use their facilities and their film and audio libraries. Ileene Huffard also deserves special recognition for spending hundreds of hours struggling with and transcribing almost forty hours of taped interviews, amounting to almost one thousand pages.

I wish to thank my family for their encouragement and moral support. To my mother, Louise Hicks, I express love and appreciation for instilling in me at an early age a love of history. To my sons, Ehren and Stephen, who went without a father much of the time because he was "chained to the computer," I offer my deep appreciation of their sacrifice, love, and understanding. Most of all, I wish to express my deep love and appreciation to my wife, Dr. Dixie Crawford Hicks, whose scholarly expertise, constant encouragement, and understanding enabled me to devote many hours and a large portion of the family's resources to the completion of this project. I sincerely hope that their support and encouragement has been sufficiently rewarded.

Introduction:
The Changing Political Landscape

The presidential election of 1980 was a watershed in American political history not because an aging Hollywood actor was elected to the nation's highest office, but because his election dramatized the political metamorphosis of the United States that had occurred since World War II. The forces propelling Reagan into leadership of the Republican party in 1980, and into control of the White House for the ensuing twelve years, reflected a significant political realignment that had been taking place during the previous two decades. The political coalition generated by Reagan exemplifies the post–World War II political complexity of the United States and serves to illustrate the continuing importance of populist and conservative ideals in American politics. In pursuit of what James Morone has called the "Democratic Wish,"[1] the populist-oriented electorate of the 1970s and 1980s invoked the values of what Samuel Huntington has labeled the "American Creed,"[2] to demand from government increased moral accountability. According to Kevin Phillips, increased political activism in the years prior to 1980 demonstrated that "populism, not conservatism, is the electoral force unique to our politics," and that, in one form or another, "American populism has gathered force and helped to give direction to the nation when it confronted various historical crossroads." The GOP victory in 1980 proved to Kevin Phillips that Reagan had successfully tapped into both the populist and the conservative ideological streams in contemporary American politics, producing not only his election victory but also the completion of the conservative transformation in American politics.[3]

Especially since Reagan's decisive victory, the influence of religion and religious values on post–World War II politics has been the focus of renewed interest among scholars of American political history. An excellent example of this type of research is Kenneth D. Wald's *Religion and Politics in the United States*, which skillfully analyzes the influence of religion on modern American political activity. Although generally undecided about the political future of the New Religious Right, Wald argues that in recent years religion has penetrated public life in many areas, but especially in politics. He concludes that the American religious tradition has significantly "contributed to some of the enduring principles that undergird the political system"; to a yet greater extent, however, "religious values and interests have helped to shape the political perspectives of individuals, probably affecting their reactions to both candidates and issues." As a result, "religious communities have entered the political process itself, in an organized effort to influence public policy on a wide range of issues."[4]

Others, such as scholars Steve Bruce,[5] Thomas Fleming and Paul Gottfried[6] and political consultant Kevin Phillips,[7] have specifically examined how the New Religious Right affected American partisan politics in the 1970s, and why it eventually jettisoned Carter and the Democrats and joined with Reagan and the Republicans. Phillips maintains that, although religion played a minor role in the 1960 election, "as with so many aspects of conservative politics, the election of 1964 was a major watershed."[8] In every ensuing election, religious groups entered the political arena, although generally they suffered from lack of effective leadership and from failure to achieve a unified nondenominational coalition which could produce significant election results.

Recent scholarship on the conservative resurgence has identified six important elements within the American political matrix that help define the sequence and relative force of the conservative Republican transformation in America after World War II.[9] First came relocation of the demographic and economic power base of political conservatism from Northeast to South and West, beginning with World War II. At the same time, the rise of the Sunbelt and the subsequent shift of national political power and prosperity enhanced long-standing southern and western opposition to the politics of eastern elites.

Intrinsic to this demographic shift was the appearance in the Republican party of populist political ideology and activity, which historically had been located within the Democratic party. Populist political activity, evident within both parties in the 1964 election, has increased in subse-

quent elections. While the Democratic party by 1960 had established itself as the "in" party and had transformed itself into the country's economically prosperous intellectual and political leadership, the electoral
process, a "bellwether of American politics," indicated a steady erosion
of Democratic political power amid the demographic and economic
changes in the nation after 1960.[10]

The second transformative element was a radical upheaval within
the Republican party, in which the political power of this new grassroots
populist ideology led the party to de-emphasize its traditional role as
defender of the status quo. Now the party fostered a resurgent activism
aimed primarily at single-issue legislation and implementation.[11] Opposition to abortion, as a partisan political issue, particularly exemplifies this
phenomenon during the 1970s and 1980s.[12]

The third identifiable element was the reinvigoration of moral conservatism, which had remained largely isolated from partisan politics until the decade following the social unrest of the 1960s. The traditionalist
reaction of Middle America to the social, moral, and racial upheavals of
the 1960s incorporated a retrograde ideology that proclaimed the restoration of old values while manifesting anxiety about the possibility that
America's hour in history had passed.[13]

A fourth element was the rise of a new Republican intelligentsia.
The neoconservative ideology that emerged during the 1960s and 1970s
in Republican circles departed somewhat from traditional political ideology, but at the same time it reemphasized many values central to Republican conservatism.[14]

The fifth element was the appearance of economic theories that expressed the frustration of the American public with the seemingly unrelenting spiral of higher prices and increased taxation. Republican conservatives touting fiscal responsibility and anti-inflationary policies argued
for reductions in government spending and espoused the merits of supply-side economics.[15]

The sixth and final piece of the complex puzzle of Republican conservatism in the 1980s was the emergence of a politically active New Religious Right which reflected the dramatic growth of religious evangelicalism
and fundamentalism within American society in recent decades.[16] The
primary impulses for the emergence of this movement were two apparent threats to its world view. In the 1940s and 1950s, the Old Religious
Right had been "exercised by the rather abstract threat of 'world communism.' By the late 1970s they were faced with the added and apparently more immediate threat of an increasingly secular state."[17]

While these elements may be more populist than conservative in the classical sense,[18] their synthesis within a Republican conservative coalition brought Ronald Reagan and the conservative philosophy an overwhelming victory in 1980. In Phillips's opinion, "Reagan's own Sun Belt politics, party insurgency, anti-Washington outsidership, religious-and-social-issue sympathies and supply-side/gold-standard economics simultaneously mirrored and encompassed all the radical transformation."[19]

Benson and the Old Christian Right

During a 1987 interview, George S. Benson casually commented that he had performed a significant role in the election of Ronald Reagan to the presidency in 1980. How could the former president of a small college in rural Arkansas, a man who had devoted a third of his life to Christian mission work, have helped influence American voters to elect the first conservative-backed president since Herbert Hoover? This question sparked my interest in George Benson and his National Education Program (NEP). Despite a plethora of new research on the resurgence of the conservative movement and the particular contribution of the New Religious Right to recent American politics, little has been written about Benson's role in this movement. My research strongly suggests that Benson, utilizing a variety of educational tools and distribution media, played a key role in this political transformation. A critical in-depth study of Benson and his various political education organizations reveals their long history of formulating and disseminating an internally consistent conservative social, political, and economic philosophy. That philosophy's broad-based appeal synthesized traditional Old Christian Right political themes, which had animated supporters of Barry Goldwater in 1964, with those of the New Christian Right which helped propel Goldwater's political descendent, Ronald Reagan, to the presidency in 1980.

As noted above, the election of a conservative Republican president in 1980 was the result of a significant transformation of conservative politics in post–World War II America. At the heart of this transformation was a new generation of American voters who had grown to political maturity during the Cold War and who perceived a rather wide disparity between the actual conditions of their nation and the largely unfulfilled promises of the New Deal and the Great Society. Many voters in this new generation came to believe that the liberal ideology espoused by moderate leaders in both parties had failed to solve most of the basic problems confronting America as a result of increased government spending, creation of new government agencies, and related attempts at social and economic restructuring. When increased government spending apparently failed to produce the Great Society envisioned by Lyndon Johnson or his predecessor, John F. Kennedy, a significant number of Americans came to believe that another course of political action was necessary. The political majority that emerged in the 1980 election, whether its members knew it or not, stood in a long tradition of conservative political ideologues who, regarding themselves as ideological descendants of the Founders of the Republic, emphasized limited constitutional government, free-enterprise economics, and religious freedom.

Historically, the philosophical difference between conservatives and liberals in American politics has gone much deeper than the argument over government spending. At its root is a fundamental disagreement over the very nature of political institutions. While generalizations concerning political ideology can be misleading, this one seems useful: in the twentieth century conservatives have tended to favor preserving old institutions, methods, and traditions; while liberals have supported reform or progress, sometimes by directly challenging the traditional order. Although proponents of both theories ultimately ground the legitimacy of a political philosophy in the will of the people, they disagree fundamentally on the appropriate power and limits of a government usually perceived to be almost constantly in conflict with the natural rights of the individual. Accordingly, a "vivid feature of American political life" since the founding of the Republic has been a preoccupation with limiting government. There has been an ever-present fear of the abuse of public power, an abuse deemed antithetical to the pursuit of individual rights.[20] Thus, at the heart of traditional American political philosophy lies a deep desire to create and maintain a perfect balance between the preservation of individual rights and the power of government to maintain civic order. Ultimately, according to this reading of American political history, government should reflect the desire of a "single, united people, bound together by a consensus over the public good which is discerned through direct citizen participation in community settings."[21] James Morone has described this unattainable and largely mythical relationship between governmental power and individual rights as the "Democratic Wish":

> The key to the ideology is an image of the people—a single, united,
> political entity with the capacity, as John Adams put it, to "think, feel,
> reason, and act." The people are wiser than their governors; they will

solve the troubles that plague the nation. This populist ideal is not simply the rhetorical flourish that strikes the modern ear. Nor is it merely a call for more responsive government. The people would be governors as well as constituents, political agents as well as principals. They will act by and for themselves. Here is nothing less than an alternative locus of political authority. Somehow, power will be seized from the government and vested in the people themselves.[22]

In a similar fashion, Samuel Huntington has described this uniquely American political ideology as the "American Creed," infused with liberal, individualistic, democratic, and egalitarian values which are basically antigovernment and antiauthority in character: "Whereas other ideologies legitimate established authority and institutions, the American Creed serves to delegitimate any hierarchical, coercive, authoritarian structures, including American ones."[23]

According to Morone and Huntington, in general, the intense struggle to promote the "Democratic Wish" or the values associated with the "American Creed," while sometimes exacerbating the tension between political ideology and political reality, over time mediated the periodic ascendancy of republican (shared civic virtue) and liberal (enlightened self-interest) viewpoints in the development of American political history. Whether motivated by enlightened self-interest or a "shared public life of civic duty," Americans demanded limited government and, at least until the development of a "modern administrative state somewhere between the two Roosevelt administrations," the development of their political institutions generally reflected this desire.[24]

At the heart of this nostalgic and sometimes distorted image of participatory democracy and limited government lies the belief, held by many modern political conservatives, in an "objective moral order based upon ontological foundations . . . derived from theistic tradition."[25] In general, this world view undergirds such conservatives' political decisions. Conservatives also hold that the pursuit of individual freedom, or enlightened self-interest, is superior to the collective will of the majority, and they reject utopianism and social planning in favor of the "free functioning of the energies of free persons, individually and in voluntary cooperation."[26]

As a consequence, conservatives today, reflecting a historic fear of governmental abuse, prefer limiting the power of the state and reject a centrally planned or directed economy. Conversely, in recent American history, and especially since 1933, the liberal world view has advocated extending the reforms of the Progressive state. Originally, arguments for government action of this type were introduced at the turn of the century as a means to restore government to the people. Franklin D. Roosevelt seized the opportunity, provided by the social and economic disorientation of the Depression, to allow government to invoke the "Democratic Wish" without first calling on the people to initiate reform. According to Morone, Roosevelt did not need to do so, since the traditional "fear of government had collapsed along with the economy."[27] Thereafter, the liberal world view which guided American politics became "essentially operational and instrumental,"[28] favoring expanding the scope of government action and spending, in the belief that only an enlarged government could have the knowledge, human resources, or money to solve the problems of modern industrial society.[29] In modern American political philosophy, the liberal viewpoint still attempts to invoke the mythical "Democratic Wish" in seeking to implement by state action a shared civic virtue derived from a democratically formulated consensus. Conversely, the conservative viewpoint argues that government never can reflect a truly democratic consensus; therefore, conservatives favor limiting the scope of government in order to maximize individual freedom. They prefer to seek direct fulfillment of the "Democratic Wish" only at the local or community level. "In the end," Morone argues,

> the government lacks precisely the communitarian sentiment that reformers repeatedly championed. The democratic ideology is legitimate and consequential partially because it offers an alternative to government. However, this means that in America both liberal and communitarian traditions eschew state action—one in favor of private choices, the other for an imaginary people. The result is that Americans have failed to institutionalize a communal spirit—an active notion of the people—within their government.[30]

With the above discussion of traditional American political philosophy in mind, this study of George Benson and his unflagging belief in traditional American values seeks to explain the recent resurgence within the electorate of traditionalist political ideals, especially limited government, free-enterprise economics, and the moral responsibility of government.[31] Benson and his traditionalist allies rejected the theory, usually associated with Progressive or New Deal ideologies, that the federal government could and should be in the vanguard of social and economic change. In addition, as most of the studies cited above indicate, the rise to prominence of the conservative political philosophy in the Republican party between 1960 and 1980 owed much to a grassroots level of political indoctrination which methodically and persistently reminded the American electorate of the differences between conservative and liberal ideologies and of the deleterious possible consequences of liberal ideals. The central claim of this study is that George S. Benson, Church of Christ missionary and educator, through the activities of his National Education Program, disseminated, at the grassroots level, a conservative philosophy at odds with the philosophy of the New Deal and what Benson called its "liberal-left" political agenda. In disseminating this philosophy, he helped to lay the groundwork for a conservative mentality and political activism that culminated in the 1980 election of Ronald Reagan.

The National Education Program (NEP), founded in 1941 by Benson, advertised itself as one of the oldest and most active organizations in America "dedicated to the preservation and advancement of the spiritual, moral, economic and political values on which this nation was founded."[32] The organization's avowed purpose was to preserve these conservative ideals against values it associated with liberalism and centralized government. As a result, the NEP consistently advocated a philosophy of government which denied that bigger was better or that fundamental change was inevitable. It argued instead for reduced governmental activity and control, more reliance on the energies of the private sector to solve persistent social problems, and renewed national commitment to "faith in God, Constitutional government and private ownership of the means of production."[33] According to Benson, an increased emphasis on the education of Americans to what he understood to be the values of the nation's Founders was vitally important because, he believed, during the Great Depression, Americans had "lost their old self-confidence and their faith in their own destiny." He felt that a whole generation had grown up accepting government handouts as a way of life and that, as a result, America was tempted to become a nation of "unblushing mendicants."[34]

Benson used the NEP to remind Americans of the values which he believed had sustained the Founders of the Republic and to convince the people of the dangers of increased government control of education, agriculture, business, and labor. This study demonstrates that the NEP, through a constant barrage of conservative "educational" materials disseminating its conservative social, political, and economic philosophies, significantly affected the emergence of the conservative activism in the

Republican party during the early 1960s. Furthermore, the NEP was an important factor in both the Republican nomination of Goldwater in 1964 and the eventual victory in 1980 of a drastically realigned coalition of conservative political and religious organizations backing Ronald Reagan.

The history of the NEP is the story of attempts by Benson and his followers to sell the American electorate on the merits of Americanism. The NEP advocated that, "no matter what the hardships or what the difficulties, the people of this country must maintain a free America, . . . where all men are free to think, free to work, free to spend their money as they please, free to engage in business at their own risk, free to own property, free to vote their convictions and free to worship God in their own way."[35] Benson and his staff preached to millions of Americans in thousands of speaking engagements, newspaper articles, radio and television broadcasts, and motion pictures their philosophy of Americanism, which effectively dovetailed with other important elements of the conservative political movement in America during this period.[36]

By examining the NEP's activities in detail, this study will show that George Benson, as an effective propagandist and political organizer, awakened and then mobilized latent conservative social and political resources. Although other political conservatives in search of the "Democratic Wish" shared with Benson the prevailing antigovernment sentiment, Benson was more successful than they. This relative success is best explained by analyzing his considerable motivational and organizational abilities and by surveying the nature of mass participation in his programs as a means of evaluating his effectiveness. In this regard, "resource mobilization" theorists such as Steve Bruce argue that the origins and effectiveness of social movements are best viewed not in terms of shared allegiance to a set of grievances to be rectified or to a set of principles to be championed (status defense or status anxiety), but rather as a function of the "existence of a skilled cadre which capitalizes on a pre-existing sense of grievance to mobilize resources."[37]

This study contends that the activity of George Benson and his NEP, as leaders in the conservative resurgence, clearly exemplifies the resource mobilization paradigm, with its emphasis on the importance of cadre leadership and new methods of sensitizing and mobilizing adherents to political activism.[38] In addition, when viewed as an effective tool for "cultural defense" of a shared world view, resource mobilization, as practiced by Benson and the NEP, provides a satisfactory explanation for the conservative political resurgence during the 1970s. This is so because resource mobilization theory emphasizes the cause-and-effect relationship between the shared world view and the political response of adherents to that view. As an effective tool for studying political responses to social and religious issues, resource mobilization theory is vitally concerned with explaining, in scientific terms, the total phenomenon.

According to Bruce, in order to validate any study of the conservative resurgence, three primary elements must be carefully examined. First, researchers should attempt to explain why there was a market for such a movement. Second, they should indicate how potential supporters were sensitized. Third, they should consider the social and political structure within which this mobilization took place, since "neither leaders nor followers act in a vacuum."[39]

In adhering to these general guidelines, this study explores Benson's accomplishments and his failures within the context of his socially and politically conservative Christian world view. Ultimately, by helping to inform and stimulate a significant number of people to political action, Benson helped to precipitate and to shape the Republican ideological transformation, and also helped to mobilize a broad base of intellectual and monetary support for various conservatives causes. For more than forty years, Benson, through the NEP, directed to the grassroots level of American politics an unrelenting and internally consistent barrage of conservative political education. This persistent barrage helped to educate and motivate thousands of political activists throughout the country. In so doing, Benson anticipated and emphasized all those transformative elements so clearly identified in recent studies of the conservative resurgence.

According to Kevin Phillips, Reagan and his conservative allies avoided stumbling over the obvious internal inconsistencies of their political philosophy, and Reagan's successful election campaign proved that a conservative synthesis within the American electorate was attainable. At the center of this synthesis of apparently contradictory political tenets was a general call for what Phillips calls an American "renaissance-cum-restoration." This freshly synthesized conservative ideology so effectively espoused by George Benson and other conservative polemicists

> provided a psychological tent for a great deal of hope and nostalgia. There was room for everyone and everything. For foreign policy hawks, the country would return to the era of Pax Americana; for supply-siders, the Treasury would take a stab at Coolidge economics; for business, a return to the days before Ralph Nader; for the New Right, a re-

turn to the days before the Supreme Court rejected God and embraced abortion, and for the neo-conservatives, a chance to dance on the political graves of the New Class [of liberal political activists] and recall the days when City College of New York students respected their professors and people like Scoop Jackson could be elected chairman of the Democratic National Committee.[40]

In the 1980 election, Ronald Reagan and his conservative allies struck a responsive chord in the hearts and minds of American voters. Reagan's success has been explained in varying degrees by researchers who not only emphasize his fortuitous appearance on an American political scene ripe for change, but who also point out his almost uncanny ability to mold traditionally divergent political groups into a workable Republican coalition.[41] This study contends that the rising tide of Republican political vitality which swept Reagan to victory in 1980 drew heavily upon a political base of grassroots activism carefully nurtured by men such as George Benson with his NEP. From 1936 to 1980, Benson had promoted political principles crucial to the Reagan success: a basic belief in a conservative, limited government as prescribed in the Constitution; a dynamic faith in the ability of the free enterprise system; and a strong belief in a world superintended by a God who has prescribed a set of obligatory, universal moral absolutes.

1

The Development
of a Rugged Individualist

Education and Commitment to Missions

George Stuart Benson was born in Dewey County, Oklahoma Territory, in September, 1898.[1] His parents were Scotch-Irish. His father moved from the Indian Territory (what is now eastern Oklahoma) into western Oklahoma, to a section of the sprawling Cheyenne-Arapaho reservation which President Benjamin Harrison had opened to white settlement. Since the government's imposition of Andrew Jackson's Indian policy, eastern Oklahoma had been a designated homeland for various Indian tribes forcibly removed west of the Mississippi River in accord with the Congressional Indian Removal Act of 1830. In April 1889, the white settlement of the central part of the territory began with the great Oklahoma land rush.

Among the fifty thousand eager settlers was the man who became George Benson's uncle, Charles Clayton Rogers, who filed the first of several family homestead applications near Kingfisher on September 12, 1889. According to his proof of residence, filed on November 28, 1894, in accordance with the rules of the Homestead Act of 1862, "Clate" Rogers affirmed that he and his family had resided and farmed continually on the 160-acre section and had made the required improvements.

In September 1891, and again in April 1892, the federal government made additional homestead tracts available farther west, in newly organized Dewey County. However, over two-thirds of the land available went unclaimed for various reasons, and in 1897 an unmarried Stuart Felix Benson filed a homestead claim on a quarter-section of land next to a homestead occupied since 1894 by Clate's father and Emma Rogers, Clate's sister. Stuart Benson and Emma Rogers renewed a friendship begun earlier in eastern Oklahoma and soon married. George Stuart Benson, the second of five children born to this couple between 1897 and 1914, came into the world in a newly constructed log cabin on this frontier homestead.

His parents were typical of the hardy pioneer stock on the American frontier. They taught their son the value of hard work, diligence, and thrift. Years later, Benson fondly recalled the frontier spirit of neighborly cooperation and hard work. He remembered that, in spite of the hardships, "people were very neighborly and morale was high. Nobody went hungry and nobody felt poor and nobody complained. I have never seen people anywhere who were more contented or happier than were the people of those frontier days when neighbors joined freely to solve one another's problems and stood firmly behind one another."[2]

George's parents instilled in him at an early age the potential rewards of self-reliance and hard work. He was the oldest boy in the family, and by the age of eight, his father expected from him a full day's work on the farm. Young George learned at first hand the meaning of self-sufficiency. Stuart Benson soon bought the adjoining farm, made available by the death of Emma's father. This acreage required George to spend even more time in the fields. Although his parents continued farming until their deaths, money was always scarce, and soon the lad began to hire himself out for odd jobs in the community, in addition to keeping up his regular chores on both farms. From an early age he nearly always provided for himself in this fashion.

The Bensons lived three miles from the one-room community schoolhouse at Bonto which George attended in first through eighth grades. The family's farm was twelve miles from the nearest sizable community, Seiling, where the young teenager frequently sold firewood, and fifty miles from the nearest railroad, at Kingfisher. George graduated from the eighth grade at Bonto School, but, because it was not accredited, he and his sister took examinations for their diplomas at Taloga, the county seat. George worked the next year on the farm and at odd jobs, saving a little money so that he could start high school the following fall in Seiling, where he completed his first year.

At age fifteen, George went away from home for his second year of high school, to the U. S. Government Indian School a hundred miles east at Claremore, Oklahoma. There, he first set up housekeeping. Several other times during his childhood, Benson had lived on his own, away from the rest of the family, as he worked at various odd jobs. At Claremore, as he had done previously at Seiling, George provided for his own education and paid his living expenses by working at various odd jobs in the community. His father had arranged for the boy to live with an old gentleman who had promised room and board in exchange for chores around his farm. However, when George arrived in Claremore, the old fellow had changed his mind, and, rather than return home empty-handed, the youngster became the school janitor for sixteen dollars per month. With the money he had already saved, George rented a small furnished house and resolved to finish the school year. It was during this year that the fifteen-year-old boy learned his greatest lesson in self-sufficiency. Benson grew to believe that his experience in Claremore established the foundation for personal characteristics of the adult he was to become. Much later, Benson reflected on the importance of that year: "I had the love and care of wonderful, God-fearing Christian parents, and they had done the first groundwork, but the foundation that is laid only by the individual himself began to be laid in Claremore."[3]

After his sophomore year at Claremore, Benson returned home and taught elementary school the following two years, while also farming and completing his high school program. Because of the limited educational opportunities available in this frontier setting, the youth demonstrated great dedication in pursuing his education diligently while under the financial hardships imposed by extended periods away from the family farm. Without doubt, much of George Benson's dogged determination developed during this period. In his view, the fact that he had had the opportunity to finish high school and to go to college, despite his humble rural upbringing, demonstrated "that anybody could get an education who wanted to work hard enough for it." That led him to believe that "probably most any other goal could likewise be attained through perseverance and hard work and that strict honesty always pays off in the long run."[4] Years later, this attitude resurfaced during Benson's tenure as president of Harding College. There he demanded that, to remain in school, every student must spend several hours each day in service work for the school and community.

Benson's parents were dedicated Christians, and he learned very early in life the value of living according to Christian moral principles. The family attended a nondenominational community church meeting in the Bonto schoolhouse. Deeply influenced by the Christian message, George at an early age dedicated himself to spreading the Gospel. He had decided early in life to commit himself to the Lord and had determined that, above all else, he was going to serve Him. That would be his life's goal, regardless of where it might lead him or what hardship it might entail.[5] At age sixteen, George took a leadership role in the local church and even preached on occasion. However, his strongest early Christian influence came from Ben Elston, a traveling evangelist from a locale in western Kansas near Harper College, a two-year junior college founded and supported by members of the Churches of Christ.[6]

Elston appealed for a nondenominational Christianity, based only upon the Bible and not on creeds or religious doctrines not plainly stated in Scripture. Benson discovered something new and exciting in Elston's religious instruction. Benson said later that he had been

> wondering about the Methodists and the Baptists and the Presbyterians and the Pentecostals and the Mormons and the Adventists. We had all of those coming around and holding meetings in the school house. I thought, 'How do I know which one is best?' I thought, 'Well, I'm going to study the creeds of all of them and I'm going to decide which one of them is the best.' Well, I listened to Elston preach and I saw I didn't need to do it that way. I could just take the Bible and work through the Biblical pattern of the Lord's church.[7]

At twenty-one, Benson finally graduated from high school. Then, after farming for two more years, at age twenty-three, he enrolled at Harper College in preparation for foreign mission work. Much older than most other students, George quickly became a leader on campus, coaching the track and field and baseball teams, while serving on the college's finance committee under President J. N. Armstrong.[8] Many other students at Harper were driven by the same religious motivation as Benson, and he soon encouraged others to prepare for the mission field also. Throughout his two years at Harper, he met regularly with other students to learn, on their own, Christian mission methodology. They decided that service in China presented both the greatest potential for Christian mission work and some appealing challenges. Consequently, as George involved himself in oratorical competition on campus[9] and continued to preach the Gospel, he rededicated himself to missionary education, with the idea that evangelizing the Chinese would be his life's work.

After graduating from Harper in 1923, Benson enrolled at Oklahoma A&M University in Stillwater, because he discovered that he could complete his bachelor's degree in only one academic year and one additional summer session. While there, he continued to preach as he raised funds for a local church building. It was in Stillwater that Benson began a phenomenal career raising money for worthy church-related causes. Eventually he would raise millions of dollars for Christian education, domestic evangelization, and foreign missions.

At Oklahoma A&M, the young evangelist also cultivated a persuasive oratorical style while leading the college debate team in national competition. Among his many speech topics was one entitled, "The Seventh Nation." Here he identified the former six as Egypt, Assyria, Babylonia, Persia, Greece, and Rome, all of which he claimed had been destroyed by internal decay. He affirmed that America would not fall in such a fashion because it had a broad educational program involving a larger proportion of her people than any one of those countries had had. He concluded that "America would have enough educated people that we would never follow the road of those ancient countries." In that speech, too, he boasted that America's constitutional government and free enterprise system made it possible for Americans to "exercise the privilege of dreaming dreams and setting about to fulfill those dreams."[10] These themes greatly influenced the direction of his life's work and animated his public service career.

Benson had planned to finish his degree at Oklahoma A&M during summer 1924. However, at the end of the school year he received an invitation to join the faculty of the newly created Harding College, in Morrilton, Arkansas, as principal of the campus high school.[11] Benson eagerly accepted the position at Harding College, where he continued his academic pursuits, completing a bachelor of arts degree in 1925. After Harding became accredited, he transferred those academic credits back to Oklahoma A&M and received a bachelor of science degree with a double major in history and economics. Benson later recalled how this struggle to complete his undergraduate work positively affected his future philosophy. He realized that "anybody could get an education if they were willing to put forth the effort required to get it. That led me to believe that probably most any other goal could likewise be attained through perseverance and hard work."[12]

Missionary to China

Despite his successful year as the principal of the high school in Morrilton, Benson was determined to teach the Gospel in a foreign field. He married Sally Ellis Hockaday in July 1925, and the couple left Harding College within the week to be missionaries to China. With only a vague promise of thirty-five dollars per month support, solicited from several Oklahoma churches, the Bensons left for Canton.

While traveling to Canton, the Bensons met two missionaries serving in China under the auspices of the China Inland Mission, Mr. and Mrs. W. G. Smith. One of the most successful mission efforts in China, the China Inland Mission had been founded in 1865 by the Englishman, J. Hudson Taylor.[13] The Smiths suggested that the Bensons leave Canton and move inland if they wished to do effective work with the Chinese people. They advised the Bensons to learn the language by living in the interior, where they would be forced to learn the customs and to speak only Chinese. As a result, in spring 1926, the Bensons went with the Smiths out of Canton and up the West River five hundred miles, to the city of Kwei Hsein in Kwangsi province. There the Smiths had built an orphanage and school for blind children.

It was on this trip upriver that George Benson was introduced to what he called the "treachery of Communism." According to historian Robert C. North, since 1923, Russian Communist agents led by Mikhail Borodin had been using the Kuomintang (the Chinese Nationalist Party of President Sun Yat-sen) as a Trojan horse through which to gain the backing of Chinese peasants for an effort to overthrow the provincial warlords. Chiang Kai-shek, at the request of Sun Yat-sen, had traveled to Russia to observe at first hand the operation of the Communist system, and Chiang and Sun had decided that Communism was the best system for uniting and modernizing China. After Sun Yat-sen's repeated attempts to organize a truly national government free from foreign control at Peking, civil war erupted, involving unstable coalitions of various political and military factions.

By the time of Benson's arrival in 1925, the power of the national government had diminished greatly in Kwangtung and Kwangsi provinces, and the region was ruled primarily by provincial warlords fighting attempts at national unification. To meet this challenge, a Nationalist army—based in Canton, led by Chiang Kai-shek, and partially supported by Mikhail Borodin—attempted to curb the power of the warlords in southern China and to replace their leadership with a central government under the Kuomintang coalition.[14] Around Canton, the warlords maintained nominal allegiance to the government in Peking, but the Kuomintang considered them "Chinese arms of imperial power." On May 23, 1925, the Kuomintang Central Executive Committee at Canton adopted a resolution "severing all connection with the Peking Government and proposing that the Party thereafter should devote its efforts toward cooperation with the Soviet Union."[15] As a result, Chinese Communist soldiers, acting under the orders of Sun Yat-sen and later of Chiang Kai-shek, battled the warlords for control of Canton and the surrounding districts.[16]

While the Benson party was traveling up the West River, Kuomintang soldiers, who had taken control of the river valley near Canton, accosted the Bensons and the Smiths and threatened to throw overboard the supplies needed so badly by the orphanage. Since the Smiths already owned property in the interior, the brief detainment ended with the Americans' being allowed to travel without much difficulty once they got farther away from Canton and into the interior, where warlords were in control.[17]

During the first six months of 1926, the Bensons struggled with the foreign culture around them, while they worked with the blind orphans. At first, as they studied Chinese customs and learned the language, they were free from the general political or military harassment associated with the civil war. Much of their language instruction came from a Chinese man employed by the Smiths. He spoke no English, and the Bensons spoke no Chinese. However, by using the Gospel of Mark as a textbook for language study, the trio communicated effectively. This arrangement also gave Benson the idea that linking Bible education and language instruction could be an effective evangelistic tool. He later employed this instructional method in several schools he started in Canton.

Benson enjoyed his work in Kwei Hsein, a city of thirty thousand people. He became acquainted with the mayor and his family, who dined in the Benson home on several occasions. Subsequently, the mayor chose the young foreigner to drive the first motorized vehicle, a Ford bus, over the newly constructed twelve-mile road between Kwei Hsein and a neighboring town. The citizens of the town had constructed the road by hand, carrying the dirt and rocks in baskets. They were very proud of it, so Benson felt deeply honored to be asked to drive the first vehicle over it: "It obviously gave us exposure and credibility we could not have otherwise gained. How important it is to be a part of the community in which we live if we are to expect people to become interested in what we have to share."[18]

However, the cordial feelings between the American missionaries and the townspeople deteriorated rapidly when Communist-dominated Kuomintang soldiers established control in the town.[19] According to Benson, the Communist soldiers turned the townspeople against all foreigners, especially the missionaries, blaming them for China's poverty.[20] Apparently this antiforeign and antimissionary sentiment spread rapidly inland with the success of Kuomintang troops in the area. Thereafter, local military and civil authorities often "stimulated attacks on Christians both foreign and Chinese. All British and most Americans were 'imperialists,' Chinese Christians were their 'running dogs,' and they and their property were fair prey for 'patriotic' citizens."[21]

One missionary related that, after having

> taken a town, a group of Communists began immediately to placard the town and especially the mission compound, chapels, etc., with anti-Christian posters and cartoons, some of which are too vulgar to mention. Others read: "The Church is the headquarters of murders and incendiaries"; "The missionaries have love in their mouths, but hate in their hearts"; "Drive out the missionaries who are making slaves of us"; "Christianity is poison"; "Christianity is the friend of Imperialism, kill Christianity." "Those who are willing to become Christians are traitors to China."[22]

As a result of this violent change in attitude on the part of local citizens stirred up by the Communist soldiers, the Bensons and the Smiths were in constant danger, as the anti-Western and antimissionary elements grew stronger and angry citizens threatened their lives.

After several perilous weeks, during which the Bensons were unable to secure passage downriver because most captains were afraid that angry mobs would burn their boats, their situation rapidly deteriorated. Their friend, the mayor, offered to help them get back to Canton. In fact, the mayor only was able to help them get out of the city unharmed, but the Bensons luckily found a boat captain who had been to America and felt grateful for the kindness Americans had shown him. As a result, this man risked his life to return the Bensons to Canton, where they hoped to secure passage on a British ship to Hong Kong. To their surprise, the turmoil inspired by the Communist-controlled Kuomintang was much worse in Canton. Furthermore, on orders from the Communist soldiers, the Chinese porters refused to move Benson's heavy baggage from one ship to another. The soldiers already had burned several boats in Canton harbor, apparently for conveying the luggage of foreigners. Eventually, after paying the exorbitant fee of seventy-five American dollars for the reluctant assistance of an American, who demanded that Benson not inform the American consul of this payment, the Bensons' luggage was transferred, and they secured passage on a British ship bound for Hong Kong. This adventure made Benson extremely leery of possible Communist control of any government, especially the American government. During much of his next ten years in China, he refused to pay bribes to inefficient government functionaries.

Peace did not soon return to Canton. The Bensons were unable to return to Canton until 1929 because, after the 1926 summer uprising, the Communist-controlled Kuomintang government, fearing unwanted foreign influence, drove all missionaries from the Chinese mainland.[23] On hearing nothing more from the Smiths, who had remained in Kwei Hsein during the fighting, the Bensons assumed that they had been killed.

While living in Hong Kong from late 1926 until spring 1929, the Bensons began to evangelize in their neighborhood but found the citizens unresponsive. Happily, Benson secured a teaching position at a British school in the city, enabling him to support his family. Soon he stumbled upon a tremendous opportunity to establish a new mission work in the Philippines. While on a world sightseeing tour, George Pepperdine, the founder of the Western Auto Supply stores in the United States, met with Benson in April 1928 and offered to finance an exploratory effort at evangelization on Mindoro Island. Pepperdine advanced four hundred dollars for a three-month campaign but allotted none of this money to support Mrs. Benson, who remained in Manila with the Bensons' young daughter, Mary Ruth. The personal support continued to come from the Morrilton Church of Christ in Morrilton, Arkansas. The money for the mission effort in the Philippines went for traveling expenses, purchase of a tent, and other necessary expenses that naturally would arise in addition to Benson's personal support.[24] Since the Bensons were unable to return to mainland China due to the political upheaval, Benson accepted Pepperdine's offer and preached in the Philippines in summer 1928.

Both Pepperdine and Benson believed that the Philippines presented a "remarkable field for successful evangelistic work," since the people already were familiar with Christianity. They were, according to Benson, nominal "Romanists." However, no priest lived in the towns where Benson worked. Perhaps once a year, a priest came to say mass, to baptize the babies, and to collect the fees for such services. Benson explained to the Morrilton church that the people's "attachment to Rome is usually quite loose, and many of the people feel little allegiance to such a system, and are very open to proper religious teaching."[25]

On Mindoro Island, Benson preached what he believed to be the "proper conception of baptism," baptized seventy-nine Filipinos, and established several congregations.[26] In Pinamalayan, according to Benson,

> the brethren furnished the materials and erected their chapel with only four dollars help from us. . . . At Paglasan the brethren brought in materials and erected their own chapel without a cent from me. The buildings were not elegant. You might [believe] them only suited for wagon sheds. Personally, I think that a chapel, ever so humble, which they have supplied themselves is worth more to the Cause in Mindoro than a temple supplied by foreign money.

On a return trip to Mindoro Island in 1960, Benson was delighted to find that some of these churches apparently were still meeting and even gradually growing.[27]

While in the Philippines, Benson learned important lessons about spreading the Christian message, but it was after his return to Canton in 1929 that he discovered what he saw as the key to successful evangelization in China. Even though American missionaries were allowed to return to China in 1929, most Chinese remained suspicious of missionary intentions and would not accept the Christian message from these "foreign devils." Even after political turmoil in Canton subsided, the anti-Western and antimissionary attitudes did not abate. During his first year back in Canton, Benson discovered the intensity of this feeling. In later years he recalled how much the Chinese disliked foreigners: "We learned the name of a foreigner when he was not present was 'Fan Kwai' [foreign devil]." According to Benson, the Chinese adults might be very polite to the missionaries, but the children always would identify foreigners as "Fan Kwai." "Thus," commented Benson, "these innocent little ones always called us 'Fan Kwai' even to our faces, revealing the real attitude of the adults."[28]

Despite such social ostracism, Benson secured a position teaching English at the National Sun Yat-sen University in Canton, where he became close friends with his department chairman. Although this influential Chinese gentleman had been educated in America, he knew very little about Christianity. Yet apparently he was not a devout Confucian either. Even though Benson's new friend was neither a preacher nor a teacher of religion, their many discussions over religious topics led Benson to the conclusion that education was the key to effective Christian evangelism in China. Benson learned from his friend that most Chinese from upper-class families wanted to study English, because "it opened doors to the knowledge of the world."[29] As a result, the Bensons and other missionaries who had joined them, Lewis T. Oldham and his new wife, Grace opened the Canton English Finishing School and, simultaneously, a separate Bible school. With the almost immediate success of these two schools, Benson believed that he had discovered one of the secrets of evangelizing the Chinese effectively.

The missionaries now directed their English finishing school toward the upper classes of Chinese society. Benson was told by his Chinese university acquaintances that their society was divided into five major classifications. Benson understood them to mean that these classes were not strict social castes along Hindu lines, but classes in which upward mobility was possible. In China the educated gentry were the most respected and occupied the highest classification, followed by farmers, merchants, artisans, and government functionaries.[30] Benson felt he had discovered a very important insight into traditional Chinese society. He learned at that time what other scholars since have discovered in their studies of Chinese society. Mary C. Wright argues that the "dominant Chinese tradition, in marked contrast to Western tradition, had always held that men are by nature good and that although their talents vary, the variation has nothing to do with class. Hence, education, on which an enormous value was placed, was theoretically as desirable for the lower classes as for the upper."[31] Even within what traditionally had been the lowest class of ordinary government functionaries, education made upward mobility possible.

Benson hoped to use his newfound discoveries about Chinese culture to influence the quality of Chinese society and its local government, and to wean the Chinese away from Communism through education, particularly Christian education. Benson, like some historians, discovered that, "since the abolition of entrance tests for Chinese Civil Service in 1905, the quality of performance and honesty of government bureaucrats had taken a decided turn for the worse," and he was determined to remedy this situation through Christian education.[32]

By enrolling in his English finishing school the children of the most respected members of the society, Benson enhanced the credibility of the Christian message being taught at the adjoining Bible school. This heightened prestige rapidly produced dividends. Almost immediately, Benson modified his course of instruction to induce many of the students who had come to learn English to attend the Bible school also, where the Bible was the only textbook and English was the language of instruction. The lesson learned during language study in the Smiths' home in Kwei Hsien six years earlier had not been wasted. For Benson it became the key to effective Christian evangelism in China.

Compared with their earlier evangelistic failures, the Bensons regarded as almost phenomenal the success of this new mission method, which centered on learning to teach secular subjects as a means of preparing students to support themselves as well as teaching the Bible.[33] George and Sally Benson soon envisioned erecting a permanent building for the school, and, by the fall term of 1936, the Bensons' last year in China, the new Canton Bible School building was complete. The school had over fifty full-time students and had graduated some twenty-five others.[34] By then the Bensons' missionary team included Lowell Davis, Roy Whitfield, Odessa White, and Ruth Gardner, recent graduates of Harding College whom Benson had encouraged to become missionaries when he taught there during a furlough in 1931–32.[35]

For the major building project in 1932–33, Benson solicited money from many American churches, but soon he was reminded by their lack of support that, historically, the Churches of Christ had exhibited a strong antimission bias. As Sydney Ahlstrom recounts, beginning before the American Civil War with the teachings of Alexander Campbell, antimissionism emerged as a "powerful new force" within many religious groups born on the frontier. Since the majority of the Churches of Christ retained their "frontier" characteristics until after World War II, they, like other predominantly rural fundamentalist denominations, developed a "widespread, popularly based opposition to organized evangelism."[36]

Despite very limited monetary support from home, it appears that Benson's indomitable determination to achieve what he believed to be God's work in China, along with his remarkable ingenuity and self-sufficiency, carried him to success in the mission field. Most of the money needed to buy property and to construct the new school building came from the combined earnings of Benson's missionary team in Canton and the remainder from his own meager family savings. The team saved additional money by doing much of the construction themselves, with Benson acting as general contractor. The total spent for the purchase of the land and the construction was about $6,000 U.S.; less than half of that came from American contributions.[37] According to Benson, "The family was broke at the end of practically every week because the Chinese workmen had to be paid weekly, but somehow there was always enough for the next week, and when the building was finished, the payments were finished."[38]

It was a sturdy brick building in which students and teachers lived and studied together. According to Benson, the boarding school environment gave the students both stability and security, helping to focus their minds on the Christian message and improving their ability to teach it to others. In 1981, when Benson returned to Canton with an American tour group, he secretly visited with several faithful Christian converts who had taught in the school in the 1930s. He also found the Canton Bible School building intact and in use, though converted to government offices.[39]

In December 1934, the Canton Bible School moved into its new headquarters. It prepared students to support themselves by teaching elementary school, much as George Benson had done in Oklahoma twenty years earlier. The pupils learned history, mathematics, English, geography, and the Bible, and many of these students became successful evangelists and teachers who started their own schools in other parts of the city or in outlying villages. The Canton Bible School was a very successful teaching and evangelistic tool used by the missionaries to introduce Christianity to the Chinese people, and Benson and his family planned to spend their lives in Chinese mission work. However, in 1936, Benson undertook a new challenge, when he became president of Harding College.

During the summer of 1930, the Benson family returned to the United States on furlough. George spent 1930-31 studying East Asian history at the University of Chicago, where he received a master's degree in August 1931.[40] The completion of his studies fulfilled his primary furlough plan—to learn more about the history, traditions, and customs of China. He felt that this knowledge would help him become a more effective Christian missionary in China. Between September and January, he taught courses in mission methods at Harding College, hoping to encourage others to join him in China.[41] While there, he renewed friendships with former professors and grew especially close to J. N. Armstrong, the aging president of Harding. It was probably during this time that Armstrong picked George Benson to be his successor.

President of Harding College

Despite Benson's determination to dedicate his life to Christian missions and his reluctance to leave Canton, he finally decided to accept Armstrong's offer and return to Harding College. He believed that he might do more there to promote and to support missionary education than anywhere else in the world. Benson knew from experience the lack of opportunity for formal instruction in cross-cultural evangelism within the Churches of Christ. He thought that, in his new Harding position, he might be able to remedy that deficiency. Reflecting on that fateful decision years later, Benson recalled:

> At that time we had not a single course in a single one of our colleges on missions. Consequently, our missionaries were going out unprepared, and fully half of them were coming home within less than three years and home to stay. So I finally decided I would accept the invitation and would undertake to develop courses in Missions and also to encourage work in Missions in our other Christian colleges. Really, this was the decisive argument in my own mind for coming home.[42]

Benson's first classes in mission methods at Harding met in 1931-32 on the old campus in Morrilton. In 1934, however, the school relocated to Searcy, Arkansas. Like many other Christian colleges, Harding was deeply in debt and on the verge of collapse. In addition, the administration had become embroiled in a rancorous theological debate with local churches, contributing greatly to its difficulties. In accepting the presidency, Benson was aware of the severe financial problems, but he had little idea of the rapidly deteriorating reputation of Harding College within the denomination. Nor did he know much about the impact of a growing premillennialism controversy which threatened to undermine the school's ability to recruit new students in training as preachers and teachers for the Churches of Christ.

Harding College's heavy debt stemmed in part from its 1934 purchase of the Galloway College property at Searcy from the Methodist

Church for $75,000. Since the appraised valuation was approximately $500,000, it appeared the purchase price had been a bargain. By 1936, however, the college had repaid none of the principal or the interest on the debt. Because the interest was accumulating at approximately $4,200 a year, the college's prospects were bleak. Even so, when Benson arrived on campus, he found faculty and student morale remarkably high, all being as eager as he was to eliminate the debt.

The college had about two hundred and fifty students, in addition to roughly one hundred elementary and high school students on the relatively large campus. Benson, however, viewed the dedication and ability of the permanent staff as the college's chief asset. After conferring with the outgoing president and his staff, Benson decided to establish four primary goals for the coming year: (1) to attain North Central Association accreditation, (2) to pay off the debt and to add to the college plant, (3) to increase salaries and to build a stronger faculty, and (4) to retain this dedicated faculty, with its deep spiritual commitment to cultivating genuinely Christian character in students.[43]

When the fall term opened in 1936, many of the teachers had no stipulated salaries and were paid whatever the school could afford. One young student, though, remembered that the faculty's priorities were in the proper order: "There was no doubt that their love for God was the compass that gave direction to their lives," and "they didn't make speeches about the need to sacrifice, they sacrificed. They did not talk about the work ethic; they worked until they were bone weary."[44]

Benson immediately established a workable salary schedule and promised to pay the faculty each month. It called for faculty with a doctoral degree to receive eighty-five dollars per month; those with a master's degree, seventy-five; and those with only a bachelor's degree, sixty-five. Benson hoped to raise additional funds to meet these obligations and to retire the short-term college debt. Further, Harding's budget management under Benson reflected lessons learned living on the edge of poverty on the Oklahoma frontier and in China. One contemporary recalled fondly that when "oldsters allege that [Benson] used to go around standing brooms on their handles to make them last longer, he simply has a twinkle in his eye, without admitting whether the example was real."[45]

To alleviate Harding's long-term debt, Benson publicly announced, on October 5, 1936, plans for a fundraising drive targeted at local churches. His initial efforts focused on members of the Churches of Christ and other citizens of Searcy. From them Benson secured a pledge of $10,000, while Harding's student body pledged another $7,000.[46] Benson

also selected thirty-three other Arkansas locations for fundraising meetings and quickly moved to solicit donations in these areas.[47] In November, Benson organized rallies at Newport and Pocahontas, Arkansas,
which netted pledges of $375.[48] By the end of November, pledges had
reached $15,000, with larger meetings boldly scheduled for Chicago, De-
troit, Denver, and Los Angeles.[49] Benson's fundraising among local
churches, however, was greatly hampered by the continuing denominational premillennialism controversy, which apparently had been a key
factor in the resignation of Benson's predecessor, J. N. Armstrong.

Division within the Churches of Christ

While president of Cordell, Harper, and Harding colleges, J. N. Armstrong
frequently contributed articles to religious journals and preached and lectured in Churches of Christ circles. His standing fell dramatically, however, when some church members felt that he sided with R. H. Boll,
another popular writer and preacher, on the issue of millennial prophecy. Periodically in the nineteenth century, this highly charged issue had
been the focus of theological controversy within many American religious movements. It had been one of several points of difference which
by 1906 had prompted the Churches of Christ to separate from the Disciples of Christ.[50] It is important to understand the nature of the controversy because it greatly affected Harding's relationship with local churches
and ultimately altered George Benson's fundraising methodology.

First, one must understand the profoundly rationalistic world view
shared by members of the Churches of Christ, which strongly shaped
how they viewed their place within Christian history. The early-nine-
teenth-century Restoration movement in American religious history embraced and advocated rationalistic, postmillenarian theology. This theology reflected the optimistic anthropology and the republican world view
of important movement leaders such as Alexander Campbell and Walter
Scott. Campbell and Scott were Scottish Common Sense Realists who
relied heavily upon the philosophical tenets of Francis Bacon, John
Locke, and other Enlightenment philosophers to explain the acquisition
of human knowledge, including religious knowledge, or "truth," as these
philosophers described it. In particular, Campbell, Scott, and other American thinkers championed the philosophical thought of, among their con-
temporaries, Thomas Reid (1710–96) at the University of Glasgow and of

Dugald Stewart (1753–1828) at Edinburgh University. Drawing heavily upon the earlier writings of Francis Bacon (1561–1626), an outspoken advocate of the inductive research method, Reid and Stewart had developed Common Sense Realism, or "the Scottish Philosophy," to rebut the religious skepticism of David Hume, another widely respected Scottish philosopher.

In the early nineteenth century, this "Scottish Philosophy" became very popular with American theologians and educators. Reid and Stewart's theories of knowledge, government, and religion were tremendously influential in most American colleges. The Scottish texts, "often adapted specifically for American use, quickly and decisively replaced the older eighteenth-century texts and were established as the center of the philosophical portions of the curriculum."[51]

Scott and Campbell adhered firmly to the rational epistemology of Bacon and John Locke, as refracted through the lens of Scottish Common Sense Realism, or "Baconianism," as it was popularly called. Baconianism argued that all knowledge, even abstract ideas, originated in sensory experiences. This argument contrasted with widely-held epistemological concepts associated with Reformed theology and deism, which posited some measure of innate or intuitive knowledge of God.

Accordingly, Scott and Campbell worked within a rational religious philosophy which proposed that revealed truth, based on the Bible, provided the only logically possible religious experience. In this view, knowledge has two sources, nature and revelation, "but the method of apprehending the truth from each is the same: a logical method which is basically inductive."[52] One could only apprehend the existence of God rationally—and then only through the evidence of Scripture. In this way, the early Church of Christ thinkers boldly applied the Lockean rejection of innate knowledge to understand the nature of God, arguing instead for a rational understanding of religious principles.

The Restoration movement also advocated postmillennialism; that is, they assumed that a "spiritual and cultural progress amounting to a millennium" was a precondition for Christ's return to reign on earth.[53] Thus, the rational theology of the Restoration movement became intertwined with cultural progress and reflected the belief that America was the divinely designated moral and spiritual leader of the world.

Late in the nineteenth century, a perspective known as premillennialism gained popularity. Like its postmillennial rival, this position ostensibly was based upon a literal interpretation of the Bible. Premillennialism, however, projected an imminent return (that is, a return that could occur at any moment) of Christ to earth, likely preceded, its adherents claimed, by political and social turmoil and by religious apostasy. This apocalyptic scenario reflected a theocentric and pessimistic view of history and of the role of Christianity within that history. As George Marsden has observed, "Modern historiography assumes that human and natural forces shape the course for history and [that] its basic model is something like a biological concept of development. Dispensationalists [premillennialists], on the other hand, start with the assumption that supernatural forces shape history."[54] So, while postmillennialism is very optimistic, premillennialism is profoundly pessimistic. The latter projects at the end of the current age divine punishment for humankind's spiritual failure, rather than rewards for cultural and spiritual improvement.

As a strong adherent of this rationally-based Restoration theology, George Benson echoed both its rationalistic and its postmillennial sentiments. Their presence is quite evident in his vigorous advocacy of Americanism—belief in God, belief in the Constitution, and belief in free enterprise—and in his equally vigorous opposition to world Communism. After returning from China, Benson resolved to prove that America was God's chosen instrument for spreading Christianity and constitutional self-government throughout the world, and to convince all Americans, and especially all members of the Churches of Christ, that it was their duty to assist in this effort.

Because he had been out of the country for so long, Benson probably did not realize the divisive potential of the premillennial argument within Churches of Christ circles. From the perspective of many adherents of traditional postmillennial Churches of Christ thought, R. H. Boll and his followers were dangerous agents of cultural modernism who taught a radical theology that threatened the fundamental world view of the Churches of Christ. As postmillennial traditionalists saw it, this deep theological divergence demanded forthright statements from important church leaders which would allow sincere church members to identify adherents of the two points of view and exclude those who espoused premillennial convictions. Many church members looked to Benson, as president of a prominent training center for future denominational leaders, to draw this line for the fellowship; to their dismay, he refused. However, since he was the new president of a financially troubled institution struggling to train future preachers and lay workers, he could not remain neutral and expect strong denominational support.

Because Armstrong would not condemn Boll's interpretation of millennial prophecy as heretical, many Churches of Christ observers decided that Armstrong was theologically unreliable. This lack of confidence in Armstrong very likely resulted in his resignation from the Harding College presidency in favor of Benson. In 1936, then, many local churches already had decided to withhold their financial support from the school. Even though he did not accept Armstrong's theological position, and in fact argued strongly against it, Benson remained loyal to his former teacher and would not dismiss him from the faculty. This loyalty made it increasingly difficult for Benson to raise funds from local congregations. The young college president argued that some of the brotherhood

> went along with the ones favoring the drawing of strict lines of fellowship. Some others, by nature more lenient, feared to speak out. Consequently, doors were closed against those soliciting either students or financial support for Harding College. While other related schools seemed to be shedding their financial troubles, Harding College was finding self-sufficiency increasingly difficult. This crisis brought a change in Harding's approach to her financial problems.[55]

Benson quickly decided to look elsewhere for financial support.[56]

Benson's New Fundraising Program

As Harding's support from the local churches rapidly diminished, Benson turned instead to several wealthy individuals within the Churches of Christ who ignored Harding's "premillennialist" label. One of the first to lend financial support was Clinton Davidson, a man who eventually would introduce Benson to many wealthy industrialists. Davidson, a prominent insurance salesman and financial counselor with business contacts in both New York and Washington, D.C., helped secure appointments for Benson with the presidents of several major oil and steel companies, as well as DuPont Chemical, International Harvester, and Quaker Oats. Additionally, Davidson's association with Washington lobbyists paved the way for Benson's appearance before the House of Representative's Committee on Ways and Means in 1941.[57] Through his personal gift of $10,000, Davidson became the first wealthy donor to contribute to Harding College out of his strong desire to help Harding promote the values of Christian education.[58]

Benson later admitted that, if the controversy over premillennialism had never arisen, Harding College probably would not have sought support from industry and consequently would not have made very much financial progress.[59]

Despite the ongoing theological controversy, Benson chipped away at the institutional debt by soliciting donations from wealthy Christians such as George Pepperdine, who earlier had sponsored Benson's mission work in the Philippines. As before, Benson's appeal to Pepperdine rested strictly on the claim that Harding College would provide an environment to better develop Christian character in its students.[60] Even though Pepperdine contributed $25,000 and Davidson $10,000 to Harding College, Benson soon discovered that Harding could provide a service to other wealthy businessmen that would encourage generous support from those not associated with the Churches of Christ.

When Benson left America in 1925 to pursue his dream of Christian evangelization, it appeared to him that the American people were happy: the government ran smoothly, railroads and highways were being constructed, rural electricity was gradually being made available in some areas, and there appeared to be very little poverty, at least compared with that seen in China. Benson had been raised on the Oklahoma frontier, one of the least economically developed areas of America, and, like many others living there, he took for granted the American free enterprise system, supported by the framework of constitutional government. On the Oklahoma frontier, there appeared to be room for everybody and a way for nearly everyone to make a living. Very few people thought of themselves as poor, and even fewer sought economic aid from any level of government. During Benson's first return trip in 1930, before the Great Depression intensified, America's economic difficulties appeared to be under control, and the general attitude of the people toward free enterprise and constitutional government had not changed significantly.

In 1936, the Benson family once again returned to the United States. This time the group traveled by way of the Suez Canal, with brief stops in India, Africa, and the Middle East. In these places, as in China, Benson discovered wretched poverty and an overwhelming lack of economic initiative. Upon his return to America, he sensed that prolonged economic calamity had drastically altered the attitudes of many Americans. Benson believed that extended periods of unemployment had robbed many Americans of hope, diminished their sense of self-worth, and eroded their faith in American government. Benson discovered a growing disdain for the government and for the American economic system, especially big business. For the first time in his life, Benson heard "severe, ugly, bitter criticism of big business," which was blamed for all of America's problems. Even from the White House, Benson heard political slogans affirming that the people running American industries were only "coupon clippers, economic royalists, and profiteers."[61] Benson had difficulty accepting the validity of these slogans, because he still believed, as he had argued in his debates at Oklahoma A&M in 1924, that the capitalistic private enterprise economy was the secret of America's high productivity and its superior standard of living.

When analyzing the relative poverty brought on by the Depression, Benson observed that Americans still lived better than most of the world's inhabitants. In the face of such widespread criticism, he wanted to convince Americans of the high quality of their economic and political system.[62] However, Benson's most pressing problem was the failing financial condition of Harding College. Happily, the need to save Harding coincided with his urge to vindicate American private enterprise and its constitutional system.

Early in his tenure as president of Harding, Benson spoke on a program along with Wallace B. Donham, dean of Harvard University's School of Business Administration, who persuaded Benson that college fundraising was more than merely soliciting donations. Fundraising actually entailed "selling satisfaction" to the donor. Benson understood Dean Donham to say that "people do not give away money. People purchase things they value. When you sell a man an automobile it is because you have made him think that the car will render him more service than the money that he must give to buy it." According to Benson, Donham suggested applying this philosophy to college fundraising: "Until you can show the prospective donor that he is going to get more satisfaction from the gift than he would from retaining the money, he is not going to make the gift."[63]

Benson readily adopted this stance and Benson proudly claimed to have raised, during each of his thirty years as president of the college, an average of one million dollars per year.[64] According to Benson, he solicited money to promote not only Christian education, but also his brand of Americanism—in particular, the free enterprise system and constitutional government. Until 1936, Harding College had been offering its Churches of Christ constituency only the satisfaction of grounding its young people in Biblical knowledge and developing in them Christian ideals and behavior. However, this constituency contained very few eminent or wealthy figures such as Clinton Davidson or George Pepperdine.[65] To broaden the college's appeal to potential donors, particularly wealthy benefactors, Benson developed the National Education Program as a part of Harding College.[66]

From its formation as Harding's Department of National Education in 1941[67] until its formal separation from the college in 1954, the National Education Program (NEP)[68] served as Benson's primary vehicle to solicit huge donations from American industry. Seizing every opportunity to address industrial and civic organizations "on the values of our American heritage," Benson touted the merits of Harding College as an educational institution dedicated to preserving such ideals. Specifically, he emphasized the importance of "faith in God, Constitutional government and the private ownership of the tools of production."[69] Since corporate management already subscribed to this credo and was anxious to promote it nationally, officials often were willing to help finance Benson's educational programs. As a result, many businessmen, out of self-interest and to promote the interests of their class, contributed both to the National Education Program and to Harding College. In so doing, they hoped to exert a strong influence "in the very field that was, in their opinion, most vital to America's future."[70]

2

The Genesis of
Free-Enterprise Education

When George Benson assumed the presidency of Harding College in 1936, his frontier upbringing and his traumatic experiences in China had decisively molded his understanding of the proper relationship among Christian education, evangelism, and social institutions. Although Christianity historically has not been limited to a particular economic or political system, Benson felt that it had a better chance to flourish within a free enterprise economic system supported by constitutional government than in chaotic China, where traditional warlords and Communist ideologues contended for power. Consequently, Benson's Christian commitments encompassed American cultural values, which he believed historically "had been able to lift the common man out of hopeless misery and despair" and had made "people . . . free"—indeed, had made them "the wonder and the envy of all the world."[1] To Benson, America's future greatness rested upon a clear apprehension of these ideals, so he set out to make Harding College an institution that exemplified this marriage of Christian ethics and faith in economic freedom and constitutional government.

He pursued this vision for Harding College on many fronts, fashioning a well-rounded liberal arts curriculum undergirded by a strong emphasis on Christian values. He worked tirelessly to retire college debts and to secure additional funding to sustain its financial health and growth. Further, Benson intended to remedy what he felt to be a great deficiency within the Churches of Christ, in the group's overall lack of dedication to world evangelism and, consequently, to effective missionary instruction. This shortcoming arose out of nineteenth-century controversies over interchurch cooperation within the Restoration movement, controversies that eventuated in separating the movement into three denominational wings—Churches of Christ, Disciples of Christ, and Christian Church.[2] Now, however, Benson acted without hesitation to strengthen the church by producing Biblical scholars and church laymen dedicated to spreading the Christian message throughout the world. With this objective in mind, the young college president set out to campaign for a clearer public understanding of what he understood to be the traditional American way of life and its heritage of freedom. This freedom, he argued, permitted the existence of institutions like Harding College.[3]

Thus, from Benson's perspective, Americanism education and Christian education were practical equivalents because each reinforced the other. Accordingly, at Harding College, Christian education and Americanism education became, in the words of one critic,

> so tightly meshed together that it is impossible to tell which is primary and which is the motivation for the other. It is probably safe to say that Christianity marked the beginning. From that point, it is not certain whether Harding College has become the tool whereby the gospel of Americanism could be preached or whether the Americanism program has been the tool for maintaining Harding College as an educational institution.[4]

As already noted, Benson returned from China to find what he considered to be a "shocking transformation" in the American spirit. America, he came to believe, had undergone a dramatic cultural and economic transformation, in which prosperity and buoyant optimism had given way to economic depression and pessimism about the future. In articulating fears generated by the economic depression, some leading analysts were expressing the belief that "the slump seemed to be the culmination of three generations of economic, social, and moral crisis."[5] Conservative religious leaders, in particular, were still experiencing the residual effects of the Scopes Trial defeat, as church attendance and income rapidly declined.[6] The Churches of Christ and Harding College were not immune to such difficulties.

At the root of Benson's concern was a basic traditionalist skepticism concerning the cultural fruits of modernity and the steady liberalization and socialization of American institutions.[7] Other prominent figures shared

Benson's apprehension,[8] and, in the early 1930s, their conservative ideology, not yet stigmatized as radical, was articulated mainly by more mainstream political figures who forcefully propounded right-wing ideology and "100 percent Americanism," in the face of a rising tide of public criticism.[9]

After his return from China, Benson was immediately caught up in the ongoing political controversy. While reinforcing his own conservative ideology, these arguments soon caused him to associate the ascendant liberal social and religious viewpoint with collectivist economic tendencies in the National Recovery Act and the Agricultural Adjustment Act of Franklin D. Roosevelt's New Deal.[10] In formulating a conservative response, Benson eschewed many of the more radical countersubversive themes used by Old Christian Right extremists. These themes had been "crystallized during the late nineteenth century, legitimized during World War I and the Red Scare, and sustained throughout the 'tribal twenties.'"[11] Even so, throughout his public career, Benson periodically was labeled an extremist, because he consistently blurred the nebulous distinction between attempts by many Progressives and New Deal supporters to effect economic and social change, and their overt complicity in conspiracies, as several far-right-wing leaders charged during the 1930s and 1940s.

While many subtle distinctions between turn-of-the-century Progressivism and New Deal policies eluded Benson, he believed that the government's response to the 1929 economic collapse was the central issue in the growing debate over increasing socialization and liberalization of American institutions. Listening to other conservatives helped to clarify his thinking.[12] To many former Progressives, the Depression demonstrated that the U.S. economy lacked self-correcting mechanisms and required regulation. Despite early support by some conservatives for the basic New Deal strategy that sought social and economic unity by providing "something for everybody, . . . the nation insistently divided into right and left." Roosevelt's economically "equivocal position became more difficult to maintain." Many of his early supporters from the "vested interests of big business," who at one time had praised him for righting the "keel of economic life" and "turning politics safely back to its normal course," became dismayed and fearful of the president's apparent growing alliance with the economic left, especially after the recession of 1937.

According to Richard Hofstadter, when the Supreme Court declared the NRA unconstitutional, Roosevelt's New Deal suddenly was forced sharply to the left. Roosevelt found it politically expedient to placate labor and to institute his own versions of popularly proposed panaceas like Huey Long's "Share-the-Wealth" plan and Francis E. Townsend's "Social Security."[13] The implementation of these programs led many former supporters to believe that Roosevelt, by spring 1938, had resolved to use large-scale government spending to cure the American economy and to redress abuses by big business: "Henceforth Roosevelt took it for granted that the economy could not operate without the stimulus of government funds."[14]

Leo Ribuffo has argued that "despite its slim prospects, a grassroots socialist alternative in the early 1900s was readily identifiable"[15] and probably had not abated noticeably by the early 1930s. In the economic and social crisis, Benson found particularly alarming the possibility that Roosevelt intended to push his economic policy still farther to the left by embracing even more collectivist solutions, thereby satisfying this increasingly popular extremist demand. Benson doubted the possibility of an immediate socialist ascendancy in Washington. However, a real possibility—one that Benson feared might be more threatening in the long run to traditional social institutions—was that ordinary Americans might be willing to accept Keynesian economic theory and its economic bromides of government regulation and deficit spending.

Although historians now concede that much of FDR's New Deal was simply an ad hoc combination of pragmatic experimentation and left-of-center sloganeering, some New Deal programs were grounded in the pioneering economic theory of Cambridge don John Maynard Keynes, who believed that full employment was the key to modern economic prosperity. According to Keynes, the rate of employment is "determined by the level of aggregate demand, which is equal to the aggregate income on the entire economy. This demand, or income, is in turn a function of consumption and investment."[16] Keynes argued that there were two ways to increase income in the economic community: to increase private investment and or to increase public consumption, even if it meant utilizing deficit spending by the state to create full employment through public works projects or direct subsidies. Central to the success of his theory was the belief that economic depressions might briefly produce fiscal deficits for central governments, but that creating and maintaining full employment was more important than balancing the budget. In any case, tax increases during the resulting prosperity would remove the deficit and balance the budget.[17]

However, in Benson's opinion, deficit spending, even during a depression, created a combination of full employment and increased government regulation that was tantamount to nationalizing American industry and socializing the economy. Although he probably did not fully understand the complexities of Keynesian economic theory—a fault he shared with most New Deal leaders—Benson's worries about the political and social implications of deficit spending were profound. To understand his willingness to speak out on political and economic issues, we must treat his concerns respectfully, even though it is now generally agreed that FDR acted to preserve the capitalistic system by using Keynesian economics to deal with its endemic flaw, cyclic fluctuation.[18]

Stung by events in China and unnerved by what he had seen and read since his return, Benson felt he could not afford the luxury of detached observation. He quickly came to the conclusion that "socialism," as he termed Keynesian economic policy, already was "knocking at the nation's front door."[19] Benson was hardly alone in his assessment of the nation's economic danger, since many of his fears were shared by a large segment of the population. As Ribuffo has observed, this segment adapted "venerable countersubversive themes [and] deemed Roosevelt's program un-American as well as unwise," and "routinely compared the whole New Deal to 'Russianized government.'"[20] In response, Benson, as well as many other "100 percent Americans" active since the turn of the century, "found in the Roosevelt administration proof that their fears had been justified all along. Freshly energized, they formed the nucleus of a now distinct far right."[21]

To heighten his worries over "creeping socialism," Benson discovered that American educators apparently had already accepted the need for socialistic economic and industrial policies. To his chagrin, he read in a 1934 report of the National Education Association (NEA) that "a dying laissez-faire [Do-Nothingism] must be completely destroyed and all of us, including the 'owners,' must be subjected to a large degree of social control."[22] At an NEA conference in Washington, educational leaders apparently had suggested to the nation that "our fragile, interdependent society, the credit agencies [banks] and the basic industries and the utilities cannot be centrally controlled and operated under private ownership." These educators therefore resolved to "join in creating a swift nationwide campaign of adult education which will support Roosevelt in taking these over and operating them at full capacity as a unified national system in the interest of all the people."[23]

Since Benson recalled that some of his University of Chicago professors in 1931 had espoused socialism and talked quite openly about the end of the capitalist system in America, the NEA report reinforced Benson's deepening suspicion that some American colleges and universities rapidly were becoming institutional vehicles for socialist propaganda.[24] Obviously the NEA committee report was not a detailed national education proposal completely endorsed by the Roosevelt administration, but Benson viewed it as an early effort to condition the public and its political leaders to accept socialism.

Additional threats of this nature loomed on the horizon for Benson, who believed that the Depression had imprinted a "relief" psychology on millions of Americans who had been forced to accept government dollars. To make matters worse, even after the return of full employment during World War II, their "children were growing up without knowledge of any other way of life."[25] To counter this trend toward dependency, Benson reminded audiences and readers of a time-honored libertarian axiom: "No matter what the hardships or what the difficulties, the people of this country must maintain a free America. They must maintain an America where all men are free to think, free to work, free to spend their money as they please, free to engage in business at their own risk, free to own property, free to vote their convictions, and free to worship God in their own way."[26]

In the face of these developments, Benson by 1941 was firmly convinced that Christian education in America faced a tremendous challenge to promote and defend the free enterprise system and its political underpinnings. Benson feared that the New Deal's collectivist economic policies made it less likely that the economy could attract investment capital. As far as Benson was concerned, New Deal policies discouraged American business investment and would lead to a deeper economic recession.

Although he was not a trained economist, Benson understood the importance in the free-market economy of national confidence in attracting and retaining capital. He had seen evidence of this economic principle in China. There he had spoken with potential American investors in a Chinese mining venture, who reported that they believed the Chinese government was then both weak and unwilling to protect their interests—indeed, it might nationalize the mines at any time. As a result, they refused to invest in the potentially lucrative coal-mining venture, even though raw materials and labor were readily available. As a result of such widespread fears, China had to import most of its coal, despite the fact that it possessed coal in abundance.[27]

Convinced that a similar loss of confidence might result in a gradual erosion of the capitalistic system in the United States, Benson vowed to reverse the trend. As Ribuffo has shown, conservative spokesmen such as Benson collected from stories such as this Chinese example what they felt to be ample evidence to argue in favor of free-enterprise economics. Additionally, these critics capitalized on growing discontent with New Deal economic programs on the part of more reactionary elements who readily appropriated traditional conspiracy themes, demanding concerted countersubversive action.

Benson, who disdained radical solutions to the growing problem, believed that a democratic political solution was still possible and that, under a constitutional system, public demand could be rallied to reverse what Benson saw as "pernicious" government policies restricting free enterprise. He argued for an unrestricted educational system to sell the general public on the merits of Americanism, or a free-market economy, and to call attention to the potential hazards of flirting with socialism. Since Benson firmly believed that the voice of the people ultimately stimulated government action, he often invoked one of the NEP's initial guiding slogans: "If you are going to move Washington to do the things it ought to do, you have got to move public opinion." His aim, according to Benson, was to "move public opinion at the grassroots in the direction of godliness and patriotism."[28]

By 1941, Benson could proudly cite Harding College as a prime example of free enterprise in action. Benson usually recounted the economic success story of Harding College to local audiences before endorsing more broadly America's traditional free-enterprise economy. Of course, Benson's prudent use of Harding's resources had played a large part in retiring Harding's debt and, at the same time, in creating student jobs. By 1948, Harding College owned and operated over fifteen hundred acres of farmland, which produced considerable food, livestock, and income for the college. The college also owned and operated a concrete-block plant that turned out five hundred blocks per day, and a campus laundry and dry-cleaning plant which did considerable business with the local community. In 1941, the college produced 158,000 gallons of milk and, according to college records, "one acre of ground produced 310 crates of strawberries valued at $1,554, while 8,160 pounds of grapes were gathered from three acres, and other individual acres produced 150 bushels of Irish potatoes and 160 bushels of sweet potatoes."[29]

The crowning economic achievement of the college in 1946 was Benson's use of $300,000 in college funds to purchase a Memphis radio station, WHBQ. According to Benson, after one year it had netted nearly $100,000 profit, which he used to reward Harding's loyal faculty with salary increases. Since the station's anticipated annual revenue of $60,000 equaled the interest on a $2 million endowment,[30] the success of this investment proved to Benson that even relatively small enterprises such as Harding College could prosper under the free-enterprise system. Benson believed that college investments in real property would produce more income than returns on stock and bonds,[31] an investment strategy seemingly vindicated when Harding later sold WHBQ for a net profit of $2.5 million.[32]

The economic success of Harding College quickly raised Benson's standing with local civic and business groups as a dynamic speaker and respected authority on conservative fiscal policies. Earlier Benson had been named an honorary member of the Little Rock Chamber of Commerce. His speech on that occasion, "Economic Condition of the Orient," broadcast over Little Rock radio station KARK, became the first of hundreds of radio "sermons" on free-enterprise economics.[33]

Benson also enhanced his reputation as a fiscal conservative by inaugurating a Harding College lecture series which attracted many prominent businessmen, at first from Arkansas and then from throughout the nation. In 1939, Benson had initiated the series of programs featuring speeches by outstanding Arkansas business executives. The next year he expanded the scope of the lecture series and induced prominent businessmen from outside Arkansas to appear. Among speakers on Harding's program in 1940 were Sterling Morton, director of the United States Chamber of Commerce; Colonel Robert S. Henry, associate to J. J. Pelly, president of the American Association of Railroads; Raymond H. Fogler, president of Montgomery Ward; and James L. Kraft, president of Kraft-Phoenix Cheese Corporation. Benson's series of economic programs was so successful that, by April 1940, he already had received letters of encouragement in this enterprise from noted businessmen Ralph Budd, F. V. DuPont, General Harboard, W. A. Harrison, C. F. Kettering, Thomas S. Lamont, David Sarnoff (the governor of Delaware), and Harold F. Swift, as well as the presidents of the New York Central Railroad, Metropolitan Life

Insurance, Eastman Kodak, Chemical Bank and Trust, Hormel, Johns-Mansville, and the *New York Sun*; and from vice-presidents of the American Bankers Association.[34]

Benson's Impact on Congress

The success of the economic lecture program, Benson's ability to engage high-quality speakers who shared his fundamental philosophy, and the personal recognition he gained as a result of the series generated positive publicity for the college and emboldened Benson to reach out by other means to the rest of the country. Though already a respected public figure in Arkansas, Benson gained national attention when he testified before the House Ways and Means Committee in May 1941 regarding a pending tax measure. Benson's well-publicized impact on that committee secured his access to a wide and receptive national audience. A full consideration of this event shows how crucial it was for Benson's future career.

Benson proposed to the committee how the government could save two billion dollars by eliminating several New Deal programs that were redundant or anachronistic. The Civilian Conservation Corps (CCC), the Works Progress Administration (WPA), and the National Youth Administration (NYA), Benson argued, had outlived their usefulness. These largely self-perpetuating agencies, he believed, existed only to provide employment for their administrators.[35]

With this appearance, Benson joined a national debate in progress, over the scope of federal spending and taxation, and over the possibility of a European war. Only six months before, in a December 1940 radio address, Franklin Roosevelt, acutely conscious of intransigent isolationist sentiment and the political pitfalls of war talk, had asked for public support of the Lend-Lease Act. "We must be the great arsenal of democracy," Roosevelt emphasized. "For us this is an emergency as serious as the war itself. We must apply ourselves to our task with the same resolution, the same sense of urgency, the same spirit of patriotism and sacrifice as we would show were we at war."[36] It was clearly a call for the American people to prepare themselves to contribute their material resources to the war effort. Subsequently, the president asked Congress to determine the most appropriate method to raise the needed revenue.

In early April 1941, John L. Sullivan, assistant secretary of the treasury, had reported to Congress that, at the end of fiscal year 1940 (July 1, 1939–June 30, 1940), the federal government had spent roughly $3.5 billion more than tax revenue collected. He estimated that, by the end of fiscal year 1941 (June 30, 1941), the deficit would be a little more than $6 billion. Furthermore, the proposed budget for fiscal year 1942, to begin on July 1, 1941, called for expenditures of a little over $19 billion, more than double the budget just two years before and 45 percent more than that for the previous year. The Treasury Department reported that tax revenues would cover two-thirds of the proposed budget, while the remaining $6 billion would be raised through bond sales. Sullivan's proposed solution to remedy this shortfall was mainly new and higher taxes.[37]

Through the national media, Benson followed testimony in the House of Representatives quite closely. On April 24, Secretary of the Treasury Henry Morgenthau appeared before the Ways and Means Committee to recommend tax increases earmarked for defense totaling $3.5 billion dollars. Since Americans understood the national emergency and since the increase equaled only 4 percent of a rapidly rising national income, he argued, Americans gladly would shoulder the burden.

Morgenthau pressed his argument further by insisting that these new taxes for national defense were "fiscally responsible and socially equitable." In addition, he proposed that Congress should "reexamine with a magnifying glass" government expenditures which were neither for "purposes of defense nor for purposes of relief and security from want." In short, Morgenthau proposed redirecting public resources toward defense production while reducing consumer spending and nondefense outlays; both these reductions would help the nation avoid rounds of wage and price inflation. The first steps, he concluded, were to increase the tax rate for the minimum income subject to income surtax, raise the excess-profits tax, and, finally, levy new excise taxes on a number of commodities not essential to the defense program.[38]

The committee questioned Morgenthau vigorously to determine exactly which nondefense expenditures would suffer most under this plan. In response, Morgenthau suggested that about $1 million might be trimmed by reducing funds for soil conservation. He also noted that over one million men had been inducted into the Army within the previous year, reducing both unemployment and the need for the CCC and the NYA.[39] He admitted that the Treasury Department had not "re-examined all of those expenditures that have been sort of grafted onto the Government during the last ten years."[40]

What alarmed fiscal conservatives like George Benson was Morgenthau's revelation that these nondefense expenditures "grafted onto government" amounted to $7 billion dollars in the proposed budget.[41] Morgenthau's testimony convinced Benson that the Treasury Department had not seriously pursued reduction of current nondefense expenditures.

Following Morgenthau's lead, Assistant Secretary Sullivan made specific tax recommendations. He proposed that roughly one-third of the needed funds come from ability-to-pay taxes (income, excess profits, capital gains, estate, and gift taxes), one-third from corporate taxes, and one-third from excise or commodity taxes. In addition, he argued for increased estate taxes, taxes on capital gains and excess profits, and various new sales taxes, to put heavier burdens on those with the greatest ability to pay. Sullivan insisted that "only through ability-to-pay taxes can tax burdens be distributed with careful regard for equity. Consumption taxes burden consumers without regard either to income or to family needs and responsibility and thus fail to meet the test of equity."[42]

In general, the committee viewed these suggestions as inflationary. Robert L. Doughton, from North Carolina, the moderate chair of the House Ways and Means Committee since 1933, had for many years consistently avoided supporting what he labeled "inflationary New Deal measures." Throughout this session, he had been encouraging reduced government spending and was especially critical of Sullivan's statement. In addition, Republican Rep. Thomas A. Jenkins of Ohio suggested to Sullivan a solution to the deficit: "Save taxes by economizing and see if we could not save a billion dollars a year."[43]

Apparently everyone on the committee agreed that, new taxes notwithstanding, the most pressing political problem for the administration and Congress was to determine what constituted essential spending. While giving lip service to economy in government, Secretary Morgenthau resolutely avoided making specific suggestions for pruning the budget. This avoidance encouraged Rep. Wesley E. Disney of Oklahoma to urge placing the responsibility for cuts squarely on the administration. "I would be most delighted," he said, "to see the fiscal head of the Government furnish the Congress his ideas through a schedule or a list of places where he thinks we ought to economize."[44]

Four days later, on April 28, the committee—apparently without significant Treasury Department input on this matter—began hearing testimony in the hope of identifying specific budget cuts deemed necessary by the public. Chairman Doughton invited witnesses "who may appear before our committee, if they oppose in part or in full the suggestions thus far made," to "suggest what, in their opinion, would be feasible ways of raising an equal amount of revenue which would be lost if the changes they make should be adopted."[45]

To the committee's displeasure, over two hundred lobbyists and other self-serving witnesses paraded before the committee and, despite Doughton's plea for help in determining where to slash expenditures, none offered suggestions for budget cuts. Instead, while generally agreeing that new taxes were required, they merely pressured the committee to exempt some particular constituency.

Twenty-eight of the witnesses recommended revising the Internal Revenue Act of 1938 to distribute the new tax burden more equitably. Ten opposed excess-profit taxes, and ninety-seven opposed excise taxes on specific items. Most of this latter group lobbied for the tobacco and liquor industries, while others opposed new taxes on records, books and journals, recreational equipment, automobiles, gasoline, furs, jewelry, musical instruments, candy, bottled drinks, and even bank checks.[46] Five additional witnesses recommended a national sales tax, and one pleaded for increased farm price supports. However, none of the witnesses seriously questioned the primary supposition of the Treasury Department, that increased taxation was preferable to limiting government spending.

At this juncture in the hearings, President Roosevelt wrote directly to Doughton, voicing the White House's concern that the committee was not taking Morgenthau's tax proposals seriously. He urged Doughton to lead the way toward new taxes: "Secretary Morgenthau has recommended that three and one-half billion of additional taxes should be levied during the coming year to defray in part the extraordinary defense expenditures. This total represents the minimum of our revenue requirements. I hope that you and the other members of your committee will act favorably on his goal." Roosevelt also reminded Doughton that he had argued for new progressive taxes in a budget message earlier in the year. "I suggested," FDR recalled, "a financial policy aimed at collecting progressive taxes out of a higher level of national income. I urged that additional tax measures should be based on the principle of ability to pay. This is still my view." Always politically astute, FDR reminded the committee chairman "that a national-defense program intended to protect our democracy is not going to make the rich richer and the poor poorer."[47]

The president's preference for higher taxes rather than a reduction in nondefense spending failed to satisfy some members of the committee. Republican Rep. Frank Crowther of New York grumbled that the president's letter contained no "guidance as to what we are to do here. It does not say a word about reduction of national expenditures in connection with writing a tax bill." Ohio Rep. Thomas A. Jenkins complained that the president "might as well not have written," since there was no mention of a reduction in government spending. A longtime conservative Republican and vocal New Deal critic, Harold Knutson of Minnesota, felt slighted. "The President," Knutson observed, "wants a bill that will not make the rich richer or the poor poorer, and that means no more taxes. . . . It probably would be helpful if the President would give the matter a little study before he writes the chairman." Knutson added sarcastically, "I think at this point it would be very appropriate to have the record show that the committee is gratified to learn that the President is willing to let Congress continue to raise the money."[48]

Three weeks of testimony from 146 witnesses, including several high-ranking government officials, suggested no new solutions to the nation's impending fiscal crisis. The problem confronting the Ways and Means Committee remained—how to increase military spending and balance the budget, without either borrowing or fueling the fires of inflation. However, on May 15, Arkansas Rep. Wilbur Mills introduced Dr. George S. Benson of Searcy, Arkansas, as witness number 147.

Benson began by describing the relative poverty of his home state, noting that "the citizens of Arkansas are interested in economy—individual economy and governmental economy. They are expert at paring expenses to the bone. They have to be. The average per capita income for all Arkansas residents is only $225 a year. For a family it is $969. If our people were not expert in eliminating unnecessary expense they could not live."[49]

Benson next described the economic lectureship program initiated at Harding College, which brought to the campus experts on state and national fiscal policy.[50] He explained how this program had piqued his interest in the economic future of the United States. He recalled how he had carefully followed the recent committee debate on the proposed tax bill and how he had discussed the proceedings with leading Arkansas citizens, "including the former Governor of Arkansas, the President of the Federal Reserve Bank, and so forth." Benson suggested that the proposals he wished to submit to the committee "are approved by the great majority of the citizens of my State, and I know that their manner of living is entirely consistent with these ideas."[51]

First and most fundamental, Benson argued, rather than increasing taxes, unnecessary government spending must be eliminated. Benson asserted that proposed tax increases, coupled with increased government spending, were dangerously inflationary and might be the first steps towards socialism, revolution, and even, eventually, repressive dictatorship. According to Benson, unless the Ways and Means Committee, the Senate Finance Committee, and the House and Senate Appropriations Committees acted wisely, the Orwellian specter just described would become a reality.[52] Benson cited recent economic developments in western Europe and Russia to illustrate and reinforce his points. Germany and France, Benson pointed out, had suffered in the early 1920s from disastrous inflation, "which completely wiped out German currency and eliminated four-fifths of the value of the franc."[53] Without strict economy in government in addition to increased taxes, Benson predicted that the U.S. national debt would reach $150 billion by the end of the war, making currency devaluation politically irresistible. Benson asked the committee, "Will not some leaders explain that by devaluing the dollar at 20 cents our twenty-two billion dollars of gold will increase in value to eighty-eight billion and then recommend that this eighty-eight billion be used to reduce the indebtedness?"[54]

Benson continued his queries: "What are the facts and where are we headed?" According to Benson, the committee's hearings had produced three important conclusions. First, administration officials were reluctant to recommend specific cuts in expenditures. Second, unjustifiable and unnecessary nondefense expenses were increasing at an alarming pace. And, third, substantial money could be saved by eliminating or reducing spending in some nondefense programs. To buttress his stance, Benson cited a report already submitted to the committee which documented monthly increases in CCC enrollment in late 1940, at a time when the Army and Navy were inducting draftees and soliciting volunteers. In Benson's view, the report provided damaging evidence of fiscal mismanagement, since draft-age CCC enrollees cost taxpayers $12.5 million to maintain.[55]

Benson proposed eliminating the CCC, NYA, federal highway construction subsidies, and soil conservation programs, which would save $1,044,000, in addition to $887,000 that might be pruned elsewhere in the federal budget.[56] He suggested a further $100 million in savings if the fiscal crisis worsened,[57] concluding his remarks to the committee in this fashion:

> I hope you will not think that any of my illustrations are extreme. To me, the questions involved are extremely serious and the danger very real. We can avoid inflation and the evils which follow it, provided the first steps are taken before the House passes the 1941 tax bill that you are planning to recommend. We are at the crossroads—where will we be five or ten years from now? That depends upon whether we continue drifting toward the three disastrous steps I have pictured or whether we change our course. In all seriousness I say, "May God help you."[58]

Present during Benson's testimony was Clinton Davidson, the individual most responsible for Benson's appearance before the committee. He later recalled that, when Benson finished speaking, the committee members stood and applauded. This, according to Davidson, reflected a generally enthusiastic agreement with Benson's recommended solution to the pending fiscal crisis.[59] Chairman Doughton commended Benson: "Not only have you made recommendations, but you have also made concrete suggestions as to how these recommendations can be effectuated." As a result, the chairman ordered Benson's remarks inserted into the *Congressional Record* and urged "every member of Congress to read it."[60]

The ranking Republican congressman on the committee, Allen T. Treadway of Massachusetts, said, "This is the most illuminating statement that has been presented by any witness to this committee." Rep. Frank Crowther of New York added, "If the rules would permit, I would move that every member rise and give the witness a vote of thanks."[61] Treadway regarded Benson's message as the single most important statement on economy in government presented to the Congress during that period; the following day he addressed the entire House, describing Benson's testimony as "the most remarkable statement I have ever listened to in my membership on the committee." He also suggested that the members of the House give Benson's suggestions "most serious consideration."[62]

As a result of these glowing reports from committee members, several national newspapers, including the *New York Times* and the *Chicago Journal of Commerce,* printed Benson's entire speech in their editorial columns on May 16. On May 19 and 20, 1941, the *Journal* ran other stories on the hearings, highlighting Benson's presentation. Eventually the *Journal* distributed over two million reprints of the speech, causing

Benson some embarrassment early the next year, as he tried to explain to the Senate Education and Labor Committee who had financed the reprints and why.[63]

At first Benson was overwhelmed by the positive response from the committee and other members of Congress and the favorable publicity generated by his testimony. However, he remained acutely aware that the most essential element of the American political system, the voting public, also had to pressure Congress to trim the federal budget. Michigan Rep. John D. Dingell reminded Benson that his "fine testimony notwithstanding," the problem must be taken up

> with your people back home. Unless and until demands from home cease, you will get no relief from the Appropriations Committee, and I will assure you of that, and all of your suggestions here will go for naught. It will be a waste of time . . . Now your first problem will be to help us reduce the entire load, to prevail upon your people back home to solve their own problems, and we will cut this Federal tax load down to a third of what it is.[64]

Although Benson had impressively advocated economy in government before the committee, he was not alone in championing this cause. Several prominent congressmen repeatedly had advocated reducing government expenditures, but with little success. Benson came to believe that he should undertake a program of national education, directed at the general public, which would argue more strongly for economy in government. The tax-paying public, he believed, then would encourage legislators to reduce spending and hopefully would defend against the "combined threats of inflation and its political corollaries—socialism, revolution, and dictatorship."[65]

Benson wasted no time before capitalizing on his well-publicized appearance before the House Ways and Means Committee. His hometown newspaper proudly reported that Dr. Benson was attracting national attention because of his strong presentation of the need for national economy. "Harding's president," it stated, "is bringing fame both to himself and the college wherever he goes. Few speakers in Arkansas are in greater demand right now than Dr. Benson and calls come from all over the United States for speeches."[66]

After his return from Washington, he received hundreds of invitations to speak further about his recommendations for economy in government. In his next local speaking engagement, at the Little Rock Rotary Club on June 12, Benson reiterated the gravity of the situation and urged the assembled businessmen to use their influence with Arkansas senators and representatives to call for a reduction in nonessential government spending. He declared, "The time is right for such a movement. . . . The spendthrift psychology of the federal government has proved contagious, and somehow has come to characterize virtually the entire nation. If this is not curbed we shall incur indebtedness from which we shall never recover, and which will certainly lead us to inflation, Socialism, and dictatorship." However, he added, the "greatest value would not be merely the billions of dollars saved, important as that is. The greatest value would be the example of thrift and economy set before the nation and which would help in restoring determination for economic independence on the part of the masses." To emphasize this point, Benson added that Congress at the time was "besieged with appeals for appropriations which ten years ago we would never have thought of carrying to the federal government. This is because the impression has been given all over the nation that the head is off the barrel at Washington and that money is being poured out and that somebody is going to get it."[67]

He made similar pleas for economy in government before the Advertising Clubs of Kansas City on June 23; the Bureau of Public Roads in Washington, D.C., on July 2; the Chambers of Commerce in Nashville, New Orleans, and Kansas City in August; and the State Public Expenditures Survey in Milwaukee and the Rotary Club of Joplin, Missouri (a speech broadcast over local radio) in September. In October, he spoke to the Rotary Clubs of Birmingham, Shreveport, and Little Rock; the County Taxpayers Association of Council Bluffs, Iowa; and the Rotary Clubs of Minneapolis and St. Paul, Minnesota, and Baltimore, Maryland. Later in 1941, he spoke to the Lions Club of Enid, Oklahoma; the Rotary Club of Chicago; the combined Civic Clubs and the Rubber Manufacturers of Akron, Ohio; and civic clubs in Joliet, Illinois; East St. Louis, Illinois; Long Island, New York; New York City; Wilmington, Delaware; Lincoln, Nebraska; and Boston. He also spoke to the State Bankers Association in Des Moines, Iowa; the Lumbermen's Association of Spokane, Washington; the Rotary Clubs in Kansas City and Tulsa, Oklahoma; and the Chamber of Commerce in Nashville.[68] At each meeting, Benson hammered home his key themes: the current fiscal crisis, excessive government spending, and the associated threat of socialism. He issued a barrage of figures, warnings, and threats of political disaster, unless, as he urged, the public demanded from Congress significant spending restraint.

Benson's newfound notoriety received an additional boost when the

Scripps-Howard Newspaper Alliance asked him to write a series of articles on economy in government. Accompanying them were "two feature stories, one concerning the college and another about Dr. Benson."[69] The central ideas contained in these articles were distilled in Benson's rousing speech, "America at the Crossroads," which, given repeatedly, became his standard exposition of economy in government. In November 1941, this speech was aired twice on radio stations in Baltimore and New York City. The stations distributed copies to approximately six hundred other NBC affiliate stations for rebroadcast.[70] In Texas, Benson delivered this speech to civic clubs in Lubbock, to the student body of the University of Houston, and to the general public on the Lone Star Radio Network. Additionally, in an interview broadcast to the nation over NBC, Benson was interviewed by Oklahoma Rep. Wesley E. Disney, a member of the House Ways and Means Committee.[71]

During his whirlwind speaking tours across the United States, Benson met and gained the respect of several very wealthy and influential corporate executives. While in New York City during the first week of December, 1941, Benson addressed the National Tax Foundation, where he received a large silver medal in recognition of his efforts to encourage economy in national government. Among approximately 750 people from twenty-eight states attending were Alfred P. Sloan, chairman of the board of General Motors, and Louis H. Brown, president of the Tax Foundation and head of Johns-Manville Corporation. Brown presented the medal to Benson, lauding his committee testimony: "A number of you present know well that committees of Congress are difficult to impress. But George S. Benson went before the Congressional Ways and Means Committee last May and made the most remarkable impression in recent years, with a plain common sense appeal. This common sense appeal for economy found immediate nationwide recognition."[72]

Benson's national publicity, multiple speaking engagements, and radio broadcasts finally bore fruit in spring 1942, when he again appeared before Congress to argue for fiscal responsibility. He had made a second congressional appearance before the Senate Finance Committee on August 21, 1941, as it was considering the Tax Bill of 1941. He told the committee that he believed any new revenue should be raised in the form of an income tax. However, he strongly argued against any new taxes and in favor of a drastic reduction in nondefense spending, to produce an additional $2 billion to be used for defense.[73]

During this third appearance in Washington, Benson spoke before the Senate Committee on Labor and Education, which was debating abolition of the CCC and the NYA. His leading supporter in the Senate during this period was Harry Byrd of Virginia, who earlier had been instrumental in amending the Tax Bill of 1941 to establish a joint congressional committee on economy in government. Byrd had arranged Benson's appearance before the Senate committee.[74]

George's testimony once again received front-page headlines in most national newspapers. It set off a flurry of debate within Congress that eventually included the administration. In late January 1942, a group of twenty Harding College students who had been receiving funds from the NYA involved FDR in the debate over abolishing the NYA and CCC. They wrote to Roosevelt, Secretary of the Treasury Morgenthau, and Sen. Harry Byrd, asking that their names be taken off the NYA rolls, effective February 1, 1942. They recommended that their allotment instead be appropriated for national defense. They stated:

> We have been anxious to do our part to assist in the great defense program of our Nation. Being working students at first we did not know just what we could do. We have also thought of the growing national debt which we understand is expected to reach $110,000,000,000 by the end of the next fiscal year.
>
> We have also observed a scarcity of labor which now affects our own community very noticeably. Accordingly, it occurred to us that we could secure employment and make our way in college without receiving National Youth Administration assistance. Finding that it is possible for us to secure other employment by which we may continue in college, we feel that it is not right for us to accept the National Youth Administration assistance in the face of this great emergency.
>
> We desire, however, that our allotment not be used to increase the allotment of some other college, which probably needs the assistance no more than our own college, and where the students could likely find other employment just as we have found that we can get other employment here. This sacrifice is being made as a contribution to the defense of our Nation.
>
> We are indeed happy that work is now abundant, that we do not longer need the National Youth Administration assistance, and that we can offer this contribution to the defense of our Nation.[75]

After reviewing the letter, NYA Director Aubrey Williams ridiculed the suggestion.[76] If Harding College students did not require NYA assistance, he noted, their allotment would not be given instead to national defense, but to students in other colleges. In defense of the NYA, Williams claimed that

> the NYA student work program has made it possible for 204 students
> to work their way through Harding College, Searcy. It has come to our
> attention that students at Harding College . . . are now able to remain
> in school without NYA jobs. We are very glad to learn that this is the
> case, since in the last four weeks we have received reports from re-
> sponsible officials of 1,249 colleges certifying that 14,416 students are
> being forced to drop out of college and universities because of curtail-
> ment of NYA funds . . . In other colleges in Arkansas 179 students are
> being forced to drop out because of curtailment of NYA funds, accord-
> ing to reports received from college officials in the state. Transfer of
> funds from Harding will enable 20 of these students to continue their
> education.[77]

Williams also issued a highly critical press release, in which he labeled Benson the "ring leader of a so-called economy drive," apparently
viewing with suspicion Benson's motives for advocating fiscal restraint.
Benson retorted through the press that he was "honored to be called
'ring leader' of an economy drive" and that he believed "everyone should
be soberly interested in preserving the American way."[78]

Senator Byrd quickly rose to defend Benson and the Harding students. In his speech to the Senate on February 3, 1942, he attacked Williams as "an arrogant and dictatorial bureaucrat" who inexplicably had
condemned efforts to save government money. Byrd added, "One would
think Mr. Williams would welcome such a statement as that made by the
students at Harding College, who said they would save and work so
they could pay their way through college and not be dependent on the
federal government. Director Williams evidently prefers to destroy the
initiative and the self-reliance of the American youth and to condemn
those who attempt to make themselves self-sustaining."[79]

The flap over the NYA continued on Capitol Hill for several months.
It kept Benson and his economy-in-government program constantly in
the news and elicited numerous supportive editorials.[80] A Chicago editor
applauded the Harding students for supplying "a cheering episode in an
otherwise dreary period of our national history. Only Aubrey Williams,"
he noted, "head of the NYA, whose job would be abolished if a few
more students followed the example of those at Harding, has denounced
the action."[81]

The adverse publicity may have prompted Roosevelt to pressure Williams to soften his stance. With a noticeable change of heart, ten days after his initial response, Williams complimented the students: "You are indeed fortunate in finding such employment, and I am deeply appreciative of the fine spirit you have exhibited."[82] This national front-page publicity surrounding the NYA and Harding College preceded Benson's testimony before the Senate Committee on Education and Labor. Apparently in response to a joint House and Senate recommendation, Tennessee Sen. Kenneth D. McKellar introduced Senate Bill S. 2295 on February 23, 1942, proposing to terminate both the NYA and CCC.[83]

In response, on March 24, 1942, Federal Security Administrator Paul V. McNutt introduced into the hearing record a supportive letter from Franklin Roosevelt, in which he applauded the efforts of the NYA and CCC and defended their continuation as part of a comprehensive war effort.[84]

Despite this open White House support for the programs, the committee heard reports favoring abolition of the two agencies by the National Education Association, the American Association of School Administrators, and the American Farm Bureau. These groups argued that vocational education and defense training should be administered by the local schools and that state and local agencies should have full responsibility for and control over all public education, including vocational training.[85]

On the other hand, three prominent college presidents—Dr. Edward C. Elliott, Purdue University; Dr. James H. Richmond, Murray State Teachers College, Murray, Kentucky; and Monsignor James F. Kelley, Seton Hall College, South Orange, New Jersey—testified in favor of retaining the disputed programs. They argued that many students at their institutions could not continue their education without federal assistance. Kelley claimed that an informal poll of college presidents at a New Jersey meeting had showed unanimous support for restoring the NYA's pre-1941 budget and increasing appropriations for it in the 1942–43 budget. In reply to Kelley's testimony, Sen. Robert A. Taft of Ohio presented a stinging rebuttal after he spotted an apparent misuse of NYA funds; he questioned Kelley pointedly about his choice of words. Obviously feeling that the primary benefit from NYA funds should be derived by the students and not by the school itself, Taft said, "You referred to this as assistance to universities and colleges. Is that the way the group generally looks on it?" President Kelley apparently noticed his poor choice of words and admitted that the funds were simply "assistance to the individual students, . . . who might otherwise not have the opportunity of attending a college or university," and not a source of revenue for the college.[86]

The debate intensified during the testimony of President Richmond, when Senator McKellar introduced into the record the now-famous letter from Harding College's NYA students, along with a second letter from D. M. Scott, an aroused citizen of New Smyrna Beach, Florida. Scott blasted NYA Director Aubrey Williams, charged college students supported by NYA with cowardice, and proposed eliminating the NYA. Scott fumed that to "buy Bonds for Defense" fell rather flat

> on many ears and fails to register in many pocketbooks when such things are known and nothing being done to stop them. "Buy a Bond" to pay the fat salary of an Aubrey Williams that they may, at your expense, pay spineless young men and women to remain in college and thus be deferred from military service. The truth is pretty damned raw isn't it? Thanks a million, Senator McKellar; we are backing you to the limit. When the enclosures have served your purpose, please return them for my files. I'd like my grandchildren to know, if they lose their liberty, why they lost it.[87]

Obviously irritated by hearing these letters read before the committee, Richmond turned his wrath on Benson, whom he depicted as a demagogue who probably wrote the students' letters for them to gain publicity for himself.[88]

Because of the earlier public controversy over the NYA letter, committee members who were hostile to Benson, including the committee chairman, Utah Sen. Elbert D. Thomas, strongly objected to Benson's characterization of the CCC and NYA as "weights about the ankles of America while she was trying to win a war."[89] Thomas personally viewed Benson as a "publicity hound" for Harding College. As evidence, Thomas voiced his strong suspicion that the *Chicago Journal of Commerce* would not have reprinted two million copies of Benson's May 1941 speech before the House Ways and Means Committee without some motive other than public service.

In rebuttal, Benson testified before the committee that many different groups had circulated those reprints to satisfy public demand and to exhibit support for abolishing the CCC and the NYA. Benson claimed that "90 percent of the public now believes that there is no good or sufficient reason for continuing these agencies created to furnish relief for men of military age."[90] Indeed, Benson viewed his warm reception by the House Ways and Means Committee, the Senate Finance Committee, and the American public during the previous ten months of speaking engagements as reflections of this growing public sentiment. "There are things that the public has begun to have a feeling about and believe in," Benson intoned, "and they are immediately moved by it, and they are behind it."[91]

Although the Senate Committee on Education and Labor did not laud Benson's testimony as had the other two congressional bodies, the tacit condemnation of Benson by some committee members did not signal a major shift in the position of Congress, which voted in July 1943 to abolish the NYA and CCC. As far as Benson was concerned, the entire affair had proved that, at last, the American people had shaken off their lethargy and persuaded their congressmen to vote against inflationary legislation.

Benson was extremely gratified that his efforts to eliminate waste in government were beginning to show results. Success stiffened his resolve to organize a program to warn the American people about the dangers of creeping socialism and inflationary New Deal programs. Squarely in step with the ideological arguments of what Leo Ribuffo labels the Old Christian Right,[92] Benson joined a rising chorus of bitter critics of the New Deal, who feared that these social and economic programs were leading the United States in the wrong direction. In particular, Benson sensed that Americans were losing sight of the ideals which he felt had made the country great—belief in God, constitutional government, and the free-enterprise system.

While speaking to the Arkansas Bottlers of Carbonated Beverages, Benson called on them to "use their influence to see that a foundation is laid now for the preservation of the American way of life after the war is over." Benson offered four suggestions for laying this foundation. He urged the bottlers to insist upon (1) a tremendous reduction in nondefense spending, (2) effective price controls, (3) re-education of the American people concerning the values associated with the American form of government, and (4) the election of a strong Congress composed of men "with backbone who will stand up against pressure groups in the interest of the American way."[93]

As a result of his crisscrossing the country in 1941 to promote economy in government, Benson and the NEP became well known. Throughout the war, Benson kept up a grueling schedule of public speaking engagements which eventually led him into some of the most influential corporate boardrooms in America. Benson cultivated for the NEP a corporate following as well as a popular one, and the NEP and Harding College received large endowments from big business during the war. For example, Sterling Morton, president of Morton Salt Corporation, donated money to purchase a 51-acre farm adjacent to the Harding campus.[94] Benson used the popularity of the NEP's message as a lever to pry open the coffers of major corporate sponsors such as DuPont, General Motors, Standard Oil, U.S. Steel, Bethlehem Steel, Republic Steel, Armco Steel, International Harvester, and Quaker Oats.[95]

These sizable gifts gave Harding College a solid financial base, made possible improvements in its physical plant, and launched the NEP's promotion of Americanism. Harding's endowment fund grew rapidly during the war years, at a time when the student body was shrinking. During 1943, for example, gifts to the school totaled over $100,000. Many came "as a result of Dr. Benson's activity in behalf of national economy, and represent[ed] expressions of appreciation on the part of many donors for his work and service to the college."[96]

After Congress abolished the NYA and the CCC, Benson, through the NEP, tackled the broad issue of increased government spending, attempting to prove that inescapably it brought greater government control. Benson warned that federal aid for farmers, public education, or other social programs eventually would erode the public morale and push the nation farther down the path toward socialism. To him such aid was a political remedy worse than the disease—"like strychnine," Benson intoned, "you just try it once."[97] What was in view, Benson predicted, was the destruction of the free-enterprise system. Federal aid, he charged, led directly to "federal control within a decade, to be followed within one more decade by nationalization of industrial production, transportation, utilities, and agriculture."[98] The United States, Benson believed, was already well down the road to state socialism because "we've allowed the propagandists to criticize competition and criticize private ownership of the tools of production, so that we've gotten to where we're afraid to tell the truth about our American way of life."[99]

Benson privately decided that the NEP should combat "subversive elements" who misled young people with false claims that capitalism was socially destructive.[100] To correct this misinformation, Benson decided to preach the traditional doctrines of political and economic conservatism and to avoid openly partisan politics. Having learned in 1941 that, if "you are going to move Washington to do the things it ought to do, you have got to move public opinion," Benson envisioned a grassroots campaign for "Godliness and Patriotism."[101]

His primary vehicle for this assault on public opinion and belief in behalf of Americanism was the NEP. According to Donald Garner, who conducted a detailed study of Benson's speaking program, Benson's aggregate average yearly audience for his speaking engagements was sixty to eighty thousand, not including his radio audiences. Garner also found that, between 1941 and 1963, Benson averaged two hundred speeches per year.[102] From its inception, according to Benson, the NEP was not designed to be a political organization to advocate partisan political ideals or to endorse political candidates or parties.[103] Instead, its sole purpose was to educate the American people about the potential dangers of increased government control over the everyday lives of American citizens. Benson believed that the most recognizable element in the battle for control of government was the unrestrained federal spending implicit in New Deal philosophy and slogans. He argued that increased government control inevitably would accompany increased accountability; "the question involved whether or not we want to keep a decentralized government with states rights and local responsibilities and local freedoms, or whether we want to become a highly centralized government with a regimented people." Benson later disclosed to the House Committee on Education that his earlier fears gradually were being realized. He reminded the committee that "a Supreme Court decision has already declared that the Federal Government may control that which it subsidizes. Consequently, only a directive would be necessary at any time to establish Federal control over the public schools of the nation after they have once been subsidized by the Federal Government." As far as Benson was concerned, "individual freedom and prosperity go hand in hand, while regimentation and poverty likewise go hand in hand."[104]

While World War II demanded a reallocation of federal funds and caused the termination of most New Deal "make-work" programs, it did not alter the pace and extent of Benson's one-man campaign on behalf of Americanism. The Beech Aircraft Company of Wichita, Kansas, gave Benson a small airplane which allowed him to tour the nation speaking to hundreds of civic groups[105] and on various radio shows. Thus, by means of rebroadcasts and printed transcripts in at least 250 weekly newspapers, Benson's message was disseminated to millions of people during the war. Beginning in 1942, Benson had his own weekly radio program on KARK in Little Rock, Arkansas, and on WMC in Memphis, Tennessee. By October 1943, when radio station WKW in Akron, Ohio, was added, the number of major stations using Benson's programs totaled eleven.[106]

Benson had seized the opportunity to exploit further the printed page. Beginning in March 1942, he wrote a syndicated newspaper column, "Looking Ahead," which the Western Newspaper Union sent at first to three thousand mostly weekly newspapers, but later to many larger daily metropolitan newspapers also. In Arkansas and Missouri, roughly 150 newspapers, with a combined circulation of 127,000, used his articles.[107] According to Philip S. Rose of the *Saturday Evening Post,* by June 1944, "Looking Ahead" appeared in over 2,500 small-town newspapers in 46 states, either on the front page or in the editorial section, with Benson's picture and byline.[108]

Benson's speaking itinerary for fall 1942 included stops in Chicago, New Orleans, Little Rock, and Memphis to address business and civic groups. In the next few years, he added Boston, Cincinnati, Cleveland, Dallas, Houston, New York City, Philadelphia, St. Louis, and Wichita, as his audiences grew in size and in financial and social prestige.[109] With a dynamic and persuasive speaking style born of years of preaching, and with an evangelistic economic message geared to his conservative audiences, Benson reiterated to these business leaders the importance of free markets and constitutional government. At the Iron and Steel Institute's fifty-fifth annual meeting at the Waldorf-Astoria Hotel in New York, he pleaded for it to take the lead in "reselling our own people on the fundamentals of our way of life." "For the last fifteen years," he observed, "a trend has been accelerated in this country which criticizes private ownership of the tools of production and brands owners of capital as 'profiteers, coupon clippers, and economic royalists.'" Defending the prosperous with this thinly veiled stab at the theme of many of Franklin Roosevelt's "Fireside Chats," Benson asserted that individuals who had been willing to take a risk should reap the rewards.[110]

Speeches to thousands of such prominent and influential businessmen, his congressional testimony, and the rapidly growing media coverage made George Benson and the message of his NEP increasingly popular. Invitations to speak multiplied, as did financial gifts to Harding College. A climax was reached in January 1946, with the receipt of what Benson claimed was the largest single contribution to Harding College by an individual. Since George Pepperdine already was on record as having contributed $25,000 in 1936 to help pay off the existing college debt, the new record sum must have exceeded that generous gift. Appropriately, this sizable contribution came from sources outside the Churches of Christ, having been solicited by Benson while he was defending free enterprise.[111]

Encouraged by his success, Benson in January 1945 championed a new cause before the House and Senate Committees on Education and Labor. In both appearances, Benson opposed increased federal aid for state and local education. To these committees he voiced his concern about the ability of local school districts to control their own programs and supply their own funds. The real need, according to Benson, was for local school districts to "set our own house in order, rather than ask for Federal aid to keep a disorderly house supplied with unnecessary funds." Benson complained that one of the "greatest fallacies in regard to Federal aid is the implication that Federal aid does not cost the states anything, but that on the contrary, they are receiving something for nothing."[112] Benson cautioned:

> It should be remembered that Washington has no money to give anybody. Washington can only tax the states to get money with which to aid the states. We should remember, moreover, that such "aid" will always be weighted with a group of bureaucrats and political hangers-on, to be paid by the same states that are getting the aid. So in the name of economy and common sense let us keep local responsibility and operate as economically as possible.[113]

This testimony, and Benson's growing reputation among some congressmen as a skillful college administrator,[114] made Benson sought after as a major national speaker opposing federal aid to education.[115] In November 1946, Benson debated Dr. Ralph Norton, head of the Education Department of Columbia University, on federal aid to education. The debate was heard nationwide on the Mutual Broadcasting System.[116] Two years later, Benson debated Louisiana's Sen. Allen J. Ellender over WGN Radio in Chicago, on the same subject.[117] And in December 1948, prior to another appearance before the House Committee on Education and Labor, he again opposed federal aid to education in a speech broadcast over the American Broadcasting Network.[118] On each occasion, Benson reemphasized that the real danger implicit in federal aid to education was increased control by the federal government. It was Benson's firm conviction that, "should we start federal aid to our public schools now, we would see virtual federal control within a decade, to be followed within one more decade by nationalization of industrial production, transportation, utilities, and agriculture."[119]

By the end of the decade, Dr. George S. Benson and the NEP had generated a tremendous amount of favorable publicity selling Americanism. Benson parlayed this favorable publicity into the resources needed to construct an effective propaganda organization. Such a stunning degree of success must have been very gratifying to Benson personally and surely stimulated his already ample ambition. Further, Harding College, once financially beleaguered, benefited greatly from the growing support of wealthy and powerful business patrons. To thousands of Americans at the beginning of the 1940s, including hundreds of Benson's new friends in important positions, his message championing economy in government struck a responsive chord. It resonated more strongly as the decade progressed. Regardless of his original motives, Benson's program had mushroomed into a financial bonanza for the college, and at every opportunity he took advantage of his newfound fame. The success of his campaign exceeded his greatest expectations, and the augmented income and generally favorable notoriety for the college further stimulated his appetite for hard work and increased his dedication to preserving American free enterprise and constitutional government.

During World War II, Benson transformed what were essentially patriotic and nostalgic platitudes about America's political heritage and accomplishments into a convincing defense of the free-market economy. Defending this economy in turn became a worthy motive for winning the war. Benson proclaimed economy in government to be a patriotic duty; as a result, the NEP at Harding College represented an idealized image of what many Americans demanded of their own government—fiscal responsibility, extreme self-sacrifice, and undying loyalty and patriotism.

Throughout the 1940s, Benson gained important allies in the business community. His initial successes, however, did not diminish the magnitude of the threats he believed faced the American nation and its free institutions. To preserve the American way, Benson believed, much more remained to be done.

3

Freedom Forums
and an Informed Citizenry:
The National Education Program's
Post–World War II
Anticommunism Crusade

As a forceful and articulate conservative spokesman known throughout the nation, George Benson depicted the United States' entry into World War II as the beginning of a crusade to preserve the American political and economic systems. However, he could equate military victory with the triumph of Americanism only as long as the war raged. The end of the war forced Benson to replace the imperative for Allied victory over fascism with the threat of Cold War Communist aggression, as a psychological, religious, and historical motive for reaffirming the basic tenets of Americanism. The substitution was not difficult for Benson, who viewed an apathetic and war-weary public as easy ideological prey for what he believed to be "self-deceived liberals."[1] These liberal elements, Benson felt, at best were unknowingly introducing socialism in the government and at worst were betraying the country to a worldwide Communist conspiracy.[2] Accordingly, Benson invested NEP with a new mission—to expose America to the potential dangers of Communism. Not only would this effort enlighten the American voter, but also it would reinforce the legitimacy of private property and profit ethics, which Benson deemed crucial to the American economic community, especially big business. Combining the affirmation of free-enterprise economics with anticommunism made it possible for NEP to utilize directly the efforts, skills, and monetary support of major American businesses to educate their employees about Benson's brand of Americanism. This combination began a long-lasting, mutually beneficial relationship between conservative activism and institutional self-interest. Benson's ideology of Americanism strengthened the nation's positive perception of big business; and big business, in turn, contributed million of dollars to Harding College and its NEP program.

The NEP's most effective tool for direct political education of the general public, and the beginning of its formal relationship with big business, was the "Freedom Forum," initiated at Harding College in 1949. The forum meetings were designed by Benson to serve two purposes. First, they provided information about the merits of Christian morality, constitutional government, and the free-enterprise system to employees of corporate sponsors. At the same time, the forums were workshops in which NEP guest speakers and instructors exposed conferees to history, comparative economics, and government; to new methods of disseminating adult Americanism education; and to "inspirational speeches to return home and to reach the people with the freedom philosophy."[3]

The NEP's plan for what it hoped would be "informative workshops highlighted by inspirational persuasive speakers" grew out of a wartime cooperative effort by the federal government and big business to sell to the American public various domestic programs that the government deemed essential to the war effort. Business and government had urged the formation of a joint committee of the Advertising Council, composed of representatives from the Association of National Advertisers and the American Association of Advertising Agencies, to conduct nationwide publicity and advertising campaigns to urge collecting scrap metal, to sell war bonds, and to prepare the public for food rationing and other restrictions thought essential for victory.[4]

After the war, the joint committee predictably sought to perpetuate its usefulness through an appropriate peacetime project. Its chairman, Don Belding, president of Foote, Cone, and Belding, one of the nation's largest advertising agencies, met with George Benson in fall 1948 in Los Angeles. He proposed launching a "nationwide seminar to attract business, industrial and professional leaders to discuss the basic internal problems of America" and to "plan an educational campaign to reach the public."[5]

The Advertising Council probably chose NEP as an appropriate vehicle to initiate the proposed seminar and educational campaign because of Benson's national reputation as a conservative spokesman. An editorial in the archconservative *Oklahoma City Times* appraised Benson as the "leading individual figure in thinking America's battle to preserve the American way of life." According to the editor, Benson had been "allotted more newspaper space, given more addresses and radio time, and attracted larger audiences than any other living American, and he has battled sturdily to jar this country back into a sense of fundamental realities."[6]

The Advertising Council's proposal meshed perfectly with Benson's plans for an educational program directed at the grassroots level of American politics. With initial sponsorship by the joint committee, in February 1949 Benson held the first of many successful Freedom Forums on the campus of Harding College.[7] Although Benson already had begun an adult education program on America's economic heritage, the new seminars were not limited to the economic education of local businessmen. Instead they encompassed "economic education, factory programs, and the teaching of the American way of life," to give "top business management executives [throughout the nation] detailed knowledge of the principles underlying the American economic system."[8]

By directing this new program to top business management executives and by providing them with the tools to educate their own employees concerning the benefits of the free-enterprise system, Benson anticipated strong corporate response and financial sponsorship, not only for his future Freedom Forums but also for the audiovisual educational programs NEP was developing. Eventually, each of these forums drew several hundred business and civic leaders who then were responsible for transmitting the information received from NEP back to their local civic organizations, businesses, and schools. Such a mutually beneficial arrangement encouraged continued corporate sponsorship of the forums.[9]

Further, Benson hoped that corporate sponsorship of the forums might help to insure the financial security of Harding College. As a result, many of his critics, such as consumer advocate Vance Packard, viewed the forums as merely a cynical ploy to raise money.[10] Whether or not Benson's motives were entirely altruistic, he firmly believed that the Freedom Forums were the best way to reach the voters of America with "the facts about our economic system, our constitutional government, and our spiritual heritage."[11] Statistics suggest that he succeeded. As the acknowledged "thought leaders" of their companies, they in turn helped to educate over nine million employees. Announcements and invitations for the first forums were sent to most major corporations, to business and advertising organizations, to many labor unions, to faculty from other colleges and universities, and to many fraternal and civic organizations in the nation. In short, the Freedom Forums were open to a cross-section of American society; but, from the outset, they were aimed at and attended primarily by middle-management executives from American industry who came as guests of Harding College and the City of Searcy, Arkansas. Because of the limited facilities on the campus, enrollment in the first forum was limited to 160. Most people who attended stayed in the homes of Harding College faculty members or other citizens of the city. In attendance at later forums were officers and members of the major labor unions, representatives of hundreds of educational institutions, and clergymen from many different denominations.[12] Most of the subsequent forums accommodated more participants, and most of those attending were top executives representing some of the nation's largest corporations. According to NEP files, during the next fifteen years, over 3,600 executives representing over one thousand companies and organizations attended the educational forums.[13]

From its inception, NEP's program focused on "building an informed citizenry." According to Benson, the responsibility to carry out this task fell on the shoulders of the business, political, and educational leaders present. Typically, in an opening forum address, Benson warned that "high ideals of government do not live from generation to generation just because they are right nor because the pattern of government had been well legislated. . . . We need to build ideals into the hearts of each oncoming generation and . . . into the hearts of those in control of the government. In America, this means the general public." These ideals, Benson warned, had a deadly enemy in the international Communist movement, which openly sought to destroy the religious and moral foundations of the "constitutional government and private enterprise" backbone of America. More alarming for Benson was what he saw as the increasing evidence of Communist "Fifth-Column" activities within the United States borders. Forum supporters, Benson believed, had a solemn duty—not to mention a strong self-interest—to make employees, friends, and associates aware of this ideological challenge. On one such occasion, Benson commented on a recent disclosure that more than "150 Communist leaders in America have been convicted of teaching the overthrow of the government by force. This should indicate what they [the Communists] have in mind."[14]

Despite such strong anti-Communist statements, Benson claimed that he always attempted to allow those who did not necessarily agree with his position opportunity to speak freely at the forum programs. Although there is little evidence to support this claim, in his opening statement at the forums, Benson almost always presented to his audience a disclaimer regarding his position on the subject at hand. He proudly stated that NEP was bringing to the meeting people from various parts of the country to discuss the many sides of the issue. He emphasized to the audience that NEP did not necessarily

> assume responsibility for everything that everybody says, nor is it a foregone conclusion that we will agree with everything that everybody says. But this is a forum. We are bringing men who we believe will challenge your imagination and stimulate your thinking. We expect this to be a great forum. We invite questions at the close of addresses and there will be opportunity for comments from the floor. We need your participation to make this a really effective forum.[15]

With the implementation of "scholarly" methodology, Benson found an ample supply of willing conservative spokesmen, as many prominent scholars, newsmakers, and government officials participated in the NEP's numerous Freedom Forums. Dr. Robert Millikan, a Nobel Prize–winning physicist from the California Institute of Technology and a strong supporter of the free-enterprise system, was the keynote speaker at the first Freedom Forum. Millikan's philosophy corresponded closely to that of the NEP, and in his autobiography he illustrated his belief in the free-enterprise system by stating that a "janitor in the laboratories of CIT receives a real wage which is somewhat more than one-third of the salary of the average full professor's at the institute. In the laboratories of the Soviet Union, for example, where the so-called 'dictatorship of the proletariat' prevails, the janitor gets less than one-fifteenth the salary of the full professor."[16]

T. C. Kirkpatrick, formerly of the FBI and then editor of *Counterattack,* a prominent anti-Communist journal, also spoke at the first Freedom Forum, along with the director of the forum, Ken Wells, and the regular participants from Harding College, who were George Benson, Dr. Clifton Ganus, and Dr. J. D. Bales.[17] Other NEP staff members assigned to the Freedom Forums included Glenn "Bud" Green, a former United Press International war correspondent; General William P. Campbell, a former military attaché in London during World War II who eventually became the U.S. Army's assistant finance chief; and Howard W. Bennett, a former executive with General Electric.[18] In addition, speaking on the merits of the free-enterprise system and constitutional government at the first few forums were representatives of Arkansas Power and Light, Armco Steel, J. I. Case Company, Caterpillar Tractor, General Electric, General Motors, International Harvester, Kellogg Foods, Pepsi, Quaker Oats, and Republic Steel.[19] Making regular appearances at the forums also were almost all of Arkansas's state and nationally elected officials, including Gov. Orval Faubus, Sen. John L. McClellan, Rep. Wilbur Mills, and future governor Winthrop Rockefeller, each of whom made several appearances at the Freedom Forums in the early 1950s.[20]

As Leo Ribuffo and M. J. Heale have argued, in the late 1940s and the early 1950s, Benson and NEP were perfectly positioned to capitalize on the long-standing cultural fear of government-imposed restrictions on individual freedom. Benson's NEP echoed the message of many other activist groups in America who did not consider themselves ultraconservative but who saw, in the "creeping socialism" of the New Deal, a conspiracy between powerful forces outside and inside the country to undermine the basic values of the American system.[21] Many Democrats as well as Republicans pictured an America in imminent danger of becoming a "godless, socialist society just one step removed from Communist dictatorship." In all of this, Benson saw a "calculated plot and organized onslaught of propaganda being made by subversive groups against our system of private capital and profit."[22] As far as Benson was concerned, education in favor of Americanism and against Communism was of primary importance to the defense of the nation, and his financial backers were in complete agreement. As the Cold War intensified, so did the rhetoric of NEP propaganda against Communism, until an equally vicious counterattack by its opponents reached fever pitch in the years before the election of 1964.

From NEP's inception, Benson had felt a sense of urgency to reeducate the American people about traditional values, and post–World War II events intensified his concern to propagate Americanism. In the early 1950s, Benson's growing fears concerning the "Communist menace" and his intense desire to warn Americans about its dangers surfaced in NEP's printed material, films, and Freedom Forum agendas. In fact, in step with the increasing complexity of the Cold War between the United States and the Soviet Union, the forums not only became increasingly anti-Communist but also acquired a decidedly more negative tone, in contrast to the generally affirmative character of the early NEP.[23]

The NEP's pointed anti-Communist attacks drew a great deal of criticism in the media, especially in the late 1950s and the early 1960s, but national and international events convinced Benson and his associates that the criticism was largely unfounded. Further, Benson determined that NEP should remain an outspoken voice against the perceived spread of Communist influence in America. The seemingly endless conflicts and apparent losses that American prestige suffered during the Cold War, according to Benson, had a dramatic effect on America's self-image and on public opinion. The NEP staff believed that the latter could be rallied to resurrect traditional values and to blunt the threats of socialism at home and communism abroad.

By the early 1950s, news reports of Communist victories over America's former allies in the Balkans, Eastern Europe, China, and North Korea made Benson's charges of domestic Communist infiltration and subversion seem more credible to a wide range of Americans. As Ellen Schrecker has observed, both

> Democrats and Republicans threw themselves into the domestic Cold War against the American Communist party. Local Communists suddenly became potential Soviet agents, who, if they were not about to take over the government, could nonetheless subvert it in more subtle ways, or at least, send vital secrets back to Moscow. Each politician had his own assessment of the extent of this conspiracy and his own formula for fighting it. But almost everyone agreed that the danger was immense.[24]

The NEP rode the tide of this growing awareness of alleged Communist infiltration by informing Americans directly about this conspiracy. Thus NEP sought out those speakers whose oratory and profoundly anti-Communist messages articulated a conspiratorial mindset. If there had been a sense of urgency in the message of the NEP, it certainly intensified during the anti-Communist "hysteria" of the 1950s. It was this issue more than any other that bonded the leading ultraconservatives in the Republican party and the leaders of NEP in the eyes of their opponents. These critics claimed that, by the 1960s, Harding College had become "perhaps the most prolific center of aggressive anti-Communist propaganda in the United States."[25]

Stimulated by the increasing criticism of its activities and opposition to its message, the tenth Freedom Forum featured several outspoken anti-

Communists. The keynote speaker, Dr. Louis Budenz, a Fordham University professor, was a former editor of the Communist *Daily Worker* and author of numerous exposés of domestic Communist subversion. He had been the government's chief witness against eleven Communist party leaders who had been deported after a sensational trial in New York in 1949.[26] Budenz praised Wisconsin Sen. Joseph McCarthy for ferreting out Communists in government, an effort that in Budenz's opinion was timely, since the "infiltration of the Communist Party in the State Department has had a drastic influence on our foreign policy in that China and Korea have been taken over by the Reds, due largely to delay in taking a stand against Russia."[27]

Herbert Philbrick, another popular lecturer and virulent anti-Communist, first came to Harding in 1954. By then he was well known throughout the country for his popular weekly dramatic television series, *I Led Three Lives*, which graphically depicted his nine hectic years as an FBI double agent. During those years, while working in a critical defense industry position with top national security clearance, he passed sensitive defense information to the Soviet KGB. At the same time, he gleaned important secret information from the Russians and passed it back to the FBI. At the fifteenth Freedom Forum, when Philbrick told of his years as a counterspy, a capacity crowd gave him a "standing ovation that signified the emotions that each individual felt for the many hazardous and nightmarish incidents that the speaker was forced to accept during his period with the Communists."[28]

Philbrick became a regular participant in the Freedom Forums and never failed to stress the dangers of a budding Communist conspiracy in America. At Harding in 1965, Philbrick even raised the issue of alleged Communist complicity in the assassination of President Kennedy. He echoed national criticism of the Warren Commission's findings and stressed the role of the alleged Communist conspiracy in both the assassination and an alleged coverup.[29]

In his speech, "The Inside Untold Story of the Assassination of President Kennedy," Philbrick reiterated familiar NEP anti-Communist rhetoric. Benson had long claimed that an atheistic Communist movement and its propaganda were the source of major problems in the United States. Philbrick pressed the point further by identifying the three-pronged attack of Communist propaganda. First, Philbrick revealed, came Communist propaganda intended "to lull the American people to sleep by promoting defeatism and pacifism." This strategy, Philbrick asserted, was designed to "continue to win while the American people do nothing." Second, said Philbrick, Communist infiltrators intended "to cause disrespect for the laws and officials of the United States." Lastly, their "leftist" propaganda tried to discredit and thereby negate the effectiveness of important anti-Communist organizations in America. Vilification, Philbrick pointed out, was a recent strategy used to blunt the influence of budding anti-Communist organizations. Philbrick cited Benson and NEP as examples of such propaganda targets.[30]

During the fifteenth Freedom Forum in 1954, Dr. Nicholas Nyaradi, chairman of the Department of Economics at Bradley University (in Peoria, Illinois) and former minister of finance of Hungary, made the first of many appearances at the Freedom Forums. Addressing the topic of "America's Economic Future," Nyaradi contrasted the positive and beneficial aspects of the free-enterprise system with the regressive economic and political consequences of collectivism and communism. In post–World War II Hungary, Nyaradi had led the democratic anti-Communist Small Farmers party. According to NEP press reports, Nyaradi was one of only a few non-Communist statesmen and diplomats who had penetrated the secrecy surrounding the plans, goals, methods, and personal lives of top Soviet leaders.[31] As Hungary's undersecretary of the Treasury and later as minister of finance, Nyaradi had traveled to Moscow to negotiate with "members of the Politburo, a Soviet claim of 200 million dollars against Hungary." During his seven-month stay in the USSR, Nyaradi claimed to have reduced the Russian assessment "to less than one-fourth of its original amount," while, more importantly, learning much about important Russian leaders.[32] Nyaradi told the forum audience how he had "fought a desperate battle in his own country against the encroachment of Russian sponsored Communism," and how, when his "position became untenable on account of increased Soviet pressure, he and his wife fled Hungary and came to the U.S."[33] The Soviet invasion of Hungary in 1956, apparently designed to crush that country's nationalistic and democratic aspirations, enhanced Nyaradi's credibility and guaranteed future invitations to address forum audiences.

Another Hungarian émigré and an equally loyal supporter of the Freedom Forums was Melchior Palyi, a distinguished economist who held a doctorate in public economics from the University of Munich. Palyi had taught for several years in various German universities before he fled the country in the late 1930s. In the United States, he taught at the University of Chicago with other leading conservatives. According to one recent investigation of the conservative resurgence in America, "the University of Chicago played a formative role in creating a conservative movement as well as a conservative world view." At Chicago, students in political economy as well as social and political philosophy were strongly influenced by defenders of free-enterprise economics who attacked value relativity as "the mortal sin of the American intelligentsia." These men emphasized putting "sound teachings into political practice, and their students went into government as well as academic careers."[34] In addition, over the years, several other speakers cemented the connection between NEP and conservative activists from the University of Chicago, where Benson had studied in the early 1930s. Nobel Prize–winning economist Milton Friedman spoke at the dedication of the George S. Benson Auditorium at Harding in 1980; and, on the eve of Friedman's emergence as one of the leading theorists of President Ronald Reagan's controversial economic program, he addressed Harding's American Studies program.[35]

Palyi, an early participant in the Freedom Forums, eventually joined the NEP staff in 1952 and later taught in Harding's American Studies program. The author of a dozen books and numerous magazine and pamphlet articles, Palyi attended all the forums, even though he was not always on the program.[36]

Other notable anti-Communist and Old Christian Right[37] figures spoke at the Freedom Forums. These included the Minnesota congressman, Dr. Walter H. Judd, an internationally noted statesman; conservative syndicated newspaper columnist Drew Pearson; Gen. Albert C. Wedemeyer, U.S. commander in China during World War II and former chief of staff to Chiang Kai-shek; Admiral James A. Van Fleet; Richard Arens, staff director of the House Un-American Activities Committee (HUAC); Dr. Howard Kershner, editor of *Christian Economics*; Dr. Clarence Manion, former dean of Notre Dame University School of Law and host of a popular radio program, "The Manion Forum"; Leonard E. Read, director of the Foundation for Economic Education; Captain Eddie Rickenbacker, World War I flying ace and president of Eastern Airlines; John Noble, an American who had spent over nine years in Siberian prison camps; Dr. William E. Mayer, an expert on Communist brainwashing techniques; Louis B. Mayer, president of Metro-Goldwyn-Mayer; and Cleon Skousen, who successively served as professor at Brigham Young University, chief of police of Salt Lake City, FBI agent, and author of the best-selling book, *The Naked Communist*. Dr. J. B. Matthews previously had been a "fellow traveler" of the Communist party (Matthews even claimed to have coined the term "fellow traveler") but had become an author, a political science professor at both Fisk and Howard universities, and a special investigator for HUAC. Gen. Edwin A. Walker was a NATO commander who had resigned from the Army over administrative decisions against his promoting anti-Communist education for American troops in Europe. U.S. Vice-President Spiro T. Agnew keynoted the Freedom Forum in April 1973, speaking on the forum's overall theme, "The Responsibility of the News Media in a Free Society."[38]

Australian Dr. Fred Schwarz, who had founded the Christian Anti-Communist Crusade in 1953, lectured to forum audiences on "The Heart, Mind, and Soul of Communism" and "Why Millionaires, Teachers, and Ministers Become Communists."[39] For conferees, Schwarz effectively combined militant anticommunism, Christian faith, and homespun prescriptions to avoid socialism. Such Freedom Forum exposure helped catapult Schwarz into the rightist mainstream. Bolstered by generous financing, Schwarz's organization in 1958 moved to Long Beach, California, where it drew heavily on like-minded supporters, receiving slightly over $1 million per year in donations during the early 1960s. Future President Ronald Reagan received early attention for his anti-Communist and conservative political ideology by appearing as a guest speaker for Schwarz in the late 1950s and early 1960s.[40]

The flood of anti-Communist speakers throughout this period did not diminish Benson's enthusiasm for and commitment to free-market economics and a Christian world view. Both were, from his perspective, practical and fundamental barriers to central government planning and the seductive appeal of socialism and communism. Accordingly, Benson's forums hosted other influential free-market advocates, such as Dr. Walter E. Spahr, New York University professor and executive vice president of the Economists' National Committee on Monetary Policy, who labeled New Deal and Fair Deal economic policies unconstitutional.[41]

Because of rapidly increasing financial support, Benson and his NEP associates achieved the forum's almost immediate success by reaching the corporate community. The NEP's ultimate purpose, however, was to nurture a free-market-oriented and anti-Communist grassroots constituency. This effort required wide dissemination of material presented at the forums. Harding College published the texts of forum lectures in book form, aimed at the general public, in the early 1950s. The purpose was to encourage people to "rise to the challenge to our Way of Life and actively promote its advantages to everyone who can be interested in his own economic, social and political future." Benson implored audiences to multiply the forum's influence by passing the books "on to someone who you think would benefit from its contents."[42]

By 1964, NEP claimed to have instructed, through its biannual Freedom Forums on the Harding campus, more than 7,500 conferees from organizations and industries with a combined membership of nearly fifteen million people.[43] In addition, in the same period, NEP staff members on other campuses had conducted another eighty-three forums.[44] The NEP message reached many millions of additional employees of other supporting corporations as well.

The tireless efforts of Benson and NEP during the latter's formative years ultimately drew the attention of a hostile opposition press. *The Nation,* long the country's leading liberal journal, gave Benson's NEP a backhanded compliment in 1952, when it admitted that an "obscure college in the Southwest may well be exerting a greater influence on the economic thinking of the American people than most of our great universities."[45] The article described the various NEP methods used to spread its message. "Drop into a movie house anywhere, or into a women's club meeting or a Main Street lecture hall, or pick up a small-town newspaper, and you are likely to be introduced to hoary economic theories adapted to modern use by the sage of Harding College at Searcy (population 4,000), Arkansas."[46] In reality, this "compliment" from Benson's adversaries indicated their grave concern over the "radical" nature of NEP's economic program, but it also pointed out—in glowing terms, as far as NEP was concerned—the breadth of NEP activity.

Probably NEP's most effective method for confronting the American public was its use of audiovisual materials. Films from its educational film library and its popular television series, "The American Adventure," were widely distributed. At the first Freedom Forum, NEP introduced the first two of ten animated cartoons in its "Adventures in Economics" series, "Make Mine Freedom" and "Going Places."

"Make Mine Freedom" stresses the preservation of the free-enterprise system and the American way of life. Its leading character, Dr. Utopia, peddles his patent medicine "Dr. Utopia's Ism" for curing political ills. "Those who take it soon find themselves living under totalitarian government with troubles far worse than those they're trying to cure," the narrators warn.

In a highly simplified form, "Going Places" explains the theory and workings of the profit motive and the capitalist system of free enterprise.

As a boy, the main character, Freddy Fudso, helps his mother make soap and becomes interested in improving the method of production so as to increase his leisure time at the fishing hole. Soon Freddy discovers that his ideas for increased production bring in increased profits. From that moment, Freddy, as his own boss, confronts many opportunities and difficulties. The point of the film is that the desire for profit spurs Freddy, who eventually tries to establish a monopoly, but, as the film happily concludes, competition and government restrictions block his efforts.[47]

The NEP's film efforts, however, were not confined to distribution at the forums. As early as 1940, Benson had experimented with producing educational cartoons on the free-enterprise system. During World War II, Benson had consulted with Walt Disney about a series of cartoons on this subject. Disney steered him to a former Disney Studio executive, John Sutherland, who greeted Benson's project enthusiastically.[48] However, Sutherland estimated the production costs at $80,000 per film. Although he lacked funds for such a large production budget, Benson was undeterred and quickly contacted Alfred P. Sloan, whom Benson had met after delivering a speech to the National Tax Foundation in New York in December 1941. Sloan, the retired chairman of the board of General Motors Corporation and head of the Sloan Foundation, personally and philanthropically wanted to disseminate economic information. Sloan agreed to fund Benson's project because he felt it was precisely the sort of educational effort his foundation had been created to support. With over one million dollars from the Sloan Foundation, and with additional support from the Falk Foundation of Pittsburgh, Sutherland and Benson set out to produce ten animated cartoons which soon captured the imagination of the American public.

These films were very expensive, but the product seems to have justified the expense. When Metro-Goldwyn-Mayer's short subjects editor, Fred Quimby, saw the first NEP cartoons in Sutherland's studio, he immediately contacted Benson and asked that MGM be permitted to distribute the films through its five thousand theaters across America. Permission was granted, and, according to MGM, "the Harding cartoons became the most popular short subjects ever distributed by MGM."[49] Quimby publicly applauded the entire film series and insisted that MGM's audiences enthusiastically demanded more. According to Quimby, "Never in the history of MGM's shorts department have so many letters been directed to his desk praising an effort." Every exhibitor, Quimby claimed, begged "for more of their type, . . . promising not only more playing time but more important billing" for wildly enthusiastic audiences.[50]

In 1950, *Business Week* favorably reviewed the first of the NEP series. The magazine admitted that "anyone who has tried to teach the economic facts of life to mass audiences knows what a waste of time it can be. Few people find interest, much less entertainment, in discourses on things like the element of risk in business. And certainly subjects like prices, wages, and taxes never made anybody laugh, except possibly in a hollow way." *Business Week* praised the NEP films as high-quality productions and claimed that the reason why more than 25 million people had viewed them favorably was that the pictures were as entertaining as they were educational. "Instead of a drum-beating approach to the American free-enterprise system, they take a light-hearted, good-humored view." Even though, admittedly, they were propaganda, their detractors had been few, "for two major reasons. (1) The pictures deal with facts rather than with ideals; and (2) they frankly point out the imperfections in the system without trying to justify them. All parties involved feel that this kind of honesty is the only way to sell an idea."[51]

The Sutherland studios and the NEP staff completed the animated cartoon series within the next few years, but their attempt to increase the audience for the Americanism message extended beyond the movie theater. Benson recognized the growing influence of television as a communication tool and guided NEP into pioneering educational efforts in that medium. Since Harding College owned WHBQ Radio in Memphis, Benson also obtained a television license for the station. The NEP utilized WHBQ as an effective tool to teach free-market theories by telecasting its film series first. However, by January 1952, "Going Places" had been aired on 63 out of the total of 107 television stations in the nation, giving at least 6.7 million people a visual lesson in free-enterprise theory.[52] By 1955, NEP had made all its audiovisual programs available for television, including the updated and popular flannel-board illustrated lecture presentations. Over one million television viewers saw "This Is Our Problem" in the early months of 1952. Over one hundred of the flannel-board presentation kits were mailed to various women's clubs in the Fort Worth area to be used as the centerpiece for a program entitled, "What Women Can Do."[53] By 1964, NEP had turned out over fifty films on various topics concerning free-enterprise economics and anticommunism which played to a nationwide television audience. It is important to remember that many American businesses contributed heavily to promote NEP's educational program. Without such financial support, NEP would not have been able to produce such a broad educational program. Production costs for the fifty film titles totaled more than $1.5 million, and NEP and its supporters invested another $1 million in sale and rental prints.[54]

In 1942, Benson started a syndicated radio program, recorded in Little Rock and Memphis studios, making editorial comments on current national problems. By the end of the war, the format of the program had changed into a thirty-minute radio drama, "Land of the Free," recounting the story of some of America's greatest historical figures. By June 1951, over 362 radio stations serving more than twenty million people weekly broadcast the program, which featured Broadway actors who dramatized the stories of well-known and extraordinarily successful Americans.[55] The purpose, of course, was to underscore the crucial role of virtue in the success of these historical figures. This was a theme George Benson preached throughout his life. The program ended each week with a Benson editorial.[56] Even though the "Land of the Free" radio programs were a popular NEP feature throughout the 1940s, eventually television eclipsed radio, requiring that the subject matter be presented in a visual format. The "American Adventure" series, which won an award from the Freedom Foundation, presented "Land of the Free" material for television.

While expensive NEP programs targeted radio, television, and movie theater audiences in the 1950s, Benson continued to write his weekly editorial newspaper column, "Looking Ahead," which reached millions of weekly readers at relatively low cost. During the early 1950s, a shorter version of this column, written especially for industrial workers and labor union members, appeared in over fifteen hundred industrial organization newsletters and trade papers. Frequently employers placed copies in employees' pay envelopes. At the same time, Benson transformed the *Grass Roots Report* into the monthly *National Education Program Newsletter* and sent it to forty thousand homes in 1952. In addition, millions of individual reprints of Freedom Forum lectures were published and sold. One NEP report stated that U.S. Steel alone used 13,500 copies, which presumably went into employees' weekly pay envelopes.[57]

Eventually, military leaders became aware of NEP's adult audiovisual presentations, and throughout the 1950s, NEP sold thousands of copies of its films and printed materials to the armed forces. In addition, Benson and his staff produced a version of the Americanism materials suitable for junior high and high school civics programs. In the early 1950s, NEP film programs were part of the regular weekly academic schedules of millions of American high school students. Eventually a standardized Americanism education program was developed, which NEP sold to many large school districts. In addition, thousands of school districts supplemented their civics programs with NEP materials. In Los Angeles alone, over 750,000 high school students received Americanism education through NEP's ever-expanding services. In addition, NEP developed new programs for Texas schools, as well as both high school and college programs in the San Francisco area in 1951. Under an arrangement with the Extension Service Film Library of the University of California, NEP movies became available to 200,000 film users in six western states, including colleges and high schools.[58]

Another popular NEP program developed for high school and college audiences was the kit "For Young Americans." This material was developed in response to a growing need expressed by some students to organize their own Americanism programs on campus. The kit was designed as an educational and orientation tool to help students stand up for Americanism against all forms of collectivism. Stuart Manly, a Los Angeles industrialist, proposed the original idea to NEP because, in working with youth groups in five separate Los Angeles schools, he found the students "very anxious to start organizations in these schools which will 'pitch' the American way of life in opposition to various campus groups promoting one form or another of collectivism."[59]

As the popularity of NEP program grew, the demand for NEP speakers outgrew Benson's ability personally to meet these commitments. Even though Benson averaged nearly two hundred speeches per year, he could not fill every request. To solve this logistical problem, NEP organized a nationwide Speakers Bureau. While the regular staff members of NEP were all capable speakers and attempted to fill in for Benson, even they could not meet the demand. As a result, the NEP staff recruited hundreds of Americanism speakers from all over the nation. The NEP became a clearinghouse for anti-Communist and free-enterprise speakers. When contacted for a speaker or for audiovisual material on a particular subject, NEP staff members channeled the request to a local speaker. In this way, hundreds of local organizations directly benefited from NEP materials and made contact with qualified Americanism speakers. Along with the many films and flannel-board presentations, the NEP clearinghouse distributed to local organizations reprints of over one thousand speeches, mostly from Freedom Forums. Included most often was a speech by Maj. William Mayer on Communist brainwashing techniques used on American prisoners of war in North Korea. It had a record distribution of over one million copies.[60] In addition, over one hundred tape-recorded speeches, including speeches by Ronald Reagan and other noted conservatives, were distributed widely by NEP during the 1950s and early 1960s.[61]

Another development in Benson's Americanism program that greatly influenced the dissemination of his views to the voting public was the development at Harding College of one of the first academic American Studies programs in the country. Harding's School of American Studies, which opened in 1952, included courses in history, social science, political science, economics, and government in a four-year degree program. This program was to train America's future leaders for "responsible positions in industrial, educational, and public service." As a multidisciplinary program, it did not require the creation of a new department.[62] In the first year, twenty-five scholarships were available for qualified high school seniors. There were also internships for fifth-year students. According to Benson, the curriculum was "based on a thorough foundation of general education in the first two years, and the junior and senior years will offer specialization with the B.A. Degree in either of three fields: business administration, public administration, or educational administration. The general approach in the new school will be the case method, in which problems and issues" would be studied "rather than subjects and courses." Benson chose a protégé, Dr. Clifton L. Ganus, NEP vice-president, to administer the new program, and Benson raised the funds to construct a large three-story building on campus to house it.[63]

In 1955, NEP began its longest continuous Americanism program—the Summer Youth Seminars, which are still being held. This particular program resembled the adult Freedom Forums, except that it accepted youthful participants chosen by local high schools and sponsored by local civic organizations. According to NEP guidelines, the conferees were "chosen because of their ability. Many of them are orators, class officers, and contest winners. At Harding they engage in a concentrated study and discussion of the American way of life contrasted to other political systems of the world."[64] These Youth Citizenship Forums at Harding College and Citizenship Seminars at Oklahoma Christian College, Oklahoma City, generally were cosponsored by State Farm Bureau organizations. As a result of this close connection between the Farm Bureau and the NEP, the Farm Bureau used NEP material in its adult activities as well.

Materials used in the program and purchased by the Farm Bureau included speech kits, speech reprints, audio recordings and high school course outlines.[65]

Attendance at the Youth Seminars usually numbered between 100 and 250 students. In 1964, the programs were held in seven different locations. After 1955, NEP presented several of these programs annually. In 1990, NEP, operating out of Oklahoma City under the direction of Robert H. Rowland, organized five Summer Youth Seminars in major cities of the Southwest.[66]

Through the years, many thousands of high school students had the opportunity to study the American system in these seminars. After attending a Summer Youth Seminar, Rowland argued, the student attendants were well prepared to decide for themselves the merits of the American system when they entered a college environment which might emphasize an alternative approach to government and economic planning. Although NEP critics strongly disagreed on this point, Rowland avowed that NEP did not attempt to "indoctrinate" these students, but rather simply presented an unbiased explanation of both sides of the issue. Consequently, Rowland asserted, when the students "sit down in a class with a professor who takes a leftist view, they have had a basis upon which to argue positions that they would not have had if they had not been exposed to our speakers and our programs over the years."[67]

Another important and long-standing NEP program was the Graduate Teachers Seminars. Each such program was a week-long graduate seminar in comparative economic and political systems, designed for high school teachers. As a result of attending the seminars, these teachers "go back to the classrooms and have a better grasp of what this country is really all about. What makes it function. What's good about it as well as what's bad." Once again, according to Rowland, no attempt was made to "indoctrinate" conferees in Americanism; rather, the goal was to teach the truth and to let intelligent citizens form their own opinions.[68]

Throughout the first twenty-five years of the Harding College National Education Program, this tiny band of dedicated staff directly influenced millions of Americans to take pride in their American heritage and more forcefully to defend the American system. However, the Harding College program was not the only product of the vision of George Benson. By the mid-1950s, a score of other Americanism programs existed on college campuses scattered throughout the nation. In these other programs, Benson was directly involved in establishing Freedom Forums,

Youth Seminars, and American Studies programs similar to those of NEP and producing suitable NEP-type materials. Beginning with Oklahoma Christian College, Oklahoma City, in 1959, Benson established effective Americanism programs at several colleges, mainly ones supported by the Churches of Christ. Kings College in New York, George Pepperdine College in Los Angeles, Columbia Christian College in Portland, Lubbock Christian College, Alabama Christian College (now Faulkner University) in Montgomery, and, to a certain extent, Abilene Christian College in Texas, all hosted Americanism programs based on the Harding College model. Like Harding College, these schools benefited from the financial support of wealthy nonchurch donors, including those associated with American corporations.

Whether these programs were sincere efforts to promote Americanism or merely ploys to reap financial rewards from conservative businessmen cannot be determined from the available evidence. However, one must remember that Benson's Americanism program presented to the American people a consistent vision of the merits of the free-enterprise system, of constitutional government, and of militant anticommunism. Together with libertarian organizations, conservative Catholic elements of the Old Christian Right, fellow anti-Communist crusaders, and prominent ministers, Benson's program influenced a large segment of American voters. The consequences of his efforts became apparent in the 1970s, with the resurgence of conservative ideology and accompanying increases in conservative power within American politics.

4

Burdens of Responsibility: The National Education Program Weathers the Storm

More than any election since 1932, the Goldwater-Johnson presidential election of 1964 emphasized the fundamental difference in American political philosophies. Although many highly emotional issues emerged, Goldwater's campaign emphasized a very tough stance against communism and for limiting government intrusion in the private sector. Asking "Why Not Victory?," Goldwater's anti-Communist rhetoric reflected a deep belief in the so-called domino theory and, ironically, approval of Harry Truman's policy toward the USSR. An equally volatile campaign issue emerged when Goldwater argued for states' rights, while Johnson strongly favored federal government implementation of tough new standards on civil rights.[1] The 1964 election gave the American electorate a clear opportunity to choose a "big-government" or a "small-government" political philosophy.

President Johnson, who had inherited the Oval Office, was an astute politician who had accomplished much in the short time since John Kennedy's death. Johnson, more than any other contemporary Democrat, embodied the "liberal consensus initiated by Franklin Delano Roosevelt and implemented by Republican Eisenhower as well as Democrat Truman."[2]

Barry Goldwater, on the other hand, had taken over the leadership of the GOP after Richard Nixon's narrow 1960 election loss to Kennedy. Many conservatives believed that Nixon had "sold out" to Nelson

Rockefeller at the nominating convention by jettisoning a conservative platform and adding Henry Cabot Lodge to the Republican ticket in exchange for liberal Republican support. Goldwater had angrily denounced Nixon's action as a "Republican Munich."[3] Despite the fact that Nixon had lost a close election in 1960, conservatives pushed Goldwater at the 1964 GOP convention because of what historian Richard Hofstadter described as the "chronic, frustrating impotence of the minority" within that party. By 1964, Goldwater's campaign had "benefited from the efficient organization that the right wing had quietly built up" inside the party.[4]

A typical southern Democrat, George Benson espoused a political philosophy that closely resembled Barry Goldwater's. Both men believed that the conservative conscience, rather than the time-honored technique of compromise, should be the "standard for political decisions."[5] Even though Benson had refused several offers to enter partisan politics in Arkansas[6] and publicly had refused to endorse either candidate or party,[7] his political philosophy appealed primarily to conservative backers of Goldwater. Both Benson and Goldwater, in the previous decade, had advocated a marked reduction in the size and scope of government. As Benson had done earlier, Goldwater now heatedly argued on the Senate floor against the Eisenhower administration's relatively high spending levels.[8] Like Benson, Goldwater saw dangers inherent in increasing government regulation of private enterprise, and one of the political convictions most consistently held by Goldwater was that a large federal government was antagonistic to individual freedom.[9]

Benson had publicly embraced this same view as early as 1950. In a Little Rock speech, Benson had pointed out what he felt to be dangerous tendencies in our government's planning program; "under that heading [he] drove home the point that President Truman's government spending has exceeded by eleven billion dollars that of all the preceding presidents of the United States, up to and including the first eight years of Franklin D. Roosevelt's administration."[10]

Goldwater also had taken a tough stance against the advance of communism abroad and at home: "We can establish the domestic conditions for maximizing freedom, along the lines I have indicated, and yet become slaves. We can do this by losing the Cold War to the Soviet Union."[11] Quite early in the Cold War, Benson had reached the same conclusion: "The Communist threat is much greater than the public is aware. Many innocent victims are preaching the fundamentals of Communism without knowing it."[12]

While they obviously concurred about the threat of communism, the most significant philosophical tie between these two men was their insistence that moral principles were the only proper foundations for political decisions. "Moral rightness," insisted Goldwater, "not administrative feasibility," was the most important consideration.[13] Benson was in complete agreement; for over twenty-five years, he and his followers had been conducting a nonpartisan campaign for a conservative candidate such as Goldwater.

In 1964, Goldwater offered the electorate "a choice, not an echo."[14] The success of his candidacy rested on the assumption that the majority of American voters held conservative political attitudes and that a clear statement of conservative principles, "if it did not win the White House, would at least cleanse the Republican Party of 'me-tooism' and foreshadow the victory of a conservative Republican presidential candidate in a subsequent election."[15] In fact, one reason Goldwater lost the 1964 election was not a lack of conservative support, but too much support from the radical elements in the party's right wing. One may argue that it was his association with "extremism in the defense of liberty"[16] that doomed Goldwater to defeat. This is the context within which NEP received a great deal of negative publicity. Some observers even blame NEP for Goldwater's humiliating defeat in 1964, since the organization formed an integral part of what critics saw as too much vocal "ultra-right-wing" support.[17]

By 1964, NEP already had influenced millions of Americans with a conservative political and economic philosophy which by the early 1960s included a strong anti-Communist message. Harding College and NEP had become almost synonymous with free-enterprise education and anti-Communist propaganda in America. The two were recognized by the news media as the "academic seat of America's Radical Right" and as important sources of conservative education.[18] In the words of a critical report, "Any tendency to dismiss the labor of . . . Dr. Benson . . . as idle rantings on the lunatic fringe will not survive a realistic appraisal of two factors: their growing influence in the schools and their prestige among certain elements of the armed forces."[19]

Despite his increased concern over the growing influence of communism, in the years prior to the election of 1964, Benson continued to emphasize free-enterprise education also. Typically, his keynote address at the Twenty-Fifth Anniversary Convention of the National Association of Real Estate Boards dealt with "Current American Economic Issues."[20]

At the convention, Benson also continued to hammer away at communism, showing NEP's controversial new film *Communist Encirclement, 1961*. Some critics argued that the film inaccurately portrayed the relationship between socialism and communism and that it accused some politically friendly nations of socialist tendencies.[21]

Despite Benson's long-standing popularity among service, business, and industrial organizations, during this time NEP received only limited criticism from professional political organizations and the media. According to the *New York Times*, "Dr. Benson and the NEP had been virtually ignored by liberal spokesmen until recently, since they had eschewed the bigotry and racism often associated with right-wing movements."[22] During this period, in addition to national newspaper coverage, the organization received national exposure on the CBS News program, "Eye Witness," which reported on the work of NEP and Harding College in a highly positive fashion. Even so, because NEP had made a significant impact on important elements of the American electorate, criticism from liberal elements of the society and the media increased dramatically.[23]

By the late 1940s, NEP had committed considerable resources to the production and distribution of films for political education in general, and for promoting anticommunism in particular. Distribution was so successful that by 1948 Harding College proudly proclaimed itself "The College That Speaks to the Nation."[24] The films' success elicited devastating criticism from left-of-center media, whose staffs probably feared and resented nonelite competition in the process of influencing public opinion.

One example of how NEP films projected Benson into bitter ideological confrontations centered on the 1951 cartoon "Fresh-Laid Plans." The fifth of ten works in the "Adventures in Economics" series, the cartoon was a biting allegorical satire on U.S. government farm policy. John Sutherland, the former Walt Disney Studio executive turned NEP employee, wrote and produced the cartoon, and MGM distributed it as a short subject to appear between features in the company's movie theaters nationwide. This particular cartoon "aroused a controversy in the mid-western farm belt,"[25] where one St. Paul, Minnesota, newspaper farm editor labeled it a direct assault on the Brannan Plan. Conceived by U.S. Secretary of Agriculture, Charles F. Brannan, the plan provided government subsidies to American farmers, to stabilize prices and improve production. The cartoon was seen by critics of government farm policy as a timely and controversial commentary on seemingly confused and contradictory policies. Further, the cartoon broke Hollywood's "long-standing rule of avoiding political controversy as if it were the plague."[26]

Satire or not, the NEP cartoon appeared to many viewers who were in favor of increased government control of American agriculture to be "a one-sided political editorial in pictures—a clever attempt to use the movies to sway public opinion on a hot political issue affecting farming."[27] Both Sutherland and Benson denied targeting the Brannan Plan, but they agreed, "If the shoe fits they can wear it."[28] In their view, the cartoon accurately described one aspect of U.S. agricultural policy.[29] Dr. Arnold J. Zurcher, executive director of the Sloan Foundation, which underwrote the NEP production costs, claimed that the film accurately explained the principles under which the American economic systems operated and showed "the virtues and shortcomings of those systems."[30] Sutherland defended the film as a lesson concerning the impossibility of "planning our lives from a central authority." The film showed, Sutherland explained, that if the government "sets prices, or plans the economy, it restricts our freedom of action and creates confusion in which the profits go to speculators. As the alternative, [he] tried to indicate that out of free confusion comes the miraculous order of supply and demand."[31]

Indeed, the entire "Adventures in Economics" series set off waves of controversy, because of both its content and the methods by which it was distributed. The first cartoon in the series, "Make Mine Freedom," produced in 1946, dealt with the virtues of free economic opportunity and the demerits of "statism." The second, "Meet King Joe," concerned the importance of investment capital to organized labor. The third, "Why Play Leap Frog?," addressed relationships among wages, prices, productivity, and profit. The fourth, "Albert in Blunderland," satirized the Russian economic system. The remainder of the series focused on topics such as the profit structure, taxes, and inflation. Each cartoon provoked controversy; in some instances, protesters picketed exhibiting theaters. In defense of Benson's program, Louis B. Mayer, head of MGM Studios and a noted conservative activist in Hollywood, claimed that his office had received "an avalanche of letters" praising the cartoons. Benson largely ignored the criticism of the films because he had expected to draw fire from those who advocated socialism or communism. He took comfort instead from a recent U.S. Navy order for eighty prints of "Make Mine Freedom" to use in anti-Communist educational programs.[32]

Controversy over the Brannan Plan, *Communist Encirclement,* and other well-publicized aspects of NEP's ultraconservatism during the late 1950s was not the first instance of controversy surrounding Benson's program. As early as 1946, when he addressed an emotional audience of twenty thousand honoring veteran Hollywood actor Frank Fay at New York City's Madison Square Garden, Benson had emerged as a controversial figure in the national anti-Communist movement. Fay had questioned the "loyalty" of several members of Actors' Equity who, at an earlier union rally in the Garden, had severely criticized both the Vatican and the U.S. government. Fay, a Roman Catholic, had angrily demanded an investigation into the loyalty of some union members; instead, Fay had been censured for his open criticism of the unionists.[33] Fay believed that "talentless Communists" were dictating the union's political stance. The "Friends of Frank Fay" program on January 10, 1946, thus became a highly controversial anti-Communist rally. Emotional speakers "assailed the Soviet Union as a slave state" and communism as a "Godless philosophy seeking to undermine American democracy."[34] Although later reprimanded by critics who labeled the meeting covertly anti-Semitic, Benson's speech, "A Cure for Communism," opportunistically reiterated his basic Americanism philosophy. While neither defending nor condemning Frank Fay's relationship with the union, Benson's speech reemphasized the superiority of the free-enterprise system and of Christian morality over atheistic communism.

In a later *Reader's Digest* article, "If I Were a Communist," Benson repeated his Madison Square Garden anti-Communist argument and injected a subtle anti-labor note as well:

If I were a powerful Communist, trying to destroy American freedom and paralyze its prosperity, I would concentrate on three aims which ultimately will reduce any country to serfdom.

First: I would foment strikes and create just as much industrial confusion and uncertainty as possible.

Second: I would scatter biased propaganda, misrepresenting businessmen and destroying faith in business. I would try to prove Private Enterprise a failure.

Third: I would boost all wasteful appropriation bills in Congress and teach people to expect something for nothing in government—this to weaken the nation's financial structure.

These three activities, carried on persistently and long enough, would wreck any Democracy—any Republic.[35]

Answering growing criticism of NEP's evident anti-labor position, exemplified by this article, Benson responded that he had appeared countless times on programs with national union leaders (such as the Madison Square Garden rally featuring International Longshoremen's Union President Joseph P. Ryan) and had even featured prominent union leaders as Freedom Forum speakers.[36]

In fact, the persistent criticism of NEP's anti-labor position appears to have been justified. The group was strongly associated with important "right-to-work" groups and constantly supported national right-to-work laws. Oklahoma Christian College's President James O. Baird highlighted NEP's anti-labor position by simultaneously presiding over Benson's American Citizenship Center, founded in Oklahoma City in 1959, and Oklahomans for the Right to Work.[37] Furthermore, NEP's Vice-President Glenn Green resigned from the organization to head the National Right to Work Committee.[38] In the face of intensifying criticism about NEP's anti-labor stance, Benson and one of his associates, James T. Karam, president of the Veterans Industrial Association, carried NEP's anti-labor position further when they testified before the Florida legislature in favor of right-to-work legislation.[39]

Answering persistent criticism throughout this period, Benson philosophically appealed to the American free-enterprise tradition. Consistently supporting right-to-work legislation in national journals, he argued that "the only way to have freedom for employees is to have freedom for private enterprise."[40] Free private enterprise, he said, included the freedom of workers to choose their own unions and their right to work without union membership.[41] Basic to NEP's labor platform was the belief that the secret to economic improvement of American labor was not increased union strength, but the productive interrelationship of employers, employees, and the consuming public. Benson believed strongly that organized labor should realistically admit that "increased wages should be geared to increased productivity."[42]

Critics who believed that NEP was pursuing a dangerously militant political agenda had sufficient cause to fear its public appeal. They launched what NEP felt was a smear campaign against it. The NEP was described as a "tax dodge," with critics claiming that NEP had survived largely because of it association with American big business. More importantly, NEP was accused of using funds donated for Christian education for extremist political propaganda, a charge it found increasingly difficult to refute.[43]

The NEP elicited a new wave of criticism in the years immediately preceding the 1964 election with *Communism on the Map*, a film narrated by former FBI double agent, Herbert Philbrick. The NEP introduced this key anti-Communist educational weapon in May 1960; in less than a year, NEP claimed, over ten million persons had seen it.[44] The movie posited four major turning points in the history of Communist expansion. At any of these points, appropriate U.S. government action could have sidetracked the movement. The points were: (1) recognition of the USSR by Roosevelt in 1933, (2) the capitulation of Eastern Europe to communism after the war, (3) the fall of China in 1949, and (4) the fall of Cuba in 1959.[45]

On April 20, 1961, Norman Thomas, six-time Socialist party candidate for president, held a news conference at Socialist party headquarters in New York City to refute the claims of this NEP film. Thomas charged that it contained untruths about both communism and socialism. In particular, he was angered by the film's labeling socialism as the "political and ideological bedfellow of Communism."[46] Thomas was also irate that the film alleged that a "red-dominated" communications union had compromised security at the Pentagon. Another claim of the film to which Thomas took exception was that practically all of Western Europe, Greenland, and all of Asia "are in the grip of Communists who often pretend to be Socialists."[47]

During this press conference, Thomas read a letter ostensibly from a State Department employee who urged that the film no longer be used as an armed forces anti-Communist training film, because it contained "half-truths and blatant untruths" and might jeopardize some of our political alliances.[48] Thomas also claimed to have a letter from James G. Dunton, assistant to Secretary of Defense Robert McNamara, which purportedly said, "The consensus here and now is that the film is not suitable for use in the military information program and that it should not be used by military personnel in any way implying official endorsement by the Department of Defense." Thomas also threatened to write President Kennedy asking to have it banned from further use by the military.[49]

Thomas was not the only critic of the film. Earlier it had aroused a storm of protest in Seattle, when ninety-two University of Washington professors viewed the film and petitioned to have its showing banned on the campus because they claimed that it distorted history. The superintendent of the Seattle public schools also banned it, and nine members of the National Council of Churches expressed opposition to the film's content. However, Washington's state legislature passed a resolution encouraging its continued use. It was also reviewed positively by Boeing Aircraft employees, and several company executives issued favorable comments regarding the film. An editorial by William Schultze of the *Seattle Post-Intelligencer* appeared beside the petition of the university professors, and readers of the paper responded overwhelmingly in favor of the film. After a private screening of the film by over 2,300 Seattle residents, the university professors began receiving anonymous typewritten postcards protesting their stand against the film and quoting a statement they claimed came directly from Lenin: "We must secure the good will of teachers and professors in schools and universities."[50]

Benson defended NEP's controversial product,[51] suggesting to Defense Secretary Robert McNamara that longtime Socialist Norman Thomas was not fit "to evaluate anti-Communist films or other anti-Communist materials." Benson noted that many people rated the film as "factual, realistic and one of the hardest-hitting tools against Communism that are available for use in America today." He asserted that the film was concerned not merely with communism but also with creating a "better understanding of the American way of life."[52] Despite favorable publicity surrounding the controversial film, the Defense Department banned both it and the equally controversial film, *Operation Abolition,* produced by the House Un-American Activities Committee. Defense replaced the pair with a new film, *The Challenge of Ideas,* narrated by Edward R. Morrow and featuring Helen Hayes and John Wayne.[53]

Another creation of NEP's film department was a generally well-reviewed documentary film, *The Truth about Communism,* narrated by Ronald Reagan. This film was formally introduced by Benson and by Alexander Kerensky, who in 1917 had been president of the Russian provisional government that was overthrown by V. I. Lenin. Kerensky stated in the introduction to the film that the "Russian people were the first victims of the Communistic tyranny." He believed that it was time to "study the Communistic movement and to understand it; not by different legends during these years, but by the documentary sources asked for from this film." Reagan reiterated in his introduction that the film was a factual documentary and that most of the scenes "were photographed by Communist cameramen as the actual events were taking place. Communist narrators interpret some of the scenes. The words of the Communist leaders are their own."[54] Apparently NEP was trying to answer criticisms leveled at its first two documentary films, *Communist Encircle-ment* and *Communism on the Map.*[55]

The popularity of these cinematic works and their use as tools in the armed forces' educational war against communism attested to NEP's effective work. At the same time, in the minds of many in the American public, the content of the films moved NEP steadily farther to the right politically and placed it in collaboration with ultraconservative national political organizations. Norman Thomas, for example, had accused NEP of being a front organization for the secretive John Birch Society.[56]

Several of these controversial groups, such as the John Birch Society, had programs that were similar to, though decidedly more radical than, NEP's. Generally they had been created at much later dates and in major urban areas. According to critics of these organizations, the terms "Radical Right" and "Far Right" refer to those groups which, through clandestine activities motivated by a fear of the "Communist conspiracy," endanger American democratic institutions and threaten America with a "super-patriotic" totalitarian government more frightening than communism. Unfortunately, according to these critics, the clear lines distinguishing "radicals," "ultras," and plain old "conservatives" had been blurred in both the national consciousness and the national media, so that by 1962 many well-meaning conservatives, who did not foresee the dangers inherent in the radical programs, were offering support to them.[57] It was amid the American electorate's philosophically "fuzzy" 1964 mindset that NEP came to be confused with ultraconservatism and "extremism."

In the 1960s, hostile books and articles fixed in the public consciousness the image of NEP as a sinister bastion of ultraconservative propaganda. For example, Cabell Phillips in the *New York Times* labeled NEP "the most prolific center of aggressive anti-Communist propaganda in the United States." At the same time he assailed it as a source of overly aggressive and unfair propaganda against many "legitimate" liberal programs which were improperly linked to "centralized government, high taxes, Federal aid programs of all kinds, religious and educational liberalism, foreign business competition and the monopoly power of organized labor."[58]

In an article entitled "Revivalism on the Far Right," Philip Horton called NEP the "intellectual center of all the new right-wing movements." He insinuated that NEP generally agreed with the John Birch Society on most issues, and especially on Robert Welch's beliefs that liberalism, socialism, and communism were ideologically identical, and that America faced Communist infiltration and treason at home. Horton stated that, in the NEP film, *A Look at Communism,* spokesman Dr. Clifton Ganus told student audiences that "'many thousands of Communists' are in high places in the United States and are influencing the actions of 'patriotic Americans.'" Horton cited statements by U.S. senators to the effect that NEP was an ultraconservative organization. Horton asserted that "threats to our liberties can come from the Right as well as the Left." He chastised senators Goldwater, Karl Mundt, and others for introducing legislation to form a government-controlled "Freedom Academy," whose purpose would be to teach effective anti-Communist techniques. These senators were quoted by Horton as saying they wanted to "develop a science of counteraction, which enables us to plan rather than to improvise—and we have no such science. We must have trained political warfare cadres—and we have no such cadres now."[59] Horton claimed these cadres resembled the Birch Society's secret "cells." George Benson responded that his organization was not linked to any other anti-Communist program cited in Horton's article, and that NEP was "older than any of those. We have not taken our cues from any of them." He also emphasized that he was not "an extremist at all."[60]

A *Newsweek* article continued the assault on NEP. It called Harding College the "academic capital of ultra-conservatism. . . . What MIT is to engineering and Harvard is to law, Harding College is to the far right."[61] *Time* followed with an article on "The Ultras," listing the NEP along with the John Birch Society, the Christian Anti-Communist Crusade, and the Christian Crusade as "a few of the manifestations of a U.S. phenomenon: the resurgence of ultra-conservative anti-Communism." *Time* asserted that NEP had influenced twenty-five million people annually with the ultraconservative literature highly "favored by the far-rightists in their forums." In a sidebar was a picture of Benson standing with General Edwin Walker, whom the army had relieved of his European command, charging him with "indoctrinating his troops with John Birch pamphlets and attempting to influence his men to cast absentee ballots for conservative political candidates."[62]

A Dayton, Ohio, news article, "Right-Wingers Invade the Classroom," showed that regional as well as national publications viewed NEP as ultraconservative. This article was extremely critical of the Dayton School District's recent purchase of NEP's high school study outline series. According to the article, each outline pointed readers to "tracts and speeches by Dr. Benson and other ultra-conservatives."[63] In Pittsburgh, a

Columbia University political science professor, Alan F. Westin, claimed that the "Radical Right had replaced the Radical Left as the great challenge to American democracy." He accused NEP of using "'dirty tactics' against loyal Americans" and declared that "radicals have infiltrated normally conservative groups." Since NEP and the John Birch Society were the only organizations mentioned, Westin appeared to indict NEP as a "radical" organization which used "bullying methods to harass their targets."[64]

Other critics were unhappy about NEP's involvement with a touring anti-Communist program designed for high school presentation. The "Project Alert" program featured anti-Communist speakers in two days of in-classroom television teaching. Combined boards of education from several states had cosponsored the project. In New Orleans, the press blasted both the program and the local television station that broadcast it. A group of local college professors condemned "Project Alert" as "an abuse of this station's purposes and privileges, and it is an imposition upon the public to channel into their school system a package of radical right opinions and oratory under the pretense of educational orthodoxy."[65]

An article in the *Kansas City Star,* generally a balanced presentation of NEP's program, also labeled it ultraconservative. The article quoted disgruntled Harding students who accused NEP of giving the school a reputation of being the "mouthpiece for a single partisan political view." The article also assailed the Freedom Forums and their "radical" speakers. It noted, "Of all the activities at Harding, there is no doubt the Freedom Forums have come under the heaviest fire from those opponents who believe many of their participants represent 'the radical right.'"[66]

By the time of the 1964 election, the media appear to have concluded that NEP was an influential part of the political Far Right and that it was pursuing a dangerously militant political agenda. Even the memory of John Kennedy was invoked against the "ultras," as readers were reminded that Kennedy had warned Americans against such political extremism. Members of the political Far Right, he had said, "look suspiciously at their neighbors and their leaders. They call for a 'man on horseback,' because they do not trust the people. They equate the Democratic Party with the welfare state, the welfare state with socialism, and socialism with communism."[67] Thus, by 1964, various critics warned that the U.S. faced the growing power of the Far Right, or neofascism;[68] by associating Barry Goldwater with this alleged neo-Fascist ultraconservatism, the liberal media may have contributed to his presidential defeat.

The NEP certainly presented a conservative viewpoint to the American electorate, and on some issues, especially anticommunism, it was rightly classified as ultraconservative. Owing to rising concern over groups such as the John Birch Society, perhaps the most militant of the major ultraconservative organizations of the early 1960s,[69] critics unwittingly lumped together groups with distinctly different histories, contributions, and purposes.

The John Birch Society, for example, was organized in 1958 by Robert Welch, a wealthy Massachusetts candy executive, in order to resist what he felt to be the threat of a deeply entrenched Communist conspiracy in America.[70] Welch accused large numbers of people of participating in a conspiracy, and he imagined Communist subversion everywhere. He kept John Birch Society membership lists secret and conducted much of his anti-Communist operation through "front organizations." Such practices heightened media suspicions that the John Birch Society was a dangerous organization whose purpose was to infiltrate "and even . . . to dominate, other extremist groups."[71]

As the 1964 election approached, the label "extremist" was unfairly extended by the press to moderately conservative groups such as NEP. In highly critical articles mentioned above, and particularly in four books, the press grouped NEP with other "extremist" organizations combating the "conspiracy" of "socialism in domestic policy, and the sellout and softness in foreign affairs."[72] As a result of such media attention, in the public view, NEP soon was branded extremist by association.

Available evidence suggests very strongly that NEP, an organization much older than the John Birch Society and other more ultraconservative groups, in fact was only moderately conservative when compared to the highly secretive and more militant John Birch Society. Therefore the label "extremist" was incorrect. The NEP's critics even admitted that it was one of the original Americanism programs and "America's original fountainhead and clearinghouse for the development of citizen leadership to safeguard American capitalism and constitutional government."[73] Throughout this period, NEP vigorously denied adopting extremist positions; when Benson was asked at a Los Angeles news conference about NEP's "extremist" label, he replied in defense, "Our program is not new, not radical and not extreme. We've been fighting communism at Harding College for 25 years and have never been considered extreme before. I don't see why we should be now."[74]

In the final analysis, the "extremist" label was more properly borne by those militant organizations like the Ku Klux Klan, which spread racism or anti-Semitism, or the Minute Men, who advocated radical restrictions on individual liberties or the violent overthrow of the government. NEP shared with Barry Goldwater the unfair and inaccurate extremist image, and in the 1964 election, the Republicans undoubtedly lost the votes of many people who were fearful of the dangers to liberty that were associated with extremism.

Because of its insistence on militant anticommunism throughout this period and its alleged affiliation with more militant groups such as the John Birch Society, NEP was both highly visible and susceptible to the same outspoken criticism. The NEP definitely was associated with extremism in the minds of many educated Americans. Despite their statements to the contrary, NEP speakers sharing rostrums all over the nation with representatives of more radical organizations positioned themselves firmly in the extremist camp in the eyes of most voters. In retrospect, NEP probably was guilty more of idealism and naïveté than militancy and extremism, because its leaders actually expected the American public to distinguish finely between themselves and members of more radical organizations.[75] A good example of the myopic idealism which often diminished NEP's credibility in the American political consciousness comes from Clifton Ganus, NEP's leading academic spokesman and the man who succeeded Benson as Harding's president. Ganus caustically reminded NEP critics that it was not the responsibility of NEP to determine which groups used their materials: "They go to schools, newspapers, churches—and no doubt, many ultra-right-wing groups. You hear us being called the Harvard or West Point of ultra-conservatism . . . and maybe that's a compliment."[76]

With statements such as this, it became increasingly difficult for NEP to avoid the opprobrium that attached to the "extremist" label. It was fears about extremism that most analysts believe scared off potential Goldwater voters in 1964.[77] The public's association of NEP with extremism eventually set off a flurry of debate within the Churches of Christ. Church leaders resented having the denomination indirectly affected by the public's misunderstanding of the relationship between Harding College's NEP and the Churches of Christ. Ultimately, however, church displeasure failed to slow the determined NEP campaign on behalf of conservative political education or to nullify its contribution to the Reagan presidential victory in 1980.

The Storm within the Churches of Christ

Not surprisingly, the avalanche of liberal media criticism directed at Benson and NEP paralleled a mounting tide of opposition within the ranks of the Churches of Christ and even within Harding College itself. The most vivid example of this strong internal criticism surfaced during Harding's lengthy fight, waged from 1948 to 1954, to obtain accreditation from the North Central Association of Colleges and Secondary Schools.

Benson had determined early on that Harding College should become accredited by a recognized regional association, though he probably failed to anticipate how difficult this process would be. From 1941 to 1948, Benson reorganized the college, significantly strengthened faculty qualifications, increased the institution's financial resources and endowments, and undertook a costly building program. By 1948, Benson believed that Harding was ready for academic respectability. However, NEP's political and business associations proved to be formidable obstacles to accreditation.

Initially the regional accrediting body rejected Harding's application because of what it described as lingering weaknesses in "faculty competence, advanced education, library, student housing, finance, and physical plant."[78] Between 1948 and 1953, Harding made considerable progress toward alleviating these deficiencies, but each year accreditation again was denied. After several unsuccessful attempts, Benson came to believe that the accreditation committee harbored a much deeper resentment against Harding. He felt that the real reason for Harding's rejections was NEP's activities and its association with ultraconservatism and big business.

Benson felt that Norman Burns of the University of Chicago, who was executive secretary of the North Central Association, had been overly critical of NEP's political philosophy and of its relationship with the college. According to Benson, when Burns was questioned about Harding College and NEP's heavy emphasis on the merits of constitutional government and private enterprise, he responded: "Nothing is wrong with it provided you put equal emphasis on Communism and equal emphasis on socialism and not present any one of them as being better than either of the other two."[79]

As if to prove that Benson's suspicions had been well founded, the North Central Association formally notified Benson that, if he separated

Harding College and NEP financially and functionally, the agency would grant accreditation. Accordingly, in 1954 Benson established separate boards of directors for NEP and Harding College, though Benson remained president of both. Benson incorporated NEP as a private, self-governing educational institution whose mission was to foster a better understanding of the American way of life. In March 1954, the North Central Association finally granted accreditation to Harding College.[80]

Even after the separation, at national and regional academic meetings, Harding students and faculty continually had to deal with negative comments about the college's alleged lack of academic freedom. Apparently faculty and students at other institutions did not know that Harding College had developed a respectable academic program and was rapidly becoming one of the outstanding educational institutions in Arkansas. Much of the criticism revolved around Harding's association with ultra-conservatism, anticommunism, and Americanism. Many critics argued that neither Harding's faculty nor its students worked and studied in an unbiased academic environment which allowed critical examination of all sides of important political and philosophical issues. Critics assumed that this was impossible while NEP and its leading advocates were in prominent positions at the college. Some of the Harding faculty even expressed the hope that "the time will come when I will no longer have to protest to individuals whom I meet away from campus that Harding College does allow its students and its faculty members to think freely and independently, that Harding does not impose a prescribed political and economic strait jacket upon her students and faculty members."[81]

It was plausible that outsiders would make negative assumptions, particularly in light of a well-publicized controversy between Harding's administration and several faculty and student leaders.[82] In the early 1950s, a consistent pattern of disagreement with NEP philosophy emerged from within the Harding faculty and student body, coupled with increasing criticism from within the otherwise loyal ranks of the Churches of Christ.

Evidence of unrest appeared in issues of the *Harding College Bison*. For example, a 1956 article claimed that some students "have promulgated the idea that a prominent member of the administration reads each page before publication in an effort to weed out all that even in the remotest way is critical of the administration." The *Bison* editors stoutly insisted that no administrator had ever censored any student publication.[83]

Surprisingly, a venerable Harding Bible professor, who had been an early critic of Christian involvement in politics and a defender of conscientious objection to military service, emerged as a leading NEP apologist. In *Americanism Under Fire*, Dr. James D. Bales attempts to refute, point by point, a well-publicized attack on NEP by the Anti-Defamation League of B'Nai B'rith.[84] When the editors of the *Bison* questioned him as to whether Harding College was liberal or conservative, Bales replied:

> The editor has asked: "If liberals had donated the money, would Harding be a liberal school?" Since we are not for sale the money does not determine the policies of the administration and the school. If one holds certain ideals and others are sufficiently impressed with one's work to help support it, that is one thing. If one advocates certain positions just because he is paid to do it, this is an entirely different thing.
>
> If the administration, and the school as a whole, had held to liberal positions and had raised money from liberals on the basis of these convictions, obviously we would have been a liberal school. We would have been liberal, however, not because of donations.
>
> If a liberal donates money, knowing our convictions, it is not wrong to receive the money. However, it is wrong to take money under false pretenses. My letter was a plea for integrity. If the dominant view is now against the conservative position, we should openly oppose the use of a conservative image for the means of raising funds.
>
> Although I have not made a survey, it is my opinion that the dominant position at Harding is conservative. However, one would have to be deaf and blind to be unaware of the fact that, although there has always been some disagreement, the opposition is becoming more vocal, even if not more widespread.[85]

Despite Bales's contention that NEP opposition at Harding was getting stronger, such statements as these might appear self-serving until a closer look is taken at earlier *Bison* editorials which discussed at length several extremely emotional issues. The first was segregation in public and private schools. According to the editors, many Harding students wondered why the college did not admit blacks. However, they concluded that, while the administration would probably favor their admission, "the segregation problem would not be solved even if this were done." They believed the proper course of action was to eliminate student prejudices and then to act. "The *Bison* doesn't know all the answers. We can only present the issue. . . Let us all look forward to the day when human beings are judged by something other than the color of their skin."[86]

To Harding's credit, in 1963 it became the first white private school in the state to admit "non-white Americans." Even though Harding, "as a private institution, faced no legal threat," voluntary actions such as this "help greatly to ease the tensions and eliminate areas of conflict as the Negro continues his pressure for greater participation in the national life."[87] Despite their persistent criticism, the editors of the *Bison* appeared particularly proud of Dr. Benson for his leadership, both in the state and the nation, in pressing for equal opportunity for blacks.[88]

A second controversy arose in 1955 around a remark in a well-publicized Freedom Forum speech by Arkansas Power and Light's President C. Hamilton Moses, about "creeping socialism" in the Tennessee Valley Authority. In response, Harding student Randy Parks countered in a *Bison* editorial that the TVA was a "boon to free enterprise over the country, operating with amazing efficiency, forcing no one to remain in its employ (as is done in England); the TVA is no more socialism than your own home-town water system, no less American than free enterprise itself."[89] This issue aroused deep emotions. Several students soon rebutted Parks and blasted the TVA.[90]

A third issue that generated considerable controversy among students was fear that the predominance of a conservative philosophy on the campus might restrict academic freedom. According to the editors, "More and more each year college students are becoming afraid to think for themselves. Our colleges are being invaded by an atmosphere of fear and suppression created by irresponsible investigations and hysterical community and campus leaders and other self-appointed 'thought police' who have succeeded in intimidating both our students and faculties." Further, they claimed that American college students in general, and not just Harding students, were "hesitant to ask questions on controversial subjects; afraid to join or support an unpopular minority even if he believes it to be right." As a result, the American political and economic system had no effective and constructive critics.[91]

Another editorial disagreed, observing that Harding students regularly received Marxist literature from the Labor Youth League. The league pointed out that American universities claimed to have academic freedom, yet refused to have Marxism taught by Marxist teachers. In response, the *Bison* editors insisted that we do study the principles of Communism and Marx in our schools. Our libraries offer the curious reader the literature of Marx, Lenin, and Stalin. However, as we are a free people and have the ability to form our own judgments, we have found the doctrine of Communism wanting. And as a parting question it might be interesting to ask the Youth Labor League if the people under her red yoke have been offered the same opportunity to study Democracy under an impartial instructor.[92]

A fourth issue on the campus was freedom of the press and editorial integrity. In response to what the editor felt was "blatantly slanted coverage" of the April 1961 Freedom Forum by the *Arkansas Gazette*, the *Bison* editor insisted that, "regardless of how good or bad the Freedom Forum, NEP, Harding College, anti-Communism, or the John Birch Society may be, it would seem that one thing all these organizations or philosophies are entitled to is fair representation by the press." Because freedom of the press is a constitutional right, "newspapers are not compelled to give this fair representation . . . As a consequence, the Freedom Forum, NEP, and Harding College have been grossly misrepresented before the public."[93]

While maintaining that they were presenting both sides of controversial issues such as the Peace Corps, government subsidies, and progressive social legislation, other editorials appeared very one-sided when they charged that liberal legislators had used government programs "as the solution to all problems, the means to all good ends. This is collectivism—service for the monolithic American state. It is not the philosophy of individual responsibility and voluntary activity."[94]

Students at Harding College were not oblivious to the heavy criticism leveled nationally at NEP and Harding College by the media and even by influential members of the Churches of Christ. Joel Anderson, a student who later became involved in a heated controversy among Harding College faculty, lamented that NEP's ultraconservative image was unfairly forced upon Harding and the Churches of Christ.[95] Unfortunately, the negative publicity generated in the national media indicated that most people learned about Harding College "not as an institution of higher learning" but as a tool of big business and promoter of ultraconservative causes.[96]

Throughout the pre-1964 election period, the political philosophies of Harding College and NEP were sources of constant controversy. After discussing the liberal-conservative controversy at the national level, one

1962 *Harding College Bison* editorial both praised the work of NEP and lamented its negative influence on the college. While the citizenship program built a love of country and a consciousness of the dangers of communism, its location on the campus also limited the work of the faculty and placed a severe strain on academic freedom, because NEP "impresses upon the Harding students a unilateral view of politics and economics." As a result, students often were "handed a comprehensive picture of the 'conservative' side on an issue, but are left to investigate other positions for themselves." Consequently, many students came to believe that the "conservative picture constitutes complete information on the subject" and based their decisions accordingly. According to this editorial, even though liberal viewpoints "can and do find their way into the experience of students here, the total volume of material is considerably one-sided."[97] Another 1962 editorial by Joel Anderson indicated that this "overdose" of anticommunism and conservatism had worked in reverse, and many Harding students took the liberal position simply out of rebellion. Regrettably, their basis for being liberals "is no sounder or better thought-through than the basis of many students for being conservatives."[98]

If the student body perceived intellectual restrictions, some of the faculty, although slower to react, eventually engaged in acrimonious discussions with the Harding administration on the same subject. Failing to obtain a satisfactory response, several faculty members resigned in protest. One source of difficulty on the Harding campus, reflecting the situation on other college campuses, was student and faculty anger over the Vietnam War and dissatisfaction with authorities in general. Eventually the Free Speech movement, begun at the University of California at Berkeley, and other radical campus issues made their way to the little campus in Searcy which had developed a national reputation for extreme conservatism.

As a result, the administration and the older faculty, who with Benson had struggled through the Depression and the early years of Harding College's financial hardship, were pitted against some of the younger faculty, who perhaps did not appreciate the vast difference between the Harding campus of 1936 and the campus thirty years later. Older faculty members certainly were most aware that millions of dollars had been raised on a conservative appeal. To them, overt criticism appeared to be ingratitude for benefits accrued through conservative appeals. Some younger faculty concluded that at Harding academic freedom was an illusion.[99] Benson obviously believed otherwise:

We have been told that . . . an educator must consider everything as relative. We have been warned that it is permissible to educate but wrong to indoctrinate. We bow to no one in our respect for truth and fact, but we are not willing to go along in namby-pamby fashion ignoring the lessons of history. We think enough facts are in to permit some decisions. We are willing to reach conclusions and to act upon them in order to preserve the priceless heritage we possess as Americans.[100]

In reference to speculation that NEP influence limited academic freedom at Harding College, Benson countered that "a Ph.D. professor should know more about what constitutes good government than a freshman in college and . . . therefore, the professor has a responsibility to help direct the thinking of the young people to help them arrive at sound, logical conclusions."[101] Benson did not believe the Harding administration or faculty to be engaged in indoctrination. However, some faculty members felt that, at Harding, the norms for acceptable classroom conduct made objectivity impossible, and many teachers feared the disapproval of NEP. Consequently, for faculty, the choices appeared to be between "expressing views contrary to the citizenship program or expressing no views at all."[102] Most chose silence, but some spoke out strongly and elicited sharp criticism from students, administrators, and other faculty members.

The severest Harding faculty critic of NEP influence was Dr. James L. Atteberry, head of the English Department. In 1966, Atteberry published an unofficial history of Harding College, in which he praised NEP's influence on the development of the school. In this history, Atteberry concluded that the

favorable national image enjoyed by Harding College during the period of accelerated building derived primarily from two focal points. The most important was the widespread popularity of Dr. Benson. But an important concomitant element was the publicity gained through the activities of the National Education Program. . . [which] continued to win friends for the school; and many individuals initially impressed by Dr. Benson through contacts with the program ultimately became firm supporters of Harding College also.[103]

By 1969, after sixteen years of service to Harding, Atteberry evidently had completely changed his attitude about NEP. According to Atteberry, his difficulties with the Harding administration began with a speech he made to the assembled Harding faculty in September 1967. In this speech, entitled "What I Would Like to See Harding Be in 1967–1968," he voiced a sincere desire for Harding truly to become a community of scholars who searched for truth, rather than a group of pedantic obscurantists. Atteberry hoped:

> that we can commit ourselves to truth-seeking in letters, in science, and religion. I hope we can free ourselves from and keep ourselves uncommitted to any static social, economic, political, or religious views, substituting instead a constant quest for truth in all areas of human understanding. In this connection I hope we can take positive steps to change our national image so that we will be recognized primarily as a Christian rather than as a political institution.[104]

Atteberry eventually was asked to resign on April 7, 1969, rather than wait for dismissal by the Harding College Board of Directors. He rather grudgingly resigned. While his resignation may have been a direct result of philosophical and theoretical differences with the Harding administration, he insisted that he never publicly disagreed with any position taken by the administration except about NEP's negative influence on the image of Harding College.[105] In his defense, Atteberry stated:

> As far as I can remember, the only program I have ever criticized on the Harding campus is the National Education Program, which I understood over the years to be specifically and officially not a part of Harding College. I have long regretted the national image provided for Harding College because of the presence of the National Education Program offices on her campus. I have expressed myself on this point to Dr. Benson and to Dr. Ganus during their terms as presidents of Harding College. I believe my regret for this unfortunate image is shared by many other people on this campus and away from here.[106]

In the end, Atteberry's resignation polarized the faculty, and during NEP's years on the campus, several Harding faculty resigned because of philosophical differences with NEP. Included in this group were Dr. Joel Anderson, who went on to become a very outspoken critic of NEP, and Dr. Joseph Spaulding, who had unfavorably reviewed Barry Goldwater's *Conscience of a Conservative*, thereby incurring the wrath of George

Benson and of NEP supporter Dr. Frank Rhodes, who earlier had been a militant anti-Communist speaker among the faculty.[107]

Criticism of NEP and its association with ultraconservatism also surfaced within the Churches of Christ. Dr. Royce Money, president of Abilene Christian University, analyzed this dissent in 1975 and raised several points relevant to the present study. Controversy over NEP arose within the Churches of Christ after the publication of "The Politics of Harding College" in *Mission,* an independent publication that was oriented toward the denomination. In the article, Dudley Lynch, an editor of another Churches of Christ publication, the *Christian Chronicle,* repeated the criticisms already aired in the June 30, 1962, issue of the *Nation* (discussed above). Lynch brought these claims to the attention of the denomination by reminding them of the difficulties inherent in a marriage of Christianity and conservative politics. Historically, the Churches of Christ had viewed political activism very cautiously. Many early Restoration leaders, such as Alexander Campbell and Walter Scott, strongly advocated participation in civic affairs, but the position of David Lipscomb in the late nineteenth century had gained ascendancy.

Christians, according to Lipscomb's understanding of Scripture, were instructed to follow Paul's admonition to the Romans and "be subject unto the higher powers. For there is no power but of God: the powers that be are ordained of God" (Rom. 13:1 KJV). Here, however, Lipscomb made a critical distinction. Even though Christians must submit to these powers, they were specifically commanded not to support their efforts, even if the government appeared to be "just and admirable." For the governments of God and those of men were "antagonistic and rivals of each other, each contending for the rule and dominion of the world."[108]

In Lipscomb's view, Scripture divided sinful humans into those obedient to Jesus and reconciled to good, and those who disobeyed and remained God's enemies. Humanity, then, consisted of Christians and non-Christians, for whom God had established two classes of governing ordinances:

> His own government for the maintenance of His authority, the spread of His kingdom and the promotion of virtue and holiness, and the protection, blessing and salvation of His children, and [in opposition] human government, His sword, His battle ax, His armory, to punish His disobedient children, and the wicked spirits who set at defiance His authority, build up institutions to supersede His government, which

were overruled by God to punish wickedness, and in turn to be destroyed for their wickedness. In these diverse and contrary senses and characters, heaven and hell, Jesus Christ and the devil are ordinances and servants of God, to accomplish the diverse works.[109]

In the end, according to Lipscomb, all human governments will be destroyed, and the whole world eventually will return to total submission to God's authority.

At mid-twentieth century, Lipscomb's arguments remained the orthodox view among many conservative church members. Several Churches of Christ schools openly disavowed Harding's Americanism program out of loyalty and adherence to Lipscomb's philosophy of church–civil government relationships.[110] Lynch's article denouncing conservative politics on the campus of Harding College galvanized many influential members of the Churches of Christ to join in the growing criticism of NEP's philosophy. Reuel Lemmons, editor of *Firm Foundation*, a journal influential among the Churches of Christ, echoed popular church sentiment when he remarked that "he hoped it was not heretical," but he regarded Americanism programs such as NEP and the American Citizenship Center (ACC) at Oklahoma Christian College in Oklahoma City as "money-raising schemes." He felt "that much of it springs more from the need of support of these powers and sources than it springs from any inherent political feeling within the college. I think it's an external stimulus working on the colleges rather than an internal explosion of sudden patriotic interests."[111]

Despite this heated criticism from inside and outside the church fellowship, when the smoke had cleared and the conservatives had been soundly defeated in the presidential election of 1964, NEP remained alive and viable. However, by 1975, Benson had outlived most of his major financial supporters, though he still had access to enough small donations from individual families to keep his program alive. In 1990, NEP and ACC newsletters still were mailed to 23,000 homes. A careful study of NEP financial records through the 1980s revealed that Benson still received substantial financial support from several corporations, as well as thousands of individual donations.[112]

Goldwater's 1964 defeat and the heavy criticism of NEP associated with the election controversies affected Benson's schedule very little. He continued to speak out against communism and in favor of free enterprise, constitutional government, and the application of Christian values to every phase of American life. Harding's building program expanded, through the financial support of its loyal corporate sponsors. After the 1964 election, NEP did gradually shift from adult and industrial education to youth forums and Americanism seminars on college campuses. The NEP had weathered the political and social storms of the 1960s. Its image had been tarnished but not destroyed. The Freedoms Foundation at Valley Forge, a major right-wing front organization, annually singled out NEP by praising its significant contributions to the dissemination of basic American ideals. Gen. Dwight D. Eisenhower presented the first Freedoms Foundation Award to George Benson in 1949.[113] Each year from 1949 to 1985, some part of the Americanism programs started by George Benson received a Freedoms Foundation award or honor.[114] In addition, in 1954, Benson was voted "Arkansan of the Year," a contest in which he polled 67,000 out of the 100,000 votes cast. K. A. Engel, publisher of the *Arkansas Democrat,* which sponsored the competition, praised Benson at the awards ceremony as the man who "helped to put the shoes on Arkansas."[115]

Commentators on the 1964 election concluded that the political climate in America had not been ripe for a conservative victory. But there would be other elections. The faith of George Benson and NEP in the ability of the American public to respond to positive education concerning free enterprise and constitutional government had not flagged. Even though deeply embroiled in controversy, NEP consistently received a tremendous amount of publicity and generous financial support that continued, although somewhat abated, throughout the 1960s and 1970s. The conservative resurgence in American politics was quietly and gradually building a philosophical base. Its ultimate victory in American politics lay ahead. The NEP charged ahead with its well-publicized activities, prepared, poised, and eager to contribute significantly to grassroots conservative political education in the 1970s.

5

The National Education Program
and the Rise of the
New Religious Right

One of the more distinctive elements in the Republican coalition that emerged in 1980 was the New Right. Based primarily upon religious fundamentalism and oriented toward single-issue political activism,[1] this segment of the political spectrum has much in common with the aforementioned neoconservatives. Both are recent additions to the Republican party, and it appears that to them party loyalty is much less important than fidelity to moral and religious principles. However, while neoconservatism was primarily an upper-middle-class intellectual reaction to what its adherents saw as the economically and socially unwise policies of the liberal establishment, the New Right, and especially the New Religious Right, was an activist movement of the lower middle class. In many respects, the New Religious Right is more important politically than neoconservatism because, traditionally, moral and religious activists have been the groups most responsive to changing social trends within the nation.[2]

Kevin Phillips claims to have coined the term "New Right" in 1974, in reference to a coalition of populist-conservative groups who emphasized "social issues, religious and cultural alienation, anti-elite rhetoric, lower-middle-class constituencies, populist fundraising, and plebiscitary opinion-mobilization."[3] But the essence of this movement in recent years has been a morally based conservatism; it includes organizations such as the Conservative Caucus, the Moral Majority, the Religious Roundtable, and, to a certain extent, George Benson's National Education Program. These were the groups most active in the conservative religious and secular coalition that supported Ronald Reagan.[4] Oddly enough, the social orientation and political affiliation of these religious groups traditionally had been Democratic, but in the 1970s, these groups moved inexorably into the Republican camp. This shift came about, not because the GOP had maintained a consistently conservative economic and social perspective, but because the new GOP leadership understood these groups' fundamentalist belief in a set of moral absolutes transcending egalitarian value relativism and sought to enact legislation responsive to that belief.

Recent studies too indicate that the New Religious Right had been mobilized to vote in 1980 partly because, for the first time, "organizational efforts were being made to mobilize them as voters and, in addition, they perceived the government to be responsive to their particular concerns." For the first time in years, the potential political power of the Religious Right was discussed openly in the media, and these rightists themselves believed that their "voices were being heard and not ignored" by the government.[5]

According to political scientist James L. Guth, the New Christian Right strongly resisted the incursion of value relativism into American culture, which helps explains this group's sudden rise to political prominence in the 1970s. Guth's argument draws on social scientific modernization and secularization theories. These help to explain the influence of the Christian Right during this period, as a cultural defense movement which typically appears "at the conjunction of several economic, social, and political developments: a degree of social mobility creating a new political constituency, the growth of 'indigenous' leadership and communication networks, and, most important, a threat to the traditional values, beliefs, and institutions of that constituency, often from a 'secularizing' (or at least secular) political elite." Guth further notes that the rise of the Religious Right is a prime example of this phenomenon. "Industrialization and urbanization," he argues, "have created a new 'evangelical' constituency, traversed by intricate new organization and communication networks. This group is then activated by 'trigger issues' involving outside threats to its religious values and institutions."[6] The IRS assault on Christian schools in the 1970s, the proposed Equal Rights Amendment, and *Roe v. Wade* (1973) angered conservative Christians and provoked their political action on a scale far larger than had ever been seen before in American political history.[7] Despite the fact that this recent rise to political prominence of fundamentalist religious groups and their increased importance to contemporary American politics has spurred a sizable body of research, as yet "social scientists are still at a loss to explain comprehensively the phenomenon or even define the constituency."[8]

In contrast to the majority of political and social scientists, who have tended to limit their research to current data in explaining the nature and extent of the influence of the New Religious Right, many historians recently have sought deeper and much older associations among religious principles, political philosophy, and voting response. One recent development in the study of American political history is the construction of a conceptual framework that restores the study of religious influences to political analysis and thereby provides insight into voting behavior past and present.[9] Although much of this research deals with voting responses in the late nineteenth century, other researchers have applied the same paradigm to the recent influence of evangelical Christianity on American elections, with startling results.

These studies posit a cause-and-effect relationship between religious ideologies and voter response.[10] They employ voting statistics to unearth historically discernible patterns that suggest the motivations of voters that may be of interest to contemporary political observers. Paul Kleppner, an influential researcher in the history of religion and politics, concludes that "no meaningful reconstruction of American political life can result from an exclusive concentration on the activities and statements of national leaders. The focus must shift to those millions of human actors whose aspirations and actions are the central concern of historical analysis."[11]

Even though scholars of nineteenth-century voting patterns have long understood that a religiously inspired world view had fueled mass partisan loyalties, "of all the shifts and surprises in contemporary political life perhaps none was so wholly unexpected as the political resurgence of evangelical Protestantism in the 1970s."[12] As a result, only recently have serious studies been done on the influence of evangelical Christianity on the elections of 1980 and 1984. This recent political analysis makes clear the need for a careful analysis, first, of these religious influences on the politics of George Benson and his National Education Program, and, second, their relationships to the New Religious Right in general and to members of the Churches of Christ in particular. It is within this context that a study of the ethnoreligious paradigm can be applied to the work of George Benson and NEP to determine their influence on the New Religious Right.

According to Kleppner, the concrete result of applying the ethno-religious typology to an analysis of past politics "differs from the products of traditional political history. It depicts party combat in terms of antagonistic political cultures [world views animated in the electorate], and it views elections as integral parts of a larger ongoing social process."[13] To understand this process and its influence on American political history, historians must ask new questions about old information. Accordingly, "how a group voted is a factual question requiring an empirical response. Why it voted that way involves an analytical question that can be posed meaningfully only after the factual one has been answered empirically."[14]

Generally speaking, the interpretations of Frederick Jackson Turner and Charles Beard dominated American historiography in the first half of the twentieth century. Beard and Turner postulated economic rivalries, free land practices, sectional tension, and class antagonisms (exacerbated by significant levels of immigration) as the dominant motivating forces behind American political behavior. Kleppner and his associates reexamined voting statistics and asked, "Did the impact of economic class cut across and neutralize that of ethnic and religious group membership?"[15] Contrary to the economic interpretation dominant in American political history, they discovered that religious factors were demonstrably the most salient variables determining voter response.[16]

With this framework of economic determinism looming in the background, Kleppner, Lee Benson, Ronald P. Formisano, and Richard J. Jensen reexamined voting records and concluded that "the dominant forces that animated the electorate were party loyalty and, more fundamentally, religion."[17] Their work was so impressive that, by the 1970s, the "ethnocultural (or ethnoreligious) interpretation of voting behavior had become the reigning orthodoxy."[18]

The core of American religion in the nineteenth century was revivalistic and enthusiastic Protestantism, which emphasized free will and the agency of man in conversion. Influencing others to seek salvation became the object of a religiously informed society which sought to identify sin and to clamor for its eradication. This new religious perspective produced a Christian world view in which religious experience, knowledge, and belief were to be supplemented by moral living that, in turn, would reshape society under divine approval.[19] This view also meant that religious practices and principles defined and shaped self, society, and government. Religion became a mass experience and a source of values which animated all sorts of benevolent enterprises and profoundly influenced political behavior in nineteenth-century America.[20]

This powerful undercurrent left over from nineteenth-century evangelicals has become the source of contemporary evangelical religious principles, as well as their manifestation within the politics of the New Christian Right. In traditional theological terms, today's evangelicals are distinguished by "three core items of faith: (1) the belief that the Bible is the inerrant Word of God, (2) the belief in the divinity of Christ, and (3) the belief in the efficacy of Christ's life, death and physical resurrection for the salvation of the human soul."[21] In the broad context of American history, the recent rise in political activism among religious groups is not a "departure from national tradition but only the renewal of a long-standing pattern in American political life."[22]

Traditionally, the right to vote has been highly prized in America. It is the means by which the electorate hopes to direct the policies and decisions of public officials. Consequently, it represents to the average citizen the opportunity to help determine the quality of one's life and the direction of one's future.[23] Of course, elections are not "mandates directly charging public officials to pursue clear-cut policy agendas. Instead, they communicate a sense of the modal preferences of the public concerning the general direction and shape of policy."[24]

The political arguments of the 1960s and 1970s illustrate two basic modes of nineteenth-century political expression. In that age, at the polls "crusading moralism" opposed "counter-crusading pluralism."[25] In contemporary elections, "secular humanism" has replaced pluralism as the primary evil to be eradicated. Even a cursory examination of the New Christian Right suggests a rebirth of crusading moralism in modern political ideology. Central to this movement is the constellation of moral issues described by this group as the "profamily agenda," which includes "opposition to abortion, support for voluntary prayer and Bible reading in public schools, the responsibility of the government to encourage the 'traditional family unit,' the maintenance of tax exemption for churches, and noninterference by the authorities with Christian schools."[26]

As an electoral movement, this group adopted "two major goals—to get evangelical Protestants to participate in politics and to support candidates who endorse conservative programs and policies."[27] In this way, voter response can be directly related to affiliation with certain moral guidelines. "Natural Rights" exemplified in the Constitution are thus justified in religious terms: "In this view, religion provides standards for judgement that are necessary to give meaning to concepts such as fairness, justice, goodness, and dignity."[28]

According to Wald, one of the causes of the reemergence of evangelical Protestantism as a viable force in American politics is its ability to adapt to the ever-changing political landscape of America while at the same time invoking traditional values and interpretations of America's past. John Winthrop's "City set on a Hill" and America as a "Redeemer" nation are traditional religious interpretations of American history which describe American national development as an integral part of God's plan. In this view, the development of constitutional government within a prosperous Christian moral framework represents progress towards the millennium. Maintaining America as a bastion against godless socialistic societies then becomes necessary for spreading Christianity and fulfilling God's plan. As a result of this line of reasoning, opposition to Jimmy Carter's Panama Canal Treaty, support for increased military spending, and renewed anticommunism all are important planks in the New Christian Right platform.[29]

This new Americanism, as the agenda and political reasoning of the New Religious Right sometimes is called, is very similar to the traditional Americanism (belief in the Constitution, in the free-enterprise system, and in God) advocated consistently since 1940 by George Benson and NEP. Of course, Benson did not originate any of these political axioms, nor did he first propose them to the American voting public. Yet, through his relentless propaganda activities, Benson kept these ideals before the American public until political conditions within the United States allowed them to re-emerge in the late 1970s as the principal ideals of the New Christian Right.

Benson's influence within the Churches of Christ as a staunch supporter of the New Religious Right has been well documented, but for purposes of this study it is necessary to analyze Benson's direct influence on voter response within the Churches of Christ. Benson's direct influence on such influential politico-religious groups as the Religious Roundtable[30] is less well known but deserves careful consideration also. Therefore, a critical analysis of Benson's and NEP's influence on the voter responses of Churches of Christ members and of the New Religious Right is in order.

The NEP's Influence on the Politics of the Churches of Christ

Although highly critical of NEP and its negative influence on the image of the Churches of Christ within the nation, Royce Money, in his study of church-state relations within the Churches of Christ since World War II,[31] has analyzed the extent of religious nationalism within the denomination, the rationale for its existence, and its apparent short-term and long-term effects.[32] As a phenomenon observable within American denominations, religious nationalism was not unique to the Churches of Christ. According to James E. Wood, religious nationalism has increased dramatically in recent years and has "reflected a way of thinking about the state in religious and spiritual terms. During 'the Eisenhower years,' this fusion of religion and the state reached heights perhaps unparalleled in all of American history."[33] The Churches of Christ and NEP strongly reflected this trend toward religiously-based patriotism.

Like many conservative religious groups, the Churches of Christ underwent significant changes during the twenty-five years following World War II. The denomination grew rapidly to become one of the top ten non-Catholic religious bodies in North America, with membership estimated at over 2.5 million.[34] More importantly, it moved from being a sect to being a denomination, according to the analysis of H. Richard Niebuhr, who observed that such a transition involves economic mobility from rural to urban establishment, upward social mobility, and enhanced educational opportunities. However, a shift toward middle-class social and economic values usually softens the ethical distinction between sectarian and churchly moral values. Following this pattern, Church of Christ members became more closely associated with mainline theology and social ethics, in a sense becoming more "modern" and less "fundamentalist." In keeping with Niebuhr's typology, much of the controversy over NEP formed part of wider denominational debates concerning the proper relationship of the Churches of Christ with the government, social ethics, and big business. Because it was so visible, NEP became the testing ground for the denomination's changing values. According to Niebuhr, analysis of this type of denominational shift in value orientation is vitally important to our study since changing theological opinions "have their roots in the relationship of the religious life to the cultural and political conditions prevailing in any groups of Christians."[35]

As the Churches of Christ became less sectarian and more formally denominational, "they became one of the most conforming groups in their society to the mores of middle class American society. Reflecting the keystone of the middle class, they became nationalistic and strong supporters of God, family, and patriotism."[36] The essential problem, then, is to determine to what extent Benson and NEP helped to facilitate the transformation of the Churches of Christ into a denomination closely identified with the principles of Americanism and of the New Religious

Right as, in the 1970s, the denomination's members, largely for the first time, entered partisan politics.

Part of the difficulty in analyzing any aspect of the Churches of Christ lies in its autonomous congregational polity. Because there is no central denominational authority or hierarchy, centers of power are dispersed and thus are difficult to analyze. Money tried to determine denominational preferences for certain political positions by analyzing three loci of power within the denomination. He found that (1) editors of popular denominational periodicals, (2) influential preachers, and (3) colleges supported by the Churches of Christ best reflected established beliefs among church members and generally guided their behavior and attitudes. Consequently, at the time of Money's study, denominational leadership among the Churches of Christ appeared to be centered in these areas, and the views of these leaders "generally reflect the views of the general membership."[37] Conversely, if these centers of power failed to reflect the views of their constituents, "they quickly lose their influence and power, since they depend solely upon a voluntary constituency in the absence of any formal denominational framework. The fact that a center of power exists is evidence of general conformity to a consensus viewpoint."[38]

As has already been demonstrated, Benson held a leadership position unique within the fellowship since he was an influential preacher and lecturer as well as head of a prestigious church-related school. At the same time, he edited both religious and political materials made readily available to members of the denomination. Further, Benson was a well-publicized national figure who represented himself first as a Christian educator and secondly as a defender of Americanism. According to Money, the typical reader of Churches of Christ periodicals, including NEP materials, "is likely to take whatever he reads as fact (particularly in historical reporting) as long as it generally conforms to his own personal outlook." In addition, Benson served simultaneously as president of Harding College and as chancellor of Oklahoma Christian College in Oklahoma City. Both institutions, in addition to serving the educational needs of the Churches of Christ, acted as focal points for activities of churchwide concern.[39]

The difficulties involved in analyzing Churches of Christ trends notwithstanding, Money established that Benson and NEP were the driving forces behind the rise of religious nationalism, and that NEP was the primary organization advocating conservative political activism within the denomination in this period.[40] Even though the denomination was already undergoing dramatic sociological and economic changes, Benson and NEP accelerated its movement into mainline American politics. Clearly, Benson's constant barrage of political propaganda, along with the fact that it emanated from a respected denominational college, certainly stimulated discussion over the traditional position of "total noninvolvement with government" that had been established earlier by David Lipscomb. Although other sociological stimuli facilitated the challenge to Lipscomb's position, Benson's strident critique accelerated its demise as a viable denominational position.

Money concluded that, "although a majority of southern conservatives probably did not agree with Lipscomb's theory of total political noninvolvement, most did believe that Christians should limit their political involvement. Primarily, they were convinced that the church should remain silent in the areas of politics and social reform."[41] Benson believed otherwise and took the lead within the denomination in discrediting Lipscomb's philosophy. Benson actively encouraged Christians to participate in policy formulation through the political process. Moreover, in his opinion, they should assume political leadership, since in the United States "far too few citizens take part in the voting process. As a consequence, national policies are often set by small minorities."[42] Important in this context is Money's study of the development of religious nationalism within the Churches of Christ. He analyzed denominational voting trends through an extensive survey. Money developed a questionnaire concerning political views and voting habits, sufficiently comprehensive to "indicate representative opinions and trends within Church of Christ circles."[43] He found within the denomination a significant shift in voting patterns toward conservative positions in recent years.

As might be expected, Money's survey showed that an overwhelming number of church members classified themselves as conservative in both politics and religion. However, the political classification "conservative" did not necessarily indicate loyalty to the Republican party, because members usually did not regard party affiliation or loyalty as an important issue. Because of various sociological and ethnic considerations, including regional uniformity and southern loyalties, affiliation with conservative political groups might include support for both Democratic and Independent candidates. Even though the study showed that independent voters within the membership tended to vote Republican rather than Democrat,[44] especially in national elections, Churches of

Christ members, like others in the New Religious Right, generally could be characterized as members of a subculture influenced more by their religious stance toward the world than by either their economic or their partisan political orientations. Thus, Money's survey decisively indicated that party affiliation was less important to Churches of Christ members than other motivating factors, especially a candidate's adherence to the shared world view considered normative among evangelicals.

Several observers of Churches of Christ politics, including historian David Edwin Harrell and political scientist Norman L. Parks, argue that members of the Churches of Christ traditionally have voted Democratic in state and local elections and Republican in national elections. Money's findings indicate that this is a valid view. However, according to Money, "the most significant discovery from the voting chart results is the steady shift from a Democratic majority among members of the Churches of Christ to a slight Republican edge from 1952 to 1972 in local and state elections." He also discovered that, in presidential elections, members have shown a "definite preference for conservative presidential candidates and have consistently voted more conservative than the national electorate," with the only exception being the election of 1964. However, Goldwater got as many votes as Johnson among Churches of Christ members, and Goldwater's 47 percent from the denomination was far above the 34.5 percent he received nationally.[45] According to Patrick Deese, political science professor at David Lipscomb College in Nashville (again confirmed by Money's statistical analysis), the period 1960–64 formed a turning point within the Churches of Christ, as the membership shifted from being mainly "Roosevelt Democrats to Republicans."[46]

As an overall indicator of significant political change among members of the denomination, from 1952 to 1972, Democratic preference went down from 62 to 43 percent, and Republican preference within the group went up from 28 to 42 percent. Although other motives were present, Money's study indicates that George Benson and NEP had a significant influence on this change of voting attitudes within the Churches of Christ. Money's survey also suggests that Churches of Christ members are basically conservative, and that "Republicans have more accurately conveyed that image in recent years than have the Democrats, especially in Presidential elections."[47] Money's interviews and survey findings suggest that the activities and programs of George Benson and NEP significantly affected "the formulation of an extremely conservative religious, economic and social image among Church of Christ members which portrayed Christianity and Americanism as being integrally related."[48]

More recently, Mel Hailey has surveyed 198 Churches of Christ ministers regarding their ideological commitment to and political support of the New Religious Right. While he admits that his findings "must be interpreted with great caution, the findings indicate that there is a residuum of support for the New Religious Right among politically active ministers," and that his findings generally support the conclusions of other researchers who have determined that political activism among conservative ministers has increased in the past decade.[49] Overall, Hailey's research tends to support and corroborate Money's earlier finding that church leaders, while overwhelmingly rejecting Lipscomb's nonparticipation argument, are not as politically active as more theologically liberal ministers. Despite their apparent lack of political activism, Churches of Christ leaders generally support the ideological framework of the New Religious Right and the Republican party, and consistently express their support at the polls.[50] More important, Hailey's research suggests that the overall effect of the emergence of the New Religious Right on Churches of Christ political ideology, and on that of other conservative religious groups as well, is that its true impact does not rest in its limited legislative victories or electoral victories, but in its "power of reinforcing or shoring up a value system at odds with a secular society," thereby unifying the major tenets of secular and religious conservatism.[51]

Other examples from within the denomination also point to the influence of George Benson and NEP on recent electoral preferences of members of the Churches of Christ. Such influence is exemplified in Robert H. Rowland, who served for nine years as president of Columbia Christian College in Portland, Oregon, before becoming director of the American Citizenship Center at Oklahoma Christian College, Oklahoma City, in 1972.[52] Although Rowland attended Harding College as a graduate student before serving as a missionary in Alaska, apparently he then was not very interested in NEP. He considered himself a Democrat and generally voted for Democratic candidates.[53] However, after he assumed the presidency of Columbia Christian College and thus became more aware of local and national political issues and their importance, he altered his outlook on political questions.

The campaign of Barry Goldwater in 1964 was a political catalyst in Rowland's life. He listened to Goldwater's speeches; read his book, *The Conscience of a Conservative;* and decided that Goldwater's political philosophy reflected more of Rowland's own "gut reaction." He then investigated conservative issues and became a staunch Goldwater supporter. Although, as a college president affiliated with the Churches of Christ, he hesitated to take part openly in partisan politics, he did start an Americanism program patterned after Benson's NEP at Columbia Christian College. According to Rowland, the single most important quality possessed by NEP was its ability to help people to "focus those gut reactions on issues that were generalized before."[54] Rowland felt the need to help focus Oregonians on these issues. Through this NEP-type program, Rowland gained access to public forums on political issues within the state and became prominent within the local political community.

While Benson did not have a direct influence on the establishment of the citizenship program at Columbia Christian, earlier he had effectively set the stage for other conservative spokesmen, such as Rowland, to influence the community. When Rowland started the program in Portland, he soon discovered that the message of George Benson already had reached large numbers of people there. According to Rowland, "There were numerous people who got the letter, businessmen who attended our forums, students who attended the forums, who saw a side of the issues that they had never heard in the public schools or on a university campus."[55] According to Rowland, Benson's films, radio programs, editorials, monthly letters, and speeches "told the side of the story that probably would never have been told without the work of George Benson."[56]

During this same period, on college campuses associated with the Churches of Christ, Benson's Americanism program consistently presented a conservative outlook. Students influenced by Benson and his program then went out to teach or to get graduate degrees, in order to come back to Christian colleges and continue advocating the conservative position.[57]

Rowland also gave an interesting example of the influence the Freedom Forums had had on grassroots political activism in America. In midsummer, after one of the American Citizenship Center's high school Freedom Forums in western Oklahoma, Rowland received a telephone call from a young participant in the program. She told Rowland that she

> wanted to do something about what she had learned. She believed that
> she had a citizenship responsibility to tell what she had heard and pass
> it on. She wondered if I could give her some literature in the form of
> tracts, monographs, whatever else, to pass out at the state fair. She had

gotten two local banks to pay for the rental of her booth. She had a lumber yard supply the plywood to build it. Now she wanted materials. She had two or three organizations that had given her materials already printed. Could I help her? So she drove down with her mother that morning and got four or five boxes of materials on freedom and free enterprise and she spent five days or so at that fair passing out literature to everybody that wanted to take it.[58]

Rowland believed, however, that the primary influence of Benson and NEP on college campuses, especially those supported by the Churches of Christ, was considerably more subtle and ultimately more lasting. He endorsed the claim of the popular conservative columnist James J. Kilpatrick that American colleges and universities, with a few exceptions, are "little brooder houses hatching students who are ignorant of industrial life and generally hostile to the incentive system." However, colleges sponsored by the Churches of Christ are an exception. Commenting on a Harris poll of college students, commissioned by Oklahoma Christian College, Oklahoma City, under Rowland's aegis, Kilpatrick described Oklahoma Christian College as, "by deliberate design, a conservative institution. Without apology, it undertakes to inculcate certain old-fashioned values. In this aim it succeeds." The Harris poll had indicated that American college students in general were suspicious of the free-enterprise economic system and advocated government intervention to control big business.[59] However, at Oklahoma Christian that was not the case.

Rowland claimed that he used the results of this poll to solicit over $15 million to construct Enterprise Square on the college campus. Enterprise Square is a unique educational facility, a combined museum and free-enterprise learning laboratory, dedicated to teaching the merits of the free-enterprise system and to preserving the history of great contributions to the American heritage by the giants of American business. Benson had been advocating free-enterprise education of this type for many years, and Rowland brought Benson's dream to fruition.

In Rowland's opinion, thousands of people who had never heard of George Benson learned about his conservative philosophy indirectly from NEP. They translated that conservative education into political action by voting overwhelmingly Republican in the 1980 election.[60] When asked to assess the impact of forty years of exposure to NEP's philosophy on the Churches of Christ; on Churches of Christ schools, their teachers, and their students; and on students attending the Freedom Forums,

Rowland responded that, politically, George Benson had influenced large numbers of individuals directly. However, Rowland believed that Benson's influence went much deeper, especially when one included those people influenced by Benson's ideology who

> then go to university campuses and train other young people, espe-
> cially, in the field of business and economics; then you have another
> generation or two or three. They are producing educators who go out
> to the schools and teach in high school or elementary school. So those
> basic positions held by George Benson were passed on through speak-
> ers like himself and through his students. Two or three generations of
> these students have had a lot of effect on the thinking of lots of people
> that never heard of George Benson.[61]

The NEP's Influence on the Moral Majority

As already noted, the perception that a threatening "secular humanism" was being sanctioned by federal court decisions prompted large groups of conservative Christians to mobilize politically during the 1970s, to pro-tect the traditional moral values that they felt were rapidly being eroded. According to Wald, the period from 1940 to 1975 saw some significant new interpretations of the traditional church-state relationship in America. In general, the Supreme Court redefined the separation of church and state by (1) applying First Amendment restrictions on religious establishment at state and local levels in addition to the national level, (2) redefining *estab-lishment* to mean "favoring religion," and (3) prohibiting government, to a greater extent, from interfering with the free exercise of religion.[62] As a result of these changes, fundamentalists and other conservative Chris-tians came to believe that government actions were endorsing moral and religious values that were antithetical to the traditional values upon which, in their opinion, American society had been founded.

The New Right that emerged in the 1970s differed significantly from the older conservative program of the previous fifty years in turning away from the traditional "glorification of the past" conservative ideology and emphasizing social progress and single-issue morality.[63] Both the Old and New Christian Right "oppose[d] communism, support[ed] free enterprise and limited government, and respect[ed] (although they [did] not always practice) religion and 'traditional values.'" But, while the Old Right continued to emphasize anticommunism and free enterprise, the New Right developed more populist and conservative themes.[64] Perhaps the most important theme of the New Right has been its insistence upon the "profamily agenda" mentioned earlier. However, this program of alleged moral absolutes also included increased defense spending, support of anticommunism, anti-inflationary policies, efforts against street crime, and calls for a balanced budget—all of which the Religious Right considered moral issues as well.[65]

According to several analysts of the recent conservative resurgence, most notably Alan Crawford, three events during the early 1970s particularly galvanized conservative religious spokesmen into action. These were (1) a school textbook controversy in West Virginia, (2) a gay rights referendum in Dade County, Florida, and (3) opposition to the Equal Rights Amendment, led by Phyllis Schlafly.[66] Most evangelicals and fundamentalists saw the conservative responses as crusades to defend traditional Christian values (i.e., the conservative religious world view discussed earlier) and institutions against the influence of secular humanism, which they felt had become "entrenched in the government, schools, media, and other institutions that molded public perceptions."[67]

To some degree, the resolutions of these three controversies satisfied conservatives and proved to them that mobilization of religious opinion could impact partisan politics. According to Wald, the political success of these "grassroots evangelical actions did not go unnoticed by 'secular' conservative activists who were seeking popular support for a broad agenda encompassing social, economic, defense, and foreign policy issues."[68] Leaders of the conservative movement paid considerable attention to the outcomes of the controversies and the nature of the evangelical support. Howard Phillips of the Conservative Caucus, Paul Weyrich of the Committee for the Survival of a Free Congress, and conservative fund-raiser Richard Viguerie saw the potential influence of the Religious Right on partisan politics and determined to create a conservative coalition, to include the New Religious Right. This coalition could then launch a "frontal attack on 'big government' as a threat to traditional religious and economic values."[69]

It was during early meetings of Phillips, Weyrich, and Viguerie that Ed McAteer, one of Phillips's aides, became involved in the discussion. McAteer had been a regional sales manager for a large soap company but had abandoned sales to try to mobilize conservative Christians to affect public policy. According to McAteer, the primary reason for the increasing national influence of the "secular humanist" philosophy was the lack of involvement by people who "had inherited traditional family values and constitutional government." Such people needed to be "informed and involved in the political process."[70]

McAteer was an evangelical Southern Baptist who already had realized the potential of mobilizing conservative Christians to political action. Earlier he had worked for Howard Kershner as national field director of the Christian Freedom Foundation (CFF).[71] Kershner, a noted conservative activist and frequent speaker on Benson's NEP forums, directed the foundation, which received strong financial support from Sun Oil Company's President J. Howard Pew of Philadelphia. While working for the CFF, McAteer had met Howard Phillips of the Conservative Caucus, which at that time had over six hundred thousand members. McAteer eventually left the CFF and joined Phillips as national field director of the Conservative Caucus. For some time, Phillips and McAteer had been discussing how to get conservative Christians effectively involved in politics. Although both men eagerly sought support from the religious community, they discovered that it would be very difficult to approach religious leaders from a partisan political position. As a result, they decided to approach some of the most influential television evangelists and leaders of large evangelical religious denominations with a proposal to create a broadly based nonpartisan conservative religious coalition which would have significant potential to influence public policy.

In January 1978, Phillips and McAteer flew to Lynchburg, Virginia, to present their proposal to Jerry Falwell, a popular television evangelist, pastor of the Thomas Road Baptist Church, and founder of Liberty University. What had been scheduled as a one-hour meeting lasted for over nine hours; from that meeting and a subsequent one involving Weyrich, Phillips, McAteer, and Falwell, the basic framework for the coalition emerged. Phillips coined the organization's name, "Moral Majority," at that second meeting, and Weyrich first used it in a "presentation to Falwell and his associates."[72]

McAteer and Phillips had envisioned a coalition of conservative religious groups, but rather quickly theological differences among denominational participants presented a major obstacle to Falwell's proposed organizational structure. Soon McAteer observed the increasing friction within the organization between denominational leaders such as Pat Robertson, Jerry Falwell, James Kennedy, Adrian Rogers, and James Robison. McAteer decided that a similar organization decidedly more ecumenical in nature might better embody his perception of Christian involvement in politics, and the Religious Roundtable was formed. The organizational meeting was held in Washington, D.C., in September 1979. According to McAteer, over 130 national leaders were present, including many prominent political, business, and military leaders who were interested in forming a coalition with conservative Christians. Also in attendance was Dr. George S. Benson.

Prior to that meeting, McAteer had commissioned the Lance Tarrance Co. of Houston to survey the opinions of religious people in the United States towards government. Although its accuracy has been questioned by some political analysts, this survey overwhelmingly indicated to McAteer that religious groups in America were ready to become more actively involved in the political process. McAteer had considerable experience in marketing and believed that, before a new product is launched, there should be a market survey to test potential receptivity. Evidently many of those present were convinced that the Religious Roundtable's conservative message would be positively received, since, after the introduction of the initial survey findings, McAteer challenged those present to contribute financially to the new organization. According to McAteer, the first contributor was George Benson.

During the period between the founding of the Moral Majority and the creation of the Religious Roundtable, McAteer had asked many people for advice about the operation of his new program and appropriate goals for it. Among the first people consulted by McAteer was Benson, who agreed with other denominational leaders that undoubtedly there would be a "reticence on the part of religious leaders to be directly connected with a political organization."[73] As a result, McAteer intended his Religious Roundtable to be avowedly nondenominational and nonpartisan.[74]

McAteer believed that the "average American is a common sense person, and if he has the facts and knows how to do things, that he will get involved and do them."[75] With this conviction in mind, McAteer organized National Affairs Briefings, which were meetings designed to accomplish four objectives: (1) to identify, (2) organize, (3) educate, and (4) give direction to people who were concerned about moral issues and their influence on the creation of public policy. At the heart of McAteer's program were local chapters of the Roundtable, which were to present issues at the local level, identify candidates who supported the Roundtable's position, and mobilize a constituency. These local chapters were given various materials from educational associations, "Right-to-Life" coalitions, military organizations, and other social-issue groups. The NEP's materials, especially its free-enterprise materials, were among those distributed at the local meetings.[76] When asked about the impact of Benson's NEP on the conservative transformation during the late 1970s, McAteer claimed that NEP was the primary program for free-enterprise information in the nation during this period, specifically "tying in the free enterprise system with the Christian political movement."[77]

The first "briefing" was held in Tupelo, Mississippi. McAteer's idea was to bring like-minded congressmen, senators, and political organizational people from Washington, D.C., to "grassroots America." Benson spoke at the first National Affairs Briefing and distributed his free-enterprise material to the participants. According to McAteer, who personally contacted Benson and sought his advice, Benson brought three very important elements to the organization of the Religious Roundtable. First, he contributed solid organizational advice and expertise and gave tremendous personal encouragement to McAteer. Second, he was an important spokesman for the Churches of Christ. According to McAteer, Benson's affiliation with the Religious Roundtable (he was on the original board of directors) was invaluable in getting members from that denomination involved in the Roundtable. Third, Benson's free-enterprise program was "one of the real [building] blocks of what we were talking about, along with foreign policy and national defense."[78]

Benson spoke at all fifteen Religious Roundtable meetings before the 1980 election and distributed his NEP materials at each. The largest and most important of those meetings at which Benson spoke was the National Affairs Briefing held in Dallas, at which Ronald Reagan delivered the address that confirmed to the nation his position on the profamily agenda and resulted in his winning a huge following in the Religious Right. According to Wald, the National Affairs Briefing in Dallas was the point in the campaign when Reagan proclaimed his support for the Moral Majority and his status as the candidate of the Religious Right was confirmed. In summation, Wald claims that, although the Moral Majority (meaning the Religious Right as a whole) refrained from formal endorsement, it "conveyed its enthusiasm in every possible way short of outright recommendation." Manifestations of this enthusiasm included pastors' encouraging evangelicals to register to vote and impressing upon "churchgoers the necessity of expressing their religious convictions in the polling booths. These efforts led to a substantial evangelical presence in the polling booths."[79] As mentioned earlier, the entrance of large numbers of religious conservatives into partisan politics in the 1980 election was deemed by many the single most important element in Reagan's election.[80]

In summing up Benson's contribution to the Religious Right, McAteer commented, "I am not flattering George Benson. I cannot say too much for him. His absolutely wonderful cooperation helped me do some of the things that needed to be done. He supplied a vital part of my total national program as it was launched."[81] Apparently, Benson provided advice and expertise on how best to provide free-enterprise and Americanism education to the Religious Right.

Benson was in a unique position to accomplish that educational effort. By 1980, he had spent forty years disseminating conservative political information at the grassroots level. Despite mistakes in judgment, he had kept his program alive and active. When McAteer approached Benson for help and advice in 1978, Benson provided not only encouragement, but also a strong organization that could mobilize conservative Christians for McAteer and eventually for Ronald Reagan.

An important question arises here: "Did Benson help organize the Moral Majority and influence its members to vote Republican?" According to Wald, many conservative Christians already preferred the Republican party before the "New Christian Right organizations began their mobilizing efforts. The groups thus appear to have capitalized upon an underlying transformation rather than to have created it."[82] George Benson was not directly involved in the formal organization of the New Religious Right, but he most certainly was a founder of the Old Religious Right who made the transition to the New. He was one of those who laid the groundwork for the political transformation among conservative Christians, that later was capitalized upon by the New Religious Right. Although he and his program largely had been out of the public eye in recent years, they still made a significant contribution to free-enterprise education as one of the bulwarks of the Religious Right's philosophy as it moved to influence the election of 1980.

The Impact of the National Education Program on the New Right: The Election of 1980

Although he had not formally announced his candidacy for the presidency in September 1978, Ronald Reagan was campaigning in South Carolina. He took time out from his busy schedule to make a telephone call to an old friend. In Searcy, Arkansas, George Benson and a host of his friends were celebrating his eightieth birthday. Reagan's congratulatory phone call added an important dimension to the festive occasion. Reagan's accompanying taped message not only extolled Benson's accomplishments but also served to remind Benson's friends of "all that he has meant to our land."

Reagan pointed out how Benson had spent over forty years campaigning for many of the same issues Reagan was then promoting in the South Carolina campaign. Reagan asserted that he had been "out on the mashed-potato circuit now for a great many years talking about the evils of big government, the conspiracy against this freedom of ours, both from within and without." Reagan "couldn't possibly count," he said, how many times while campaigning he had quoted Benson in his own speeches.

Along with Benson's influence on his own thought, Reagan also recognized that Benson for a long time had played a leading role in shaping grassroots opinion and mobilizing voters to back conservative causes.

According to Reagan, Benson had been warning the American public of the dangers confronting their political and economic system "long before any were willing to accept the warning, or to believe that it could possibly have any bearing on us."[1]

This study has argued that George Benson, through his National Education Program, contributed significantly to the major realignment in American politics, which allowed a conservative-dominated Republican party to gain political control in 1980. This book also has reviewed the important research done by Thomas Fleming, Paul Gottfried, M. J. Heale, Kevin Phillips, Kenneth Wald, and Clyde Wilcox, which places in historical context Benson's contribution to the resurgence of conservatism that led up to the presidential election of 1980. These authors point to at least six important transformative conditions present within American society which greatly influenced this conservative political resurgence.

First, these researchers discovered a significant demographic relocation of the largest conservative constituency from the Northeast to the South and West. Accompanying this demographic shift was a transfer of populist political ideology from its historic home within the Democratic party to the GOP.

Second, the scholars observed that the transfer of important elements of populist ideology from the Democrats to the Republicans ultimately provoked an internal philosophical battle whose outcome changed each party's ideological foundations. The Republican party was no longer the party of the status quo. Instead, it became a party dominated by disgruntled activists bent upon tossing into the political arena cultural wars over what they felt were traditional moral values of Western civilization. This sort of single-issue politics, aimed at restoring moral absolutes to public policy, also served to unite many divergent activist groups under a general conservative banner which Ronald Reagan and his political supporters eventually embraced.

Third, these authors found that conservatives emphasized maintaining a strong military presence in the world. Determined to preserve America as the moral leader of the world, the conservatives demanded renewed anti-Communist activism and increased military spending. As a result, the Republican platform reflected an increased interest in foreign affairs and called for escalating military preparedness. This revived interest in foreign policy also reflected many conservatives' deep-seated fear that the Vietnam War, the Iran hostage crisis, and the Panama Canal Treaty signified that America's hour in history had passed.

Fourth, Republican conservatism benefited significantly from a revitalized neoconservative ideology brought into the party by defectors from the Democratic party intelligentsia. These intellectuals had become disillusioned with the scope and direction of Democratic party liberalism. Many of them loathed the Democrats' association with social and philosophical radicalism, which they felt was the primary cause of the dramatic increase in social, racial, and moral unrest in America.

Fifth, American conservatives renewed their traditional emphasis on fiscal responsibility through decreased government spending. This economic stance dovetailed nicely with their vital concern with reducing government regulation and business taxation. Consequently, they introduced supply-side economics as an alternative to the traditional Democratic insistence that government spending should be used to prime the American economic pump.

Sixth, conservative ranks swelled with the entrance into American politics of the New Religious Right, which had been, until the 1980 election, largely apolitical. Because of the apparent failure of the Democratic party to embody in public policy what many fundamentalists believed to be traditional American moral values, they joined with the Republicans to create a morally based conservatism.

This study has demonstrated that George Benson and his NEP made a significant contribution to the political education of grassroots America in each of these six aspects of the political transformation. Without groups like NEP arguing diligently and forcefully in favor of the aforementioned conservative ideals at the grassroots level, the conservative coalition which carried Ronald Reagan to victory in 1980 might never have materialized. Central to the argument that NEP was influential in the conservative transformation is the contention that, through the years, NEP's materials and services came into the homes of millions of Americans and thereby directly influenced American political education at the grassroots level.[2]

By 1954, NEP had amassed a mailing list of forty-seven thousand people for its newsletters and reprints of speeches. At the same time, it reached millions more through daily and weekly newspaper columns, trade magazines, and labor union publications. It also should be remembered that hundreds of companies distributed NEP's conservative propaganda in weekly pay envelopes. Simultaneously, NEP produced hundreds of radio and television programs that were distributed on more than three hundred stations. These audiovisual presentations also were widely distributed through high school and college film libraries and appeared in MGM movie theaters.[3]

However, NEP's greatest influence probably came through the Freedom Forums and associated NEP materials. While these programs directly influenced those in attendance (both students and representatives of the business community), millions of employees of almost a thousand major corporations later received these educational materials directly from representatives of their own corporations who had attended the Freedom Forums.[4]

Even though NEP aspired to distribute its message nationally, the bulk of its material circulated in the Midwest and the Middle South. The organization was especially prominent among members of the Churches of Christ in these areas, but a careful survey of newspapers, radio stations, and television stations which used NEP materials reveals that its influence was not limited to church members. While the majority of these important media centers were located in the Midwest and Middle South, NEP's programs received significant national attention as well.

The NEP had its greatest impact in those locations identified by Phillips, Gottfried, and Fleming as pivotal in the demographic shift in the conservative power base from Northeast to South and West, both within the Republican party and the national electorate as a whole. At the same time that NEP began targeting the religious and agricultural communities in the South and Southwest, an unprecedented economic transformation was taking place in these regions. As an economic group, residents of the South and Southwest gained a large new measure of influence. Dwelling in a relatively unpopulated and decidedly nonurban environment, they especially resented higher taxes to support federal social service programs in mostly urban areas in other sections of the country. Phillips believes that the generation that came of age in the 1960s has since become "even more conservative, less worried about 'social justice' and more concerned about jobs, mortgages and families."[5]

Resentment over exporting their tax dollars to urban areas led many in the South and Southwest to political activism as "populist outsiders," to use Kevin Phillips' label. While "populist outsiders" of an earlier era had crusaded against the evils of "big business," the postwar populist outsiders to whom Benson spoke campaigned against the evils of "big government" instead.

Through relentless propaganda and campaigning in the South and Southwest, Benson's NEP expressed regional opposition to runaway inflation and massive federal spending for social welfare programs, while touting the merits of a relatively unrestricted free-enterprise system to increase productivity, to reduce inflation, and to shore up the general economy.[6]

During this period of socioeconomic metamorphosis, the liberal-conservative continuum in American political philosophy changed drastically, too. Traditionally, the Democratic party had been the party of the farmer and the laborer, while its political opposition nearly always had represented businessmen and professionals. This alignment explained the pre–World War II liberal-conservative philosophical division in American politics.[7] However, the Democratic party in America after the war took on a decidedly different philosophical cast. Under Kennedy's New Frontier and Johnson's Great Society, the farmer and laborer received less political attention, as the goals and methodologies of liberalism became more and more theoretical, technological, and sociological. According to Phillips, the era found liberals

> blueprinting a war in Vietnam with computers, rearranging schools and neighborhoods to promote racial balance, philosophizing about the irrelevance of budget deficits and gold. Slowly but surely liberalism lost much of its Jacksonian and Trumanesque moorings in rural Missouri and steel-making East Baltimore and, led by the ascendant professors, urban planners, social-welfare workers, minority causists and international economists, managed to become increasingly the political vehicle and banner of *those* interests, not of blue-collar Americans.[8]

Into this political wasteland, where the needs of farmers and laborers appeared to have been largely abandoned in favor of minorities and the disadvantaged, stepped a group of conservative spokesmen and populist activists. In the 1970s they offered to end inflation, to cut government spending on social programs, and to shore up a sagging American economy, so that farmers and laborers could not only help rebuild the nation's prosperity but enjoy a larger share of it.

Conservative activists in the 1970s preached the same message that Benson and his followers had disseminated successfully for thirty years. While Benson had no control over the demographic patterns of postwar America, he was in a unique position to broadcast his message to the thousands of conservatives who were moving southward and westward during that period. To some of these transplanted Americans, Benson appeared to epitomize the very best qualities of the conservative tradition. He always fit the idealized image of an extremely hard-working, frugal, and dedicated individual who embodied the Protestant work ethic of an earlier era—an ethic that many felt had been irretrievably lost. At the same time, he convinced thousands of listeners that these principles, which he called Americanism, had been the dominant ideals of the nation's Founders and that future American governments should reflect these qualities. The financial success of Harding College seemed to prove the truth of these principles, espoused for years by other conservatives and traditionalists, and helped to point like-minded Americans toward the proper course for the future.

Simultaneously, there occurred a changing of the guard within the Republican party. One sensitive issue which polarized Republicans during these years of ideological transformation was the dispute over the apparent loss of American military power and prestige. Many conservatives within the party called for a renewed American military buildup, accompanied by a strong commitment to vigorous anticommunism. Although this was a central issue in the 1964 election, the debacle in Vietnam, under the leadership of political moderates, rallied conservatives around a stronger military commitment.

Among American conservatives, Benson and NEP were early voices for vigorous anticommunism and military preparedness. Shortly after World War II, NEP, especially through its Freedom Forums and its anti-Communist films, such as *Communism on the Map, Communist Encirclement,* and *The Truth about Communism,* emerged as a pacesetter in this area. As mentioned earlier, Fred Schwarz of the Christian Anti-Communist Crusade received early support from Benson and NEP. In 1962, Ronald Reagan, who narrated *The Truth about Communism,* participated in a Christian Anti-Communist Crusade rally in Los Angeles, at which he denounced the welfare state because it "represented a centralization of government just as dangerous for Americans as Communism."[9]

While mainstream Republican conservatives during this period still emphasized economic and social issues, the greatest source of party unity and cohesion was a profound shared perception of an internal and external Communist threat. Of course, early in his career Benson and NEP had exploited this fear and assumed a strident anticommunism stance. In the process of articulating a perception of subversion, betrayal, and passivity on the part of American political leaders, Benson and other outspoken anti-Communists had tapped into what Stanley Kutler has described as a "constant thread in the American political and social fabric since the late nineteenth century."[10] Beginning with eighteenth-century fears about the "fragility of republican institutions" and continuing through twentieth-century anxiety about subversion, Americans already insecure in a competitive economy and a democratic polity frequently heard that their Republic was imperiled by enemies within and without. As a result, according to Heale, in America no single interest "could long monopolize, and a challenge to the preeminence of a particular class or group could be interpreted—or represented—as a form of insurrection."[11]

Amid this persistent trend in American political thought, especially after the Communist takeover of Eastern Europe following World War II, virulent anticommunism captured the attention of the major political party elites.[12] Generally, Republicans blamed the Democrats for the sudden appearance of Communist sympathizers within American society, and, as the Cold War intensified under President Truman, Roosevelt's war policies were "examined anew for evidence of softness toward the emerging Russian enemy rather than the weakening German foe."[13] Many Republicans were convinced that Roosevelt's cooperation with Stalin had jeopardized America's position of strength in the postwar world. Truman, in practice a hawkish Cold War Democrat, inherited responsibility for this awkward situation. Similarly, in February 1950, when Senator Joseph McCarthy charged that 205 "card-carrying Communists" had infiltrated the State Department, blame once again fell on the Democrats.

However, as the argument over the threat of communism intensified and the "witch hunts" organized by McCarthy spread into many areas of American life, including the movie industry,[14] popular dissatisfaction with McCarthy's tactics spread to Republican party ranks. The debates became so intense that, once again, many moderate Republicans were alienated from the conservative followers of McCarthy. The party thus was threatened once again with division, this time over the anti-Communist issue.

The Republican Convention battle between the moderates and conservatives and the outcome of the 1964 election should be viewed as the culmination of two decades of anti-Communist rhetoric in American politics. Even though anticommunism does not necessarily indicate political extremism—many moderates in both parties supported it as a viable government policy—Goldwater's defeat in 1964 may be attributed to his alleged association with, and sympathy for, several extremist factions who rallied around the anti-Communist banner. Schwarz's Christian Anti-Communist Crusade, Billy James Hargis's Christian Crusade, Rev. Carl McIntire's Twentieth Century Reformation Hour, and Robert Welch's John Birch Society were the leading ultraconservative organizations which, with varying degrees of enthusiasm, supported Barry Goldwater in 1964. While these organizations denied any particular partisan affiliation, Goldwater's tacit approval of their agendas tarred him with the brush of extremism in the eyes of many mainstream voters. The extremist image grew stronger after his acceptance speech during the convention, in which he proclaimed that "extremism in the defense of liberty is no vice."[15]

Even after Goldwater's 1964 defeat, a persistent strain of anticommunism remained within the American polity, and this eventually was exploited by Ronald Reagan and his conservative allies. In his account of American anticommunism, Heale attributes the continued popularity of this message to its strong association with fundamentalist Protestantism throughout this period. According to Heale, Benson and his organization provided important leadership against communism in the South and Southwest during this era. The NEP used "broadcasts, free newspaper columns, textbooks, and school study outlines to 'immunize our people to Communist infiltration and propaganda.'"[16] However, by the late 1970s, organizations such as Benson's NEP, Schwarz's Christian Anti-Communist Crusade, and Hargis's Christian Crusade faded from the American limelight, while a "new breed of evangelist, exploiting the continued growth of the fundamentalist sects and the technology of television, kept alive some of the old preoccupations. Such 'televangelists' as Jerry Falwell, Jim Bakker, and Pat Robertson were eloquent foes of 'Godless Communism.'"[17] It is very important, then, to note that the consistent anti-Communist message they broadcast into millions of American homes during the 1970s reinforced a jeremiad that had been proclaimed by Benson and NEP as early as 1946.

Ronald Reagan, the conservative political activist in the Goldwater train, in the 1964 Republican campaign embodied an "insurgent spirit" that spawned the New Right in the 1980s. The New Right advanced a populist approach to American politics, while preserving the remnants of a classical conservative political philosophy. While George Benson struggled to stay free of partisan political entanglements, those who heard him speak during the Goldwater era easily recognized him as a Goldwater supporter. One may argue that Benson supported Goldwater's conservative ideals rather than the candidate; in practice it was impossible to make such a distinction, for the public never could grasp such subtleties. Even so, it is quite obvious that very similar political ideologies undergirded NEP and the 1964 Goldwater campaign. The press tied NEP, as well as other "extremist" groups, to Goldwater, an association that contributed to the GOP defeat. However, despite the 1964 humiliation at the polls, Benson stuck to his beliefs during the subsequent lean years of conservatism and helped to engineer a conservative resurgence at the grassroots level that dictated the dominant ideology of the Republican party in the 1980s.

At the same time that many conservatives blamed an international Communist conspiracy for American failures abroad and for increased civil rights and antiwar activism at home, other conservatives cited communism and its associated "secular humanist" philosophy as the chief sources of America's deeper social disorientation. Benson and NEP shared this nostalgic perception with millions of Americans who believed that their society was ethically disoriented and beset by unwarranted racial and social strife during the 1960s and 1970s. As far as Benson and millions of other conservatives were concerned, the twin influences of communism and secular humanism had eaten away at the moral fiber of America. As a result, Benson and NEP consistently and persistently argued for a renewed military preparedness abroad and a rededication to traditional moral values at home, as means of calming the nation's widespread social and racial unrest.

In the opinion of Carey McWilliams, who analyzed California as a social melting pot after World War II, many residents, having recently relocated there from some other state, looked back fondly upon simpler and better times in their former homes.[18] Obviously, their nostalgia conjured up an America that never existed except in Hollywood productions in which actors like Ronald Reagan busily recreated that vanishing "social utopia."[19]

A substantial number of conservatives who rallied around Reagan never understood that it was impossible to recreate America's glory years except in the movies. Benson and his followers might be classified as despairing traditionalists who mourned a decaying social order and "fumed about Federal Courts that imposed restrictions on school prayer and municipal Christmas displays while striking down restraints on abortion and nude dancing." At the same time, they viewed with alarm an economy in disarray to a "magnitude not seen since the 1930s." They were unhappy that America no longer dominated in world affairs and angry that the Japanese outproduced American heavy industry and surpassed American technological accomplishments. They were dismayed to see that America was an empire in retreat, after the loss in Vietnam and the return of the Panama Canal to a contemptible and obviously unstable Panamanian government. A Harris poll taken at the end of the 1970s revealed that, from 1966 to 1979, Americans steadily had lost faith in their own political institutions and in their power to solve civic problems. The poll also showed that the public viewed with suspicion many national institutions, particularly the press, television news broadcasting, organized labor, and even organized religion.[20]

The NEP, as part of the wider conservative movement, had focused upon virulent anticommunism in the 1950s. Now resentment rallied conservatives to a banner of nostalgia, national glory, and economic health. According to Kevin Phillips, "Our political history suggests that our country's wars do not end—not their final national impact—until they've been refought in the political arena, and the refighting can go on for more than a decade."[21] Apparently, American dissatisfaction over the Vietnam debacle, coupled with the humiliating Iranian hostage crisis, reminded conservatives that they preferred aggressive foreign policy and military strength to "détente." Reagan's campaign rhetoric made much of contemporary American military reversals. He promised to revitalize American foreign policy and to strengthen the American military, even though American relations with the Soviet Union had been improving steadily. Reagan and his conservative followers believed that negotiating with the Russians from a position of strength was far superior to being forced to the bargaining table out of weakness. Oddly enough, this very same message had been rejected by the American people when Barry Goldwater first presented it in 1964. However, in 1980, Reagan spoke with a substantially reorganized Republican party at his back and to a generally more militant conservative national electorate. In Phillips's opinion, this political nostalgia stirred the national electorate, aroused Americans who longed for a "more powerful, less sophisticated and less cynical yesteryear," and undoubtedly affected the outcome of the 1980 presidential election.[22]

Throughout this period, Benson and his supporters presented an identical message to the American public. Benson's NEP newsletter, his editorials, and his speeches continually decried America's fading glory. Generally he blamed liberal Communist sympathizers within American society and the foreign organizations which he said controlled them. While conservative activists within the Republican party played on frustrations over defeat in Southeast Asia and anger over attacks from without and subversion within, others in the new coalition became aware that for years Benson had been leading the fight against American complacency in the face of "Communist subversion." During the 1970s, more and more top-ranking conservatives listened attentively to Benson's advice.

Benson's direct influence on many of the conservative and neoconservative theorists of his day is difficult to gauge statistically. It can be argued, however, that, like Ronald Reagan, many Republican party leaders of the 1980s acquired conservative principles in part through George Benson's considerable influence. For over forty years, Benson had been a prolific speaker and pamphleteer within the conservative movement. According to Leopold Tyrmand, Reagan (and certainly other leading thinkers within the conservative movement) had been influenced greatly via cultural osmosis, as men like Benson constantly kept conservative ideals before the public.[23]

It should be remembered that George Benson had studied at the University of Chicago in the 1930s, when many of the scholars to whom Tyrmand referred had been sharpening and perfecting conservative tenets. Benson, like many others at the university, had spent considerable time abroad during the interwar period and had seen at first hand the human misery brought on by totalitarian political leadership. He found that the conservative free-enterprise economics and republican political values taught at the University of Chicago contrasted sharply with socialism and Marxism. He already had been exposed to the practical shortcomings of socialist ideology in China during the 1920s, so socialist theorists who had become more active in America's academic communities during the Depression failed to shake Benson's conservative allegiances. The open intellectual atmosphere and spirited arguments of students and professors on that campus during the 1930s produced many of the intellectual leaders of the conservative resurgence of the 1970s.

Even though many of these intellectuals made a considerable impact on conservative political ideology during the 1960s and 1970s, one historian of the Reagan revolution doubts whether Reagan actually read their works. Instead, probably "their ideas came to him via cultural osmosis, from conservative publicists and pamphleteering."[24] Nonetheless, at a 1981 meeting of the Conservative Political Conference, Reagan himself claimed to be the ideological heir of these classical theoreticians. He believed that his party's victory owed a great debt to ideologues such as Russell Kirk, Friedrich A. Hayek, Milton Friedman, and Ludwig von Mises.[25] Friedman, who won the Nobel Prize for economics in 1975, formulated Reagan's supply-side economic theory. With Hayek, Richard Weaver, and Leo Strauss, he taught at the University of Chicago, and, according to Gottfried and Fleming, "played a formative role in creating a conservative movement as well as a conservative world view."[26] Strauss, who held an endowed chair in political thought at Chicago, was another of the most influential conservative theoreticians of the era. He scored "'value-relativity' as the mortal sin of the American intelligentsia" and believed in the importance of "putting sound teachings into political practice." Among his students who went on to become important conservative apologists were such noted scholars as Martin Diamond, Harry V. Jaffa (author of Goldwater's controversial 1964 acceptance speech), and Alan Bloom, who wrote an influential critique of value relativity, *The Closing of the American Mind.*[27] Of course, these scholarly conservative political thinkers helped to transform the Republican party elite, but primarily it was activists such as Benson who motivated the grassroots political elements in America to action.

One of the three influential New Right theorists deemed most responsible for the conservative transformation within the Republican party was Howard Phillips of the Conservative Caucus.[28] He described himself as a great admirer of George Benson and admitted that he "could not remember a time since he had become politically conscious when he did not know about the work of George Benson."[29]

Even though Benson and NEP had a marked influence upon the anti-Communist movement, and to a certain extent were major contributors to classical conservative political philosophy during this period, it is their influence upon conservative economic theory and the "profamily agenda" of the Religious Right that most graphically illustrates their role in the conservative transformation.

The elements perhaps most responsible for the conservative metamorphosis and the eventual Republican ascendancy in 1980 were promises to initiate a substantially new economic policy for American society and to enforce fiscal responsibility. Fulfilling these would involve lowering taxes to stimulate consumer spending and capital investment, deregulating corporate America to improve productivity, and shifting the burden of welfare payments to the communities. Generally, the aim was "to get government off the backs of the American people."

Central to this economic philosophy was the belief that inflation was the source of America's economic difficulties. The major cause of runaway inflation was, in this view, uncontrolled government spending. Kevin Phillips asserts that "no one can understand American politics of the 1980s without first grasping the nature of a global price revolution" that has seen price indexes in the U.S. and Western Europe rise by 300 to 600 percent since World War II.[30]

The conservative synthesis in the early 1970s, formulated by activists such as Benson, mobilized the populist electorate by "postulating a new oppressive *public sector* economic elite—the bureaucrats and managers of the Inflationary State." In this view, government had "become the dominant (and an inefficient and abusive) means of production, extorting the prices of its goods and services through taxes."[31] Under the guise of Keynesian economics, the government carried the program of artificially created inflation to ease debt, for which turn-of-the-century populists had unsuccessfully argued. Even the Republican Richard Nixon, who also failed to curb government spending, excused his inability by boasting, "We're all Keynesians now."[32] Though Reagan's economic plans ultimately failed to curb government spending, even though they substantially reduced inflation, he and his conservative supporters mobilized a populist electorate dedicated to reversing the tendency to increase the size and scope of government.[33] Even though American populism had been, since the 1890s, a tool of the economic left, in the 1960s populism shifted steadily to the right.[34]

Fiscal conservatives laid the blame for prolonged economic stagnation at the feet of Kennedy's New Frontier and Johnson's Great Society, even though they grudgingly admitted that Johnson had been the last president to present a balanced budget.[35] Although Eisenhower and Nixon were equally to blame for increasing the size of government, it had taken a considerable amount of time for what the right called the governmental "spending frenzy" to outstrip the productive capacity of the American economy. As a result, "as the 1970s opened, conservative economic theories were outsider credos barely taken seriously by either the Republican administration of Richard Nixon or the business community." But, by 1981, monetarism, supply-side economics, deregulation, and gold currency convertibility were recognized as "the official economic theology of a new revolutionary conservative government."[36]

While these conservative economic panaceas produced results that were mixed at best, one still may argue that they did inject, even among liberal economic theorists, new respect for hard work and thrift. At the same time, they restored respect for business, investment, and production. The Reagan economic synthesis, as it was played out in the American economy, also rehabilitated the respect for work, faith, family, and flag, at least to a limited extent, because Americans believed that a return to economic strength would produce spiritual and military strength as well.[37]

This marriage of supply-side economic theory to fundamentalist theology had a great influence on the 1980 election. Conservative theorists like Benson invoked America's past to prove that the free-enterprise system and freedom of religion were related and mutually dependent: "theology has been a powerful ally of conservative economics," and religion could be "yoked to capitalism of yore." Both R. H. Tawney and Max Weber argued that the effort "invokes and involves two Calvins: President Calvin Coolidge and the sixteenth-century reformer John Calvin."[38] Reagan and his followers argued this linkage during the campaign of 1980, just as NEP consistently had proclaimed it earlier, because the theological legitimacy of the corporation was important not only to justify the increased role they hoped business would play in politics, but also to strengthen the ideological alliance of conservative politics, free enterprise, and fundamentalist religion.

For forty years, Benson's NEP had been promoting Reagan's economic theories, especially his pledge to "get the government off the backs of the American people." An integral part of Benson's Americanism program was the claim that the free-enterprise system had to be free from government planning and regulation. In 1980 Reagan echoed these NEP arguments while raising fundamental objections to government "interference" in the economy.

During the campaign, Reagan pledged to free the economy of inflation and slow growth, whose causes, according to proponents of limited government, were the unnecessary proliferation of government programs, regulations on the economy, and high taxes. Many conservatives, including Benson, argued that, even after fifteen years of the War on Poverty and the Great Society programs, "few of the high expectations of their proponents had been realized." They felt that "too much money was being spent on such programs, sometimes with too little effect, and that too large a proportion of the population had become dependent on federal assistance, weakening the incentives for them to make it on their own."[39]

Perhaps the most striking aspect of Reagan's program was its "coherent set of philosophical principles for addressing the nation's problems and a talent for communicating his vision of the country's future."[40] The long-term efforts of organizations such as NEP, arguing for basic conservative economic principles, formed the historical backdrop to Reagan's "revolutionary" prescriptions for America's problems in the 1980s.

The history of NEP is the story of Benson and his followers, persistently advocating their belief in constitutional government and the free-enterprise system, as well as their belief that God is active in the affairs of men, especially in the activities of America. To Benson and his NEP staff, these ideals remained supreme, undergirding American society and enabling America to assume the economic and moral leadership of the world. Beginning with his plea for economy in government before the House Ways and Means Committee in 1941, Benson consistently advocated a relatively unrestricted free-enterprise system as the best—and the only constitutional—means to increase the productivity, wealth, and well-being of individual Americans.

As noted in this study, NEP produced hundreds of television programs and movies which contrasted the merits of free-enterprise economics with the evils of collectivization. Over the years, millions of people came in contact with this conservative economic propaganda at the same time that the federal budget for social services increased at a staggering rate. Simultaneously, in the late 1970s, America experienced its worst inflation since the end of World War II.

Benson's NEP, through thousands of speeches and publications and hundreds of audiovisual presentations directed at the general public, high schools, and college students, emphasized the seemingly inarguable correlation between high levels of government spending and runaway inflation. Simultaneously, NEP advocated deregulation of American industry and supply-side economics as remedies for the problems of decreased productivity and decreased consumer buying power.

According to Kevin Phillips, the four major components of the conservative economic hypothesis were: (1) supply-side theory, (2) monetarism, (3) gold convertibility, and (4) far-reaching economic deregulation.[41] Benson's NEP had advocated each of these components of conservative economic theory since the early 1940s; as the years passed, its arguments reached an ever wider audience for its movies and lectures. Eventually the members of this audience voted for conservative economics at the polls.[42]

The sixth and perhaps the most important element of the conservative resurgence is the influence of the Religious Right. Over the years, Benson exerted a significant influence on the Churches of Christ, especially on the educational level of the denomination during its rise in economic status. Perhaps no individual had more influence on political thought within the Churches of Christ than George Benson. Whether or not they agreed with his general philosophy, many within the denomination were led to an increased political involvement through interaction with NEP.

Benson's influence within the Churches of Christ was not his only influence on the Religious Right. As Ed McAteer, the founder of the Religious Roundtable has indicated, George Benson and his free-enterprise education played a direct and highly significant role in the influence of Religious Right's "profamily agenda" during the 1980 campaign. Because the leaders of the Religious Right made free-enterprise economics a moral issue, Benson was able effectively to combine theology and economics for them—or, more precisely, to combine free-enterprise economics with a prevailing post–World War II "civil religion."[43]

In summary, NEP labored as a tireless agent for conservative political education in America. Determining just how much impact, negative or positive, it had on any given election is, at best, difficult without a careful review of the statistical evidence, much of which remains unavailable. However, from the nature and scope of the criticisms used against NEP, we can judge that it probably had a significant impact on the development of a conservative political ideology during this period. Conversely, because of the negative influence surrounding the program, NEP probably deserves some of the blame for the defeat of Goldwater in the election of 1964, in conservatism's first opportunity at national leadership. But we also can judge from the quality, persistence, and sheer volume of its propaganda and educational materials, that NEP probably contributed greatly, at the grassroots level, to the resurgent activism of many concerned citizens who maintained a deep-seated belief in conservative political ideals as the proper foundation for American institutions.

To these ends, George Benson and NEP dedicated forty years of service. Benson must be credited with a significant impact on the political education of the nation. Throughout, he never consciously strove to convert liberals to conservative positions, but rather he attempted to sensitize already "conservative Christians to political issues and to their need to get involved."[44] To a large degree, the nation's new political leadership and many of the rank and file, especially since the election of 1980, have supported the conservative values and ideals which George Benson advocated throughout his life. Benson's political education program proved most effective, either directly or indirectly, in influencing many at the grassroots level of the resurgent political right.

Notes

Preface

1. Bob Schieffer and Gary Paul Gates, *The Acting President* (New York: E. P. Dutton, 1989), 4.
2. Cited in Kevin P. Phillips, *Post-Conservative America: People, Politics, and Ideology in a Time of Crisis* (New York: Random House, 1982), 49. Phillips cited the Harris poll released on November 4, 1980. While these estimates may have been a little high and "not the monolith originally portrayed by media accounts, it was a sizable percentage of the target constituency." Clyde Wilcox, "Evangelicals and the Moral Majority," *Journal for the Scientific Study of Religion* 28, no. 4 (1989): 407. Despite a wealth of new analytical studies by political scientists attempting to disprove the contention that the New Religious Right contributed significantly to Reagan's victory, there has been no clear consensus on the subject. Most of the research has merely dissected the New Religious Right into its constituent parts, paying little attention to synthesizing statistical analysis and the many historical and sociological studies on the influence of religion in society. See, e.g., Kathleen Murphy Beatty and B. Oliver Walter, "Fundamentalists, Evangelicals, and Politics," *American Politics Quarterly* 16, no. 1 (Jan. 1988): 43; and Clyde Wilcox, "Evangelicals and Fundamentalists in the New Christian Right: Religious Differences in the Ohio Moral Majority," *Journal for the Scientific Study of Religion* 25, no. 3 (1986): 355–63.
3. Kevin Phillips, *Post-Conservative America,* 189.
4. Clyde Wilcox, "The Christian Right in Twentieth-Century America: Continuity and Change," *Review of Politics* 50, no. 4 (Fall 1988): 668.
5. On the major differences between these constituencies' participation in politics, see Beatty and Walter, "Fundamentalists, Evangelicals, and Politics"; and Wilcox, "Evangelicals and Fundamentalists."
6. Steve Bruce, *The Rise and Fall of the New Religious Right* (Oxford, England: Clarendon Press, 1988), 41.

7. Charles W. Dunn, ed., *American Political Theology: Historical Perspectives and Theoretical Analysis* (New York: Praeger, 1984), 83. Dunn cites Paul Kurtz, ed., *Humanist Manifestos One & Two* (Buffalo, N.Y.: Prometheus, 1973), 7–10.

8. Bruce, *Rise and Fall,* 30.

9. James Dunphy, "A Religion for a New Age," *Humanist* 43 (Jan.–Feb. 1983): 26.

10. Kevin Phillips, *Post-Conservative America,* 189–90.

11. Lee Edwards, "Paul Weyrich, Conscience of the New Right," *Conservative Digest,* July 1981, 2.

12. Kevin Phillips, *Post-Conservative America,* 189–90. Unfortunately, as far as some die-hard conservatives were concerned, Reagan and his successor, George Bush, never mastered fiscal responsibility. As early as the 1984 election campaign, fiscal conservatives such as Howard Phillips and Paul Weyrich abandoned Reagan and Bush in search of more conservative leadership. Ultimately, Howard Phillips found no one equal to the task, so he entered the 1992 presidential race himself, promising to reduce the federal budget to 1987 levels immediately, to eliminate the income tax, and eventually to eliminate all federal programs not in existence in 1960. From televised campaign interview in Atlanta, Ga., Oct. 23, 1992.

13. Bruce, *Rise and Fall,* 56–59.

14. Howell Raines, "Reagan Backs Evangelicals in Their Political Activities," *New York Times,* Aug. 23, 1980, B9.

15. Immediately after his inauguration, Reagan began disappointing his staunch conservative allies, who demanded almost blind obedience to altogether unrealistic and impractical ideals. Although much of the Reagan administration's policy advocated conservative solutions to the staggering problems confronting the nation, in reality Reagan bowed rather quickly to the necessity for political compromise and abandoned his conservative rhetoric in favor of more pragmatic answers. While dramatically increasing the defense budget, firing striking air traffic controllers, and deregulating the transportation industry, Reagan succumbed to demands by state and local governments for entitlements and federal grants of various types, thereby almost tripling the federal deficit in eight years. For an interesting analysis of what happened to Reagan's conservative coalition, consult Schieffer and Gates, *Acting President,* esp. chap. 1.

16. Many conservative organizers such as Howard Phillips, Weyrich, and Viguerie, although associated more closely with Republicans than with Democrats, "stressed the bipartisan nature of the movement they had helped mobilize." Bruce, *Rise and Fall,* 149.

17. John C. Stevens, *Before Any Were Willing: The Story of George S. Benson* (Searcy, Ark.: Harding Univ. Press, 1991), 391.

18. Mike Trimble, "Searcy: A Portrait of an Arkansas Town," *Arkansas Times,* July 1986, 64.

Introduction

1. James A. Morone, *The Democratic Wish: Popular Participation and the Limits of American Government* (New York: Basic Books, 1990).
2. Samuel P. Huntington, *American Politics: The Promise of Disharmony* (Cambridge, Mass.: Belknap Press of Harvard Univ. Press, 1981).
3. Kevin Phillips, *Post-Conservative America*, xx.
4. Kenneth D. Wald, *Religion and Politics in the United States* (New York: St. Martin's Press, 1987), xi.
5. Bruce, *Rise and Fall*.
6. Paul Gottfried and Thomas Fleming, *The Conservative Movement* (Boston: Twayne, 1988).
7. Kevin P. Phillips, *The Emerging Republican Majority* (New Rochelle, N.Y.: Arlington House, 1969); Kevin P. Phillips, *Mediacracy: American Parties and Politics in the Communication Age* (Garden City, N.Y.: Doubleday, 1975); and Kevin Phillips, *Post-Conservative America*.
8. Phillips, *Post-Conservative America*, 186.
9. See esp. Kevin Phillips, *Post-Conservative America, Emerging Republican Majority,* and *Mediacracy*; as well as Gottfried and Fleming, *Conservative Movement*. Although a shrewd observer of the conservative transformation, Kevin Phillips never has presented himself as an apologist for the conservative movement. Rather, he has been one of its most vocal critics. Long-time conservative analyst William A. Rusher, who, along with F. Clifton White, organized the Draft Goldwater Committee, credits Kevin Phillips, *Emerging Republican Majority,* with accurately describing the "coalition of social and economic conservatives that was just then taking power in America (and which has retained it, almost uninterruptedly, ever since)." However, Kevin Phillips, *Post-Conservative America,* "turned savagely against the coalition and its avatar, Ronald Reagan." William A. Rusher, "GOP Must Stop Efforts to Bash Reagan Era," *Memphis* (Tenn.) *Commercial Appeal,* June 27, 1990. Phillips's most recent book is described by one conservative publicist as a "book-length tantrum against the 'greed' of the Reagan Years. *The Politics of Rich and Poor* should make Kevin a potful of money by confirming the mythology of the left at the expense of both the right and the truth"; Warren T. Brookes, "Phillips's Populist Greed," *Memphis* (Tenn.) *Commercial Appeal,* Aug. 6, 1990.
10. Kevin Phillips, *Post-Conservative America*, 88–104.
11. Ibid., 37–40; Gottfried and Fleming, *Conservative Movement,* 77–82.
12. See Joseph Sobran, *Single Issues: Essays on the Crucial Social Questions* (New York: Human Life Press, 1983).
13. Gottfried and Fleming, *Conservative Movement,* 11–20.
14. Kevin Phillips, *Post-Conservative America,* 43–46; Gottfried and Fleming, *Conservative Movement,* 59–76.

15. Kevin Phillips, *Post-Conservative America,* 50–51.

16. Gottfried and Fleming, *Conservative Movement,* 82–95; Wald, *Religion and Politics,* 186–212; Kevin Phillips, *Post-Conservative America,* 46–50. William G. McLoughlin, in his classic study, *Revivals, Awakenings, and Reform* (Chicago: Univ. of Chicago Press, 1978), which preceded the rise of the moral majority, would define this phenomenon in terms of the sociological process of "revitalization." According to this theory, first advocated by sociologist Anthony F. C. Wallace, the New Religious Right attempted politically to revitalize the cultural system in order to "overcome jarring disjunctions between norms and experience, old beliefs and new realities, dying patterns and emerging patterns of behavior." McLoughlin, *Revivals,* 10.

17. Bruce, *Rise and Fall,* 22. The best in-depth history of anticommunism during this period, including an exhaustive bibliographical essay, is M. J. Heale, *American Anticommunism: Combating the Enemy Within, 1830–1970* (Baltimore, Md.: Johns Hopkins Univ. Press, 1990).

18. Kevin Phillips, *Post-Conservative America,* xviii.

19. Ibid., 51.

20. Morone, *Democratic Wish,* 3.

21. Ibid., 7.

22. Ibid., 5.

23. Huntington, *American Politics,* 4.

24. Morone, *Democratic Wish,* 3.

25. Frank S. Meyer, "Conservatism," in *Left, Right, and Center: Essays on Liberalism and Conservatism in the United States,* ed. Robert A. Goldwin (Chicago: Rand McNally, 1965), 5.

26. Ibid., 7

27. Morone, *Democratic Wish,* 26.

28. Meyer, "Conservatism," 5. James Guth has found that objection to the "thoroughgoing secularism" of "New Politics" Democrats and their ascendancy as social and political elites in the 1960s and 1970s was largely responsible for the political mobilization of religious conservatives in the 1980s. James Guth et al., "The Politics of Religion in America," *American Politics Quarterly* 16, no. 3 (July 1988): 363.

29. John L. Palmer and Isabel V. Sawhill, *The Reagan Experiment: An Examination of Economic and Social Policies Under the Reagan Administration* (Washington D.C.: Urban Institute Press, 1982), argues that the Reagan "counterrevolution," with Congressional approval, attempted to implement broad conservative remedies instead. According to *Congressional Quarterly,* Reagan's success rate at implementing these policies was 82 percent in his first year in office. Qtd. in Bruce, *Rise and Fall,* 136.

30. Morone, *Democratic Wish,* 29.

31. Sociologists such as Max Weber have identified this process as "cultural defense." "In this view, a movement such as the New Christian Right would be explained as a reaction to changes in the social, moral, cultural, and political environment which threatened to undermine the ability of a particular group to maintain its shared culture." Bruce, *Rise and Fall,* 16.

32. James D. Bales, *Americanism Under Fire* (Searcy, Ark.: Bales Bookstore, 1965), 1.

33. George S. Benson to Ted Altman, Sept. 23, 1970. Transcript in personal collection of Ted Altman, Harding University, Searcy, Ark.

34. Philip S. Rose, "Arkansas Crusader," *Saturday Evening Post* 216 (June 3, 1944): 19. This article is a distillation of research on the early history of NEP, interviews with its organizers, and observations of Benson at various speaking engagements. Rose concludes with this observation: "I came away from my visit with Dr. Benson feeling that here is a man who is good to the core. He is a basic American. He draws his inspiration from the founding fathers of the republic, from the truths of history, and from the Bible. He wants America to rededicate itself to human freedom, to divest itself of all foreign ideologies and resume its march forward. This is his platform. Win, lose, or draw, he is in the fight to the end." Ibid., 85.

35. Ibid., 84.

36. According to Bruce, *Rise and Fall,* 49, "the market for the New Christian Right was created by the interaction of a number of trends. On the one hand, an increasingly liberal state, committed to promoting interests (such as those of blacks, women, and homosexuals) which fundamentalists opposed, was intervening more and more in the sub-societies and subcultures of conservative Protestant America. On the other hand, the rise of the South and the stronger profile of the evangelical religion gave conservative Protestants reasons to feel both that they were not getting their due and that their due could be got if they organized to claim it."

37. Ibid., 16. See also Echo E. Fields, "Understanding Activist Fundamentalism: Capitalist Crisis and the 'Colonization of the Lifeworld,'" *Sociological Analysis* 52, no. 2 (Summer 1991).

38. Bruce, *Rise and Fall,* 18. See also J. Craig Jenkins, "Resource Mobilization and the Study of Social Movements," *Annual Review of Sociology* 9 (1983): 527–53.

39. Bruce, *Rise and Fall,* 24.

40. Kevin Phillips, *Post-Conservative America,* 51–52.

41. Reagan, even in his days as the "ultraconservative" governor of California, was known as a "coalition builder. From the very beginning of his first administration, Reagan chose to concentrate on issues that united conservatives: rebuilding the American economy and containing the spread of Communism." Gottfried and Fleming, *Conservative Movement,* 96.

1. The Development of a Rugged Individualist

1. Much of this early biographical information comes from three primary sources. First is L. Edward Hicks, "George S. Benson: Missionary Pioneer in China and the Philippines: 1925–1936," interviews with George S. Benson, Apr. 17, 1987 (Memphis, Tenn.: Oral History Research Office, Memphis State Univ.; and Mississippi Valley Historical Collection, Brister Library, Memphis State Univ., 1990). Second is George S. Benson to Ted Altman, June 23, 1970, and Sept. 23, 1970; letters in personal collection of Ted Altman, Harding Univ. Third is "Interview with George S. Benson," (interviewer unknown), in Oral History Office, Harding Univ., Searcy, Ark., 1985. Other citations will be noted.
2. George S. Benson, *Missionary Experiences,* ed. Phil Watson (Delight, Ark.: Gospel Light Publishing, 1987), 6–7.
3. Ibid., 14.
4. "Interview with George S. Benson," Harding Oral History Office, 3.
5. George S. Benson, *Missionary Experiences,* 14–15.
6. Most of the faculty of Harper College had helped David Lipscomb start a similar school in Nashville, Tenn. In 1901, James A. Harding and his son-in-law, J. N. Armstrong, left Lipscomb and opened Potter Bible College at Bowling Green, Ky. After encountering financial trouble there, most of the faculty, along with the library and laboratory equipment, relocated in 1905 to Odessa, Mo., as the Western Bible and Literary College. However, as financial troubles continued, the organization moved again to Cordell, Okla., and eventually to Harper, Kans. Earl Irvin West, *The Search for the Ancient Order* (Reprint, Nashville, Tenn.: Gospel Advocate Co., 1990), 3: 234–304.
7. Hicks, "George S. Benson: Missionary Pioneer," 16–17.
8. George S. Benson to J. D. Bales, Sept. 1, 1986. Transcript in NEP Files, Special Collections, Library, Harding Univ.
9. During his second year at Harper, he won the oratorical contest with a speech entitled, "The Man in Overalls," in which he described the American farmer as the man who feeds the world. George S. Benson to Ted Altman, June 23, 1970, 10; transcript in personal collection of Ted Altman, Harding Univ.
10. George S. Benson, *Missionary Experiences,* 24–25.
11. Once again financial difficulties forced Armstrong and his loyal followers to relocate. This time, the Harper College faculty was hired, and its library and laboratory equipment was purchased, by another junior college, Arkansas Christian School, which was renamed Harding College in honor of Armstrong's father-in-law, James A. Harding. West, *Search for the Ancient Order,* 4:88.
12. George S. Benson, *Missionary Experiences,* 27.

13. Stephen Neill, *A History of Christian Missions* (New York: Penguin Books, 1986), 282.

14. Robert C. North, *Moscow and Chinese Communists* (Stanford, Calif.: Stanford Univ. Press, 1963), 79–97.

15. O. Edmund Clubb, *Twentieth-Century China,* 2d ed. (New York: Columbia Univ. Press, 1972), 129.

16. North, *Moscow and Chinese Communists,* 89.

17. Kuomintang troops in Kwangsi province met heavy resistance from Liu Chen-huan, the local warlord who had joined with Yang Hsi-min in marching from Yunnan to Canton to oust Sun Yat-sen's Kuomintang nationalists. At the time of Benson's arrival in the interior, the warlords maintained an unstable peace in the interior of the province. Clubb, *20th-Century China,* 129.

18. Benson, *Missionary Experiences,* 37.

19. Chiang Kai-shek later purged his party of Communist elements and, in December 1928, turned on his former allies and began a campaign to defeat the Kuomintang [Communist] provincial governments he had helped establish. North, *Moscow and Chinese Communists,* 118–19. According to his biographers, Chiang Kai-shek's decision to marry Soong Mayling, the American-educated daughter of a wealthy Chinese Christian, strongly influenced his future political course of action. Mayling and her family would consent to the marriage only if he accepted Christianity. Apparently, Chiang became deeply committed to Christianity, which strongly influenced his later political activities. See Brian Crozier and Eric Chou, *The Man Who Lost China: The First Full Biography of Chiang Kai-shek* (New York: Charles Scribner's Sons, 1976), 107–20.

20. According to Crozier and Chou, *Man Who Lost China,* 78–79, two incidents in 1925 greatly exacerbated antiforeign feelings, benefiting the Kuomintang, who "always did well when foreigners made themselves more than unusually unpopular." The authors also claim that the Russians were considered exceptions to the rule of "deplorable foreign behavior." Both incidents involved foreign troops' firing on Chinese civilians in Shanghai and Canton and were labeled "massacres" by the Kuomintang.

21. Kenneth Scott Latourette, *A History of Christian Missions in China* (New York: Russell and Russell, 1929), 819.

22. Lewis T. Oldham, "Things Chinese," cited in *Oriental* (Canton) *Christian* 2, no. 1 (Oct. 1930): 12.

23. See Latourette, *History of Missions in China,* 812–22.

24. George S. Benson to Supporting Congregations, Nov. 20, 1928. Letter in Special Collections, Library, Harding Univ.

25. Ibid.

26. Ibid.

27. Hicks, "George S. Benson: Missionary Pioneer," 109.

28. Benson, *Missionary Experiences,* 54–55. For a complete discussion of this phenomenon, see John Pollock, *A Foreign Devil in China: The Story of Dr. L. Nelson Bell* (Minneapolis, Minn.: World Wide Publications, 1971), 131–40.

29. Hicks, "George S. Benson: Missionary Pioneer," 79.

30. Benson, *Missionary Experiences,* 56. For a detailed discussion of the importance of education in the Chinese culture, and of the Protestant missionary attempt to fulfill the Chinese's educational needs, see Latourette, *History of Missions in China,* 622–46.

31. Mary C. Wright, "Modern China in Transition, 1900–1950," in *Modern China,* ed. Albert Feuerwerker (Englewood Cliffs, N.J.: Prentice-Hall, 1964), 12.

32. Franz Michael, "State and Society in Nineteenth-Century China," in *Modern China,* ed. Albert Feuerwerker (Englewood Cliffs, N.J.: Prentice-Hall, 1964), 57–69.

33. Latourette, *History of Missions in China,* 622–24, argues that the attitude of a significant number of Chinese toward Western education changed dramatically during the early 20th century. Where mission schools and Western education once had been despised and "few if any Chinese of consequence would send their children to them, now mission schools were popular." The most popular inducement was the opportunity to learn English, which opened opportunities for employment in high-salaried jobs.

34. Roy Whitfield, "The Canton Bible School—Fall Term, 1936," *Oriental* (Canton) *Christian* 7, no. 10 (Oct. 1936): 1.

35. "Their dedication is reflected in the fact that the four of them remained in China until Mao Tse Tung took over and drove out all missionaries in 1949." Benson, *Missionary Experiences,* 63.

36. Sydney E. Ahlstrom, *A Religious History of the American People,* 2 vols. (Garden City, N.Y.: Image Books, 1975), 2:176. For a more detailed discussion of Churches of Christ antimissionism during this period, see West, *Search for the Ancient Order,* 4:187–91.

37. George Benson, "Canton Bible School Building Finished," *Oriental* (Canton) *Christian* 5, no. 12 (Dec. 1934): 3.

38. George S. Benson to Ted Altman, June 23, 1970. Typescript in personal collection of Ted Altman, Harding Univ.

39. Hicks, "George S. Benson: Missionary Pioneer," 88.

40. While at Chicago, George studied the history of antiquity, history of the ancient Orient, Far Eastern religions from antiquity to the present, and world religions, and took several courses in Chinese history, including foreign rights and interests in China, and China under a republic. Because of the strong Russian Communist influence in China, he also studied the history of Russia since 1900. His thesis was "The Interest of Foreign Nations in Manchuria" (M.A. thesis, Univ. of Chicago, 1931). Donald P. Gar-

ner, "George S. Benson: Conservative, Anti-Communist, Pro-Americanism Speaker" (Ph.D. diss., Wayne State Univ., Detroit, 1963), 39.

41. George S. Benson, "In Harding College," *Oriental* (Canton) *Christian* 3, no. 6 (Mar. 1932): 4.

42. George S. Benson to Ted Altman, Sept. 25, 1970, 3. Typescript in personal collection of Ted Altman, Harding Univ.

43. "Interview with George S. Benson," Harding Oral History Office, 7–8. Harding's charter requires that each member of the board of trustees shall be a "member of the Church of Christ in good standing, who believes in and adheres to a strict construction of the Bible and who opposes all innovations in the work and worship of the church such as instruments of music, missionary societies, Christian endeavor societies, and all other human inventions not authorized by the Word of God." This is the only connection between Harding College and any group of churches; although no student is required to belong to any particular religious group, the practice has been to restrict the faculty to members of the Churches of Christ. Gene Fretz, "Harding Observes an Anniversary and a Way of Life," *Arkansas Gazette,* May 30, 1954. This article is the product of research on the early history of NEP, interviews with its leading personalities, and observations of George S. Benson at his various speaking engagements.

44. Annie May Alston Lewis (Harding College, Class of 1939), *Harding University Bulletin,* Apr. 1990, 6.

45. "George S. Benson Announces Retirement from Harding," *Firm Foundation* 82, no. 20 (May 18, 1965): 320.

46. *Harding College Bison,* Oct. 13 and 27, 1936, 1.

47. *Bison,* Oct. 20, 1936, 1.

48. *Bison,* Nov. 3, 1936, 1.

49. *Bison,* Nov. 24, 1936, 1.

50. For a full discussion of the theological implications of this debate within the Restoration movement, see Richard T. Hughes, "The Apocalyptic Origins of the Churches of Christ and the Triumph of Modernism," *Religion and American Culture* 2 (Summer 1992): 181.

51. Theodore Dwight Bozeman, *Protestants in an Age of Science: The Baconian Ideal and Antebellum American Religious Thought* (Chapel Hill: Univ. of North Carolina Press, 1977), 22. Other recent studies of the importance of Scottish Common Sense Realism in American philosophy and theology are E. H. Meyer, *The Instructed Conscience: The Shaping of the American National Ethic* (Philadelphia: Univ. of Pennsylvania Press, 1972); George M. Marsden, *Fundamentalism and American Culture: The Shaping of Twentieth-Century Evangelicalism: 1870–1925* (New York: Oxford Univ. Press, 1980); and C. Leonard Allen, "Baconianism and the Bible in the Disciples of Christ: James S. Lamar and *The Organon of Scripture,*" *Church History* 55 (1986): 65.

52. Thomas H. Olbricht, "The Rationalism of the Restoration," *Restoration Quarterly* 11 (1968): 79.

53. Marsden, *Fundamentalism and American Culture,* 27.

54. Ibid., 63.

55. George S. Benson, "Crises in Christian Education During the Past Fifty Years" (unpublished article, 1986, NEP Files), 5.

56. L. Edward Hicks, "Interview with Dr. Billy Ray Cox, Former Vice-President of Harding College," Jan. 22, 1989; audiotape in collection of L. Edward Hicks.

57. George S. Benson, "Crises in Christian Education," 7.

58. *Bison,* Jan. 12, 1937.

59. George S. Benson, "Crises in Christian Education," 8.

60. George S. Benson to Ted Altman, June 23, 1970, 18. Typescript in personal collection of Ted Altman, Harding Univ.

61. Hicks, "George S. Benson: Missionary Pioneer," 159. Richard Hofstadter, *The American Political Tradition and the Men Who Made It* (New York: Vintage Books, 1948), 335, believes that much of Roosevelt's bitterness toward big business arose after certain conservatives publicly attacked him unfairly: "Nothing that Roosevelt had done warranted the vituperation he soon got in the conservative press or the obscenities that the hate-Roosevelt maniacs were bruiting about in their clubs and dining-rooms." Although Roosevelt had been involved in political controversy before, the "malice and deliberate stupidity of his critics made him angry, and his political struggle with the 'economic royalists' soon became intensely personal."

62. "As George Benson read the New York newspapers, and talked to people, and listened, he concluded that the American public's attitude toward many things had changed. The depression was hanging on, and the leaders and the public seemed ready to scrap some of the basic founding principles. This worried the returning missionary. It continued to worry him as the family made its way toward Searcy. He knew that he would have to do something about this, personally; it endangered, he felt, the nation's progress and security." Ted Max Altman, "The Contributions of George S. Benson to Christian Education" (Ph.D. diss., North Texas State Univ., Denton, Tex., 1971), 46. This study is mostly the product of various interviews with George Benson and is not a critical analysis of the many controversial aspects of the National Education Program.

63. George S. Benson to Ted Altman, Sept. 23, 1970, 4. Typescript in personal collection of Ted Altman, Harding Univ.

64. Hicks, "George S. Benson: Missionary Pioneer," 447.

65. George S. Benson to Ted Altman, Sept. 23, 1970, 5. Typescript in personal collection of Ted Altman, Harding Univ. Although some of the money to retire the Harding debt was solicited from church people, Benson quickly

found that many either could not or would not help further. Benson gives special credit to Clinton Davidson's role in helping to raise the funds from sources outside the churches: "He has not only been a liberal contributor, but he has put us in contact with men of means, a number of whom have contributed and some whom have contributed liberally. In fact, fully 55% of the total amount raised has been directly through his efforts and through men with whom he has put us in contact and whom we would have been unable to contact except for Mr. Davidson." *Bison,* Dec. 12, 1939.

66. Apparently Benson quickly put this philosophy to use, since he received $25,000 from DuPont Chemical, enough to retire the original debt in 1939. George S. Benson to Ted Altman, June 23, 1970. Typescript in personal collection of Ted Altman, Harding Univ. The college newspaper proudly stated, "What seemed to be fantastic three years ago became reality Thursday noon when the $68,000 mortgage on Harding College" was tossed into a huge bonfire by former President J. N. Armstrong. *Bison,* Dec. 5, 1939.

67. "With the college board's permission, Dr. Benson took $31,995.25—which was the exact amount left in the college treasury—to start the National Education Program." Frank Hughes, "$75,000 Debt Just a Memory for College: President Leads It to Fame," *Chicago Daily Tribune,* Jan. 22, 1948.

68. Hereafter the abbreviation NEP will be used.

69. George S. Benson to Ted Altman, Sept. 23, 1970, 5. Typescript in personal collection of Ted Altman, Harding Univ.

70. Ibid., 6.

2. The Genesis of Free-Enterprise Education

1. Rose, "Arkansas Crusader," 19. Other reports about NEP during this period identified these basic ideals as instrumental in the initiation of Harding's program. See Frank Hughes, "College Is a Champion of U.S. Way: 25 Million Get Its Message," *Chicago Daily Tribune,* Jan. 19, 1948. Hughes's series of articles distilled research on the early history of NEP, interviews with its organizers, and observations of Benson at work on the Harding College campus and at various speaking engagements. Other *Chicago Daily Tribune* articles by Frank Hughes include: "Work, Profit! It's Credo of This College: Students Live the American Way," Jan. 20, 1948; "How College Finds Pro-U.S. Instructors: Looks for Truth, Christian Ideals," Jan. 21, 1948; and "$75,000 Debt Just Memory for College: President Leads It to Fame," Jan. 22, 1948.

2. For a detailed examination of this argument over the direction of Christian mission work, see David Edwin Harrell, *The Social Sources of Division in*

the Disciples of Christ, 1865–1900: A Social History of the Disciples of Christ (Atlanta, Ga.: Publishing Systems, 1973).

3. Altman, "Contributions," 147.

4. Garner, "George S. Benson," 53. This dissertation was the result of over six months of personal contact with George S. Benson. Garner traveled extensively with Benson to his various speaking engagements, analyzed his public speaking style, and assessed the impact that Benson and his message had on his listeners. Overall, this study deals very critically with Benson's activities and motivation, yet treats objectively his accomplishments and shortcomings.

5. Leo Ribuffo, *The Old Christian Right: The Protestant Far Right from the Great Depression to the Cold War* (Philadelphia, Pa.: Temple Univ. Press, 1983), 3.

6. Ibid., 4.

7. Clyde Wilcox, "Evangelicals and the Moral Majority," 401, argues that "irrational forces at best played a small role in explaining support for the Old Christian Right," and believes rather that its support stemmed from a "prerequisite set of religious and political beliefs."

8. By August 1934, the most widely publicized critics of Roosevelt's policies had formed the American Liberty League, composed not only of wealthy industrialists such as William Knudsen or J. Howard Pew, but also of "illustrious Democratic politicians such as Al Smith, Jouett Shouse, John W. Davis, and Bainbridge Colby." James MacGregor Burns, *Roosevelt: The Lion and the Fox* (New York: Harcourt, Brace and World, 1956), 206.

9. Ribuffo, *Old Christian Right,* 6.

10. Burns, *Roosevelt,* 205.

11. Themes such as strident anti-Semitism, nativism, and racism were particularly appealing to some right-wing groups during this period. Ribuffo, *Old Christian Right,* 7.

12. "The Depression and, to a greater extent, the Roosevelt administration's response to it precipitated the development of a distinctive far right. As Americans weighed rival explanations of the crisis, the country's formerly amorphous ideological spectrum was divided into relatively clear segments." Ibid., 13.

13. Hofstadter, *American Political Tradition,* 335–37.

14. Ibid, 339–40.

15. Ribuffo, *Old Christian Right,* 13.

16. Robert M. Collins, *The Business Response to Keynes, 1929–1964* (New York: Columbia Univ. Press, 1981), 7.

17. It appears that Democratic New Dealers, and the Republican proponents of Reaganomics of the 1980s, were only half-Keynesian. Neither favored a tax increase in times of prosperity.

18. For convincing arguments that Roosevelt and Keynes acted to save capi-

talism, consult Robert Lekachman, *The Age of Keynes* (New York: Random House, 1966), and Paul K. Conkin, *The New Deal* (New York: Thomas Y. Crowell, 1967).

19. John L. Fletcher, "George S. Benson—His Fight: Free Enterprise," *Arkansas Gazette*, Dec. 14, 1952. This article too distills research, interviews with NEP organizers, and personal observations of Benson both on the campus and at his various speaking engagements.

20. Ribuffo, *Old Christian Right,* 15.

21. Ibid., 16.

22. Fletcher, "George S. Benson—His Fight."

23. *Proceedings of the National Education Association,* July 6, 1934, vol. 72 passim., qtd. in Fletcher, "George S. Benson—His Fight."

24. Altman, "Contributions of George S. Benson," 37.

25. Rose, "Arkansas Crusader," 84. According to historian William E. Leuchtenburg, in *Franklin D. Roosevelt and the New Deal* (New York: Harper Torchbooks, 1963), 10, the New Deal provoked extensive hostility and "hit home" because many Americans, for the first time, experienced the federal government.

26. Rose, "Arkansas Crusader," 84.

27. This story was recounted by Benson, qtd. in Gene Fretz, "Harding Observes an Anniversary and a Way of Life," *Arkansas Gazette,* May 30, 1954.

28. From one of Benson's standard early speeches, qtd. in Cabell Phillips, "Wide Anti-Red Drive Directed From Small Town in Arkansas," *New York Times,* May 18, 1961, 26.

29. Frank Hughes, "$75,000 Debt Just a Memory for College: President Leads It to Fame," *Chicago Daily Tribune,* Jan. 22, 1948.

30. "Harding Buys Memphis Radio Station WHBQ," *Bison,* May 21, 1946.

31. "Harding Investments," *Bison,* Oct. 31, 1956.

32. George S. Benson to Bud Green, June 11, 1971. Typescript in NEP Files.

33. "Dr. Benson Made Honorary Member of Little Rock Chamber of Commerce," *Bison,* Apr. 25, 1939.

34. "Lectures to Begin," *Bison,* Apr. 16, 1940.

35. George S. Benson, "Statement Before the Ways and Means Committee by Dr. George S. Benson, President of Harding College, Searcy, Ark., May 15, 1941." In U.S., Congress, *Congressional Record,* 77th Cong., 1st. sess., 1941, 87, appendix, pt. 2: A2326–28.

36. Speech by Franklin D. Roosevelt on national radio, *Vital Speeches of the Day* (New York: City News Publishing Co.), May 1941, 7:194–97. Roosevelt continued: "We have furnished the British great material support and we will furnish far more in the future . . . There will be no 'bottlenecks' in our determination to aid Great Britain. No dictator, no combination of dictators, will weaken that determination by threats of how they will construe that determination." Ibid.

37. John L. Sullivan, assistant secretary of the treasury, in U.S. Congress, *Congressional Record,* 77th Cong., 1st Sess., June 30, 1941, 87, pt. 1:481.

38. Henry Morgenthau, treasury secretary, in U.S., Congress, House, Committee on Ways and Means, *Revenue Revision of 1941: Hearings Before the Committee on Ways and Means on Revenue Revision of 1941,* 77th Cong., 1st sess., 1941, pt. 1:1–46.

39. Ibid., 1:11. *Newsweek* already had reported that, whereas a year before, there had been 9.5 million unemployed, within the past year 2.5 million of them had found jobs; it predicted that, within the next year, an additional 3 million would go to work. Furthermore, the Office of Production Management announced that it was stepping up its program of government-sponsored trainees from 1 to 2 million participants and in fact was planning to go at least 50% beyond that. *Newsweek,* May 19, 1941, 45.

40. House Ways and Means Committee, *Revenue Revision of 1941,* vol. 1: 13.

41. Ibid., 19.

42. Ibid., 47.

43. Ibid., 16.

44. Ibid., 11.

45. Ibid., 91.

46. Ibid., vols. 1 and 2, passim.

47. Ibid., 1:477.

48. Ibid., 1:479

49. George S. Benson, "Statement Before the Ways and Means Committee," pt. 2: A2326.

50. Cited in "Lectures to Begin," *Bison,* Apr. 16, 1940.

51. George S. Benson, "Statement Before the Ways and Means Committee," pt. 2: A2326.

52. Ibid.

53. Ibid., pt. 2:A2326–27.

54. Ibid., pt. 2:A2327.

55. Ibid.

56. According to Benson, those items whose cost could be cut in half included: (1) rivers, harbors, and flood control; (2) national park improvements; (3) agriculture, forests, and trails; (4) rural rehabilitation; (5) export bounties; (6) WPA; (7) departmental publicity and franking; and (8) reports of National Resources Planning and Office of Governmental Reports. Ibid.

57. Items identified under this category included: (1) Agriculture Department expenses (in addition to agricultural aids), (2) Department of Commerce, (3) Department of the Interior, (4) Department of Justice, (5) War Department (nonmilitary services), (6) miscellaneous independent offices, and (7) refugee relief. Ibid.

58. Ibid., A2328. Despite Benson's presentation before the committee, on July

2, 1941, the "nation's biggest tax bill, designed to raise an $3,504,400,000 additional was tentatively approved today by the House Way and Means Committee." "Higher Levies Added . . . ," editorial, *Searcy* (Ark.) *Daily Citizen,* July 3, 1941.

59. Reference to the committee's response to Benson's testimony was included in a speech by Davidson, cited in Garner, "George S. Benson," 74.

60. House Ways and Means Committee, *Revenue Revision of 1941,* 2:1205–6.

61. Cited in Phil S. Hanna, "Man from Arkansas Stirs Congressional Committee by Plea for Economy Now," *Chicago Journal of Commerce,* May 20, 1941.

62. George S. Benson, "Statement Before the Ways and Means Committee," pt. 2: A2325–26.

63. U.S., Congress, Senate, Committee on Education and Labor, *Hearing on S. 2295, A Bill to Provide for the Termination of the Civilian Conservation Corps and the National Youth Administration,* 77th Cong., 2d sess., Mar. 23–Apr. 17, 1942, 530.

64. House Ways and Means Committee, *Revenue Revision of 1941,* 2:1205.

65. George S. Benson, "Emergency Message to the American People," *Omaha* (Nebr.) *Morning World Herald,* Oct. 27, 1941.

66. "Dr. Benson Returns from Speaking Trip to Milwaukee," *Searcy* (Ark.) *Daily Citizen,* Sept. 29, 1941.

67. "Educator Sees Need of Thrift Object Lesson," *Arkansas Gazette,* June 13, 1941, 1.

68. *Searcy* (Ark.) *Daily Citizen,* June–Dec. 1941, passim.

69. *Bison,* Sept. 30, 1941. *Omaha* (Nebr.) *Morning World-Herald* published these articles, beginning on Oct. 27, 1941, as "Emergency Message to the American People."

70. *Searcy* (Ark.) *Daily Citizen,* Nov. 14, 1941. This particular speech was inserted into the *Congressional Record* by Sen. Harry Byrd of Virginia. U.S., Congress, *Congressional Record,* 77th Cong., 2nd Sess., Nov. 10, 1941, 87, appendix, pt. 14:A5053–54.

71. *Bison,* Nov. 4, 1941.

72. "Silver Medal to Dr. Benson for Economy Efforts," *Searcy* (Ark.) *Daily Citizen,* Dec. 6, 1941, 1.

73. *New York Times,* Aug. 21, 1941.

74. "Bearing Fruit," editorial, *Searcy* (Ark.) *Daily Citizen,* Oct. 3, 1941. Cited in Senate Committee on Education and Labor, *Hearing on S. 2295 for Termination of the CCC and NYA,* 60. According to the second witness before the committee in March 1942, Senator Byrd, creation of the Joint Committee on Reduction of Nonessential Federal Expenditures first had been suggested by Secretary of the Treasury Morgenthau. The committee eventually was composed of the Treasury secretary, the federal budget director, and chairmen and ranking members of the House Ways and Means Committee, the House Appropriations Committee, the Senate Finance Commit-

tee, and the Senate Appropriations Committee. On December 26, 1941, this new committee, with Senator Byrd as its chairman, recommended to the Senate deep cuts in the U.S. agricultural subsidy program, public works, and relief agencies. In addition, it recommended abolishing the CCC and NYA. Since Benson had become one of the nation's leading advocates for such economy measures, Senator Byrd made sure that Benson would appear. *Searcy* (Ark.) *Daily Citizen,* Dec. 30, 1941, 1.

75. Cited in Senate Committee on Education and Labor, *Hearing on S. 2295 for Termination of the CCC and NYA,* 529–30.

76. Aubrey W. Williams was one of the most controversial figures in Roosevelt's administration. Depending on the political leanings of those making the evaluation, he was either "a symbol of decency, a symbol of democracy" (Harry Hopkins) or "one of the pinkest of this pink New Deal Administration" (Sen. Hamilton Fish). Democratic Sen. Kenneth D. McKellar of Tennessee "claimed privately that this 'willful, suave, easy, generous, oily' man 'not only disbelieves in the divinity of Christ, but he disbelieves in the American form of government,' and publicly that he had turned agencies under his control over to Communist fronts." Cited by John A. Salmond, "Aubrey Williams: A Typical New Dealer?" in *The New Deal: The National Level,* ed. John Braeman, Robert H. Bremner, and David Brody (Columbus: Ohio State Univ. Press, 1975), 219.

77. Washington press release reported in "Cold Shoulder Given Student Economy Idea—NYA Head Cool to Plea Made by Harding College," *Searcy* (Ark.) *Daily Citizen,* Jan. 28, 1942.

78. Washington press release reported in "Dr. Benson and NYA Official Present Views on Controversy Concerning Aid for Students," *Searcy* (Ark.) *Daily Citizen,* Jan. 29, 1942.

79. Byrd's speech cited in "Lauds Harding Students—Hits Leader of NYA—Senator Byrd Flays Williams in Speech," *Searcy* (Ark.) *Daily Citizen,* Feb. 4, 1942, 1.

80. Benson continued to receive valuable publicity for the school and his program, as editorial writers all over the country joined Senator Byrd and "turned to their typewriters in defense of the students." Rose, "Arkansas Crusader," 83.

81. "Jobs for Youth," *Chicago Daily News,* Feb. 11, 1942, 12.

82. Cited in "Williams Writes to Former NYA Harding Students—NYA Administration States President Roosevelt Asked Him to Reply to Students," *Bison,* Feb. 24, 1942.

83. Cited in Senate Committee on Education and Labor, *Hearing on S. 2295 for Termination of the CCC and NYA,* 25. The CCC had been created by Congress in June 1933, for the purpose of "providing employment, as well as vocational training for youthful citizens of the United States who are unemployed and in need of employment." Ibid., 29. The NYA had been

established by executive order in June 1935. The CCC appropriations were made directly by Congress, while funding for the NYA originally was allocated by the president through money supplied by the Relief Appropriations Acts of 1936 and 1937. During this period, therefore, the NYA continued by executive fiat. In 1938 it was transferred from the Works Progress Administration to the Federal Security Agency. Thereafter Congress funded it directly as part of that agency. Ibid., 456. An interesting question of constitutionality was raised during Sen. Byrd's testimony before the committee. Vermont Sen. George D. Aiken asked how Congress could abolish "by legislation an agency that has not been established by legislation?" Sen. McKellar replied, "Because it has been established by Executive Order under authority that the Congress has given to the President." Ibid., 60.

84. Ibid., 72.
85. Ibid., 505–7.
86. Ibid., 205.
87. Ibid., 210.
88. Ibid.
89. Ibid., 519.
90. Ibid.
91. Ibid.
92. Ribuffo, *Old Christian Right,* 1–19.
93. "Save American Way Is Appeal of Dr. Benson—Harding College Educator Sees Danger Ahead," *Searcy* (Ark.) *Daily Citizen,* Jan. 20, 1942.
94. "Sterling Morton Purchases New Farm for School," *Bison,* Jan. 23, 1945.
95. George Benson to Dr. James D. Key, Nov. 20, 1986. Typescript in NEP Files. All these corporations consistently supported conservative causes and were early members of what John S. Saloma, III, in *Ominous Politics: The New Conservative Labyrinth* (New York: Hill and Wang, 1984), describes as the conservative labyrinth.
96. "Reports Success in Endowment Campaign Here—$12,000 Donated to Dole, Says Dr. Benson," *Searcy* (Ark.) *Daily Citizen,* Jan. 10, 1942.
97. "77th Convention of American Bankers Association," *New York Times,* Oct. 2, 1951, 39:8. Benson had told the House Committee on Education in May 1945 that one reason "so many people come rushing to Washington for relief in regard to local problems is because they have the impression that if they get it from Washington its costs nobody anything. This is a false impression which should by all means be corrected, before it wrecks our economic order." Benson, "Should the Public School System Be Subsidized by Federal Funds," *Congressional Digest* 25 (Jan. 1946): 47.
98. George S. Benson, "Federal Aid to Education," *Vital Speeches of the Day* 15 (Jan. 15, 1949): 208.
99. "77th Convention of American Bankers Association," 44:1.

100. "Benson Speaking to American Iron and Steel Institute 55th General Meeting at Waldorf-Astoria," *New York Times,* May 23, 1947, 33:4.

101. Cabell Phillips, "Wide Anti-Red Drive Directed from Small Town in Arkansas—Dr. George S. Benson, Head of College and National Education Program, Aims to Alert the Common Man," *New York Times,* May 18, 1961, 26:1.

102. Garner, "George S. Benson," 133.

103. George S. Benson, qtd. in Irving Spiegel, "Aid to Right Wing Laid to Big Firms." *New York Times,* Sept. 20, 1964, 73:1. Benson himself claimed to have been a lifelong Democrat who "votes for the man and not the party." "Benson Likes Conservative Label, Defeats Other Names," *Arkansas Democrat,* March 11, 1962, 7A:1.

104. George S. Benson before the House Committee on Education, May 3, 1945, rptd. as George Benson, "Should the Public School System Be Subsidized by Federal Funds?" *Congressional Digest* 25 (Jan. 1946): 47.

105. "Plane Donated for College Use." *Bison,* Sept. 23, 1944.

106. Benson Ends Speaking Tour." *Bison,* Sept. 29, 1942 and Oct. 19, 1943.

107. "President Will Write Syndicated Column." *Bison,* Mar. 10, 1942.

108. Rose, "Arkansas Crusader," 83.

109. *Bison,* passim. Jan. 1942 to Jan. 1943.

110. "Bison Speaking to American Iron and Steel Institute 55th General Meeting at Waldorf-Astoria." *New York Times,* May 23, 1947, 33:4.

111. "Harding Receives Largest Contribution." *Bison,* Jan. 29, 1946.

112. George S. Benson, "Should the Public School System Be Subsidized by Federal Funds?" *Congressional Digest* 25 (Jan. 1946): 47.

113. George S. Benson, "Federal Aid to Education" (Pamphlet; Searcy, Ark.: National Education Program, n.d.).

114. Benson, in July 1944, had been appointed to a 15-member Advisory Commission to the Senate Committee on Civil Service. "President Benson Appointed to Advisory Commission." *Bison,* Sept. 23, 1944.

115. When Benson testified before the House Executive Expenditures Committee in opposition to a proposed "full employment" bill, the executive secretary of the Citizens National Committee commented that "he had watched hearings for years, and has heard applause only twice. Dr. Benson is the man who caused it before." "Dr. Benson Testifies Before House Committee." *Bison,* Oct. 23, 1945.

116. "Dr. Benson to Debate Columbia University Professor." *Bison,* Nov. 14, 1946.

117. "President Benson in Radio Debate Last Tuesday Night." *Bison,* May 11, 1948.

118. Cited in George Benson, "Federal Aid To Education," *Vital Speeches of the Day* 15 (Jan. 15, 1949): 207–10.

119. Ibid., 208. Obviously Benson's prediction was incorrect, but that does not

detract from the sincerity of his effort to hold the line against what he felt to be "creeping socialism." Benson and Harding College eventually succumbed to the economic pressure on higher education from Washington and were criticized strongly in conservative circles for accepting a rather large federal education grant to conduct scientific research in space medicine in 1963. "Scientist Clark to Continue Space Medicine Research in Harding Post," *Arkansas Democrat,* Apr. 14, 1963; and "Open House for Harding New Research Annex Set," *Searcy (Ark.) Daily Citizen.*

3. Freedom Forums and an Informed Citizenry

1. For example, in a speech before the American Association of Advertising Agencies, Benson described the dangers of postwar inflation and the possibility that an economic depression might follow. He emphasized the possibility that prolonged depression might bring on nationalization of industry and described a "calculated plot and organized onslaught of propaganda being made by subversive groups against our system of private capital and the profit system, and in favor of collectivization of some type by our government." "Benson Speaks to American Association of Advertising Agencies," *New York Times,* Apr. 9, 1949, 24:3.
2. Consult Heale, *American Anticommunism.*
3. John L. Fletcher, "George S. Benson—His Fight: Free Enterprise," *Arkansas Gazette,* Dec. 14, 1952.
4. Altman, "Contributions," 67. For a different ideological perspective on this organization, see Mark H. Leff, "The Politics of Sacrifice on the American Home Front in World War II," *Journal of American History* 77 (Mar. 1991): 1296.
5. Altman, "Contributions," 68. Kenneth Wells, vice-president of Foote, Cone and Belding, was director of the first few Freedom Forums, but later he and Belding helped create the Freedoms Foundation at Valley Forge, Penn., which became a leading front organization for conservative activists. Wells became director of the foundation; President Eisenhower was its first honorary president. According to its literature, the foundation was created to provide national award recognition to individuals and organizations working to "bring about a better public understanding of the American Way of Life." Cited in ibid., 69. For a fuller discussion of the relationship between NEP and the Freedoms Foundation, consult George Thayer, *The Farther Shore of Politics: The American Political Fringe Today* (New York: Simon and Schuster, 1967), 276.
6. Editorial, *Oklahoma City Times,* Oct. 20, 1947. It was during this period that Benson gained recognition as one of America's premier public speakers. M. Norvell Young, Benson's close friend and president of Pepperdine

University, once related this story about Benson's taxing travel schedule. He was with Benson as he drove to the Memphis airport, arriving just in time to see an airliner ready to take off. According to Young, Benson "rushed into the airport and asked for a ticket so that he could make the plane which was just leaving for Chicago. The ticket agent informed him that this plane was not going to Chicago, but to Dallas. He replied, 'Just get me on that plane anyway for I have business everywhere.'" Quoted in M. Norvel Young, "Just Catch the Plane in Dallas or Nashville." *Firm Foundation* 77, no. 11 (Mar. 15, 1960): 166.

7. Although the majority of the Freedom Forums were held on the Harding campus, during the first few years several were held at different locations and attracted slightly different audiences. Freedom Forum III was held at the College of Aeronautics, Univ. of Southern California, and was sponsored by the Advertisers Association of the West; No. VI was held at Sun Valley, Idaho; No. VII at Carroll College, Waukesha, Wisc.; No. VIII at Purdue Univ., West Lafayette, Ind.; and No. XI at Cranbrook School, Bloomfield Hills, Mich., "Freedom Forum XIX to Run a Five-day Week," *Bison,* Oct. 17, 1953, 1. Freedom Forum VIII, held at Purdue Univ., featured Dr. Earl Butz, chairman of Purdue's Department of Agriculture and Economics, who spoke on "Our Current Agricultural Policies: The Mess We're In," quoted in "National Education Program to Hold Freedom Forum at Purdue," *Bison,* Oct. 14, 1950, 1. Butz went on to become secretary of agriculture under President Richard Nixon in 1971.

8. "Benson Speaks to American Association of Advertising Agencies," *New York Times,* Apr. 9, 1949, 24:3. On Jan. 20, 1949, Belding had announced the new program to a meeting of the Chicago Federated Advertisers Club and asked the group to send representatives to the February seminar at Harding College. "Meeting of Chicago Federated Advertisers," *New York Times,* Jan. 21, 1949, 36:5.

9. One attendant responded positively to the presentation of NEP material at one of these forums by presenting NEP's illustrated lecture, "This Is Our Problem" over 170 times in one year. A short time after the conclusion of Freedom Forum IX, NEP polled the 161 conferees, and 134 reported continued involvement in activities directly resulting from their forum experiences. Cited in the NEP newsletter, *Your Grass Roots Report* 5 (June 1951), edited by George S. Benson.

10. Vance Packard, "Public Relations Good or Bad," *Atlantic,* May 1958, 56.

11. Interview with George S. Benson, qtd. in Altman, "Contributions," 69. Another NEP educational program similar to a Freedom Forum was held in Houston in 1954, but it was designed more as a "trade institute" aimed at "national and foreign representatives of manufacturing, exporting, importing, banking, legal, and advertising concerns." The program, designed and presented by George Benson and NEP staffer Dr. Melchior Palyi, an eco-

nomic consultant from Chicago, was intended to "provide an opportunity for advanced study in the field of international trade for corporation, business and professional executives." Such topics as organization, promotion, and management in foreign trade; arbitration; investments; competition; and trade policies were discussed. Sponsors of the event included Philip Cortney, president of Coty International, New York; Rudolf Hecht, chairman of the board, Mississippi Shipping Co., New Orleans; Jesse Jones, chairman of the board, National Bank of Commerce, Houston; S. J. Meyers, president, Chicago Board of Trade; Gen. Robert E. Wood, chairman of the board, Sears, Roebuck and Co., Chicago; and Roy Hofheinz, mayor of Houston, Tex. "Harding to Host Trade Institute in Houston, Texas," *Bison,* Feb. 13, 1954, 1.

12. Garner, "George S. Benson," 139.
13. Don Johnson, "Benson's Years Have Boosted Harding," *Bison,* May 6, 1965, 1.
14. "Benson Opens Freedom Forum," *Bison,* Apr. 25, 1956, 1.
15. George S. Benson, ed., *Expanding American Markets: Freedom Forum XXV Lectures* (Searcy, Ark.: NEP, 1964), ix.
16. Robert A. Millikan, *The Autobiography of Robert A. Millikan* (New York: Prentice-Hall, 1950), 286.
17. "Freedom Forum to Be Held Here—Leaders of Nation's Industries Invited," *Bison,* Jan. 25, 1949.
18. "Twenty-fourth Annual Freedom Forum Gets Underway Tuesday," *Bison,* Apr. 18, 1963, 2.
19. "Forum Ends Friday After Five-day Lecture Program," *Bison,* Oct. 29, 1949.
20. Freedom Forum XXV, on the subject of "Expanding American Markets," was held in Little Rock in 1964, sponsored jointly by Sen. McClellan, Rep. Mills, and Gov. Faubus. "Twenty-fifth Freedom Forum Concluded Today." *Bison,* Feb. 6, 1964, 1. Also on the program were Edwin T. Neilan, president, U.S. Chamber of Commerce; Charles B. Shuman, president, American Farm Bureau Federation; Dr. Frank H. Sparks, past president, Council for Financial Aid to Education; Dr. William Gomberg, professor of industry, Wharton School of Finance and Commerce; Dr. John W. Kendrick, professor of economics, George Washington University; George W. Mitchell, member of the board of governors, Federal Reserve System; Frank Ahlgren, editor of the *Memphis* (Tenn.) *Commercial Appeal;* and Earnest Wilkinson, president, Brigham Young University. Ibid.
21. Ribuffo, *Old Christian Right;* Heale, *American Anticommunism.*
22. "Benson Speaks to American Association of Advertising Agencies," *New York Times,* Apr. 9, 1949, 24:3.
23. "This should not have been a surprise, considering that the American people were suffering regular mega-shocks from international and national communism." Stevens, *Before Any Were Willing,* 254.

24. Ellen W. Schrecker, *No Ivory Tower: McCarthyism and the Universities* (New York: Oxford Univ. Press, 1987), 4.

25. Cabell Phillips, "Wide Anti-Red Drive Directed From Small Town in Arkansas," *New York Times,* May 18, 1961, 26.

26. These supposed "Communist" leaders were prosecuted under the Smith Act, an infrequently used and highly controversial 1940 statute that made it illegal to "teach and advocate the overthrow and destruction of the Government of the United States by force or violence." Cited in Schrecker, *No Ivory Tower,* 6. FBI double agent Herbert Philbrick, another NEP regular, also was a government witness. For a detailed study of the Smith Act trials, see Michael Belknap, *Cold War Political Justice: The Smith Act, the Communist Party, and American Civil Liberties* (Westport, Conn.: Greenwood, 1977).

27. Sarah Longley, "Freedom Forum X," *Bison,* Oct. 20, 1951, 1.

28. "Philbrick Climaxes Forum XV Sessions," *Bison,* Apr. 17, 1954, 1.

29. Philbrick was not alone in his speculation about the Warren Commission report. Along with several others, New York lawyer Mark Lane, whose book *Rush to Judgement* (New York: Holt, Rinehart and Winston, 1966) became a bestseller in 1966, had seriously questioned the findings of the Warren Commission, appointed by President Johnson to investigate Kennedy's assassination. More recently, Oliver Stone's movie, *JFK,* has reopened this debate. For a comprehensive evaluation of both sides of the cinematic controversy, see "Through the Looking Glass: A Critical Overview of Oliver Stone's JFK," *Cineaste* 18, no. 1 (1992): 8.

30. "Philbrick Speaks on Communist Role in Kennedy Assassination," *Bison,* Mar. 11, 1965, 1. Philbrick was sufficiently impressed with Harding College's overall program that he sent his daughter to school there in 1965.

31. "Editorial," *Oklahoma City Del City News,* July 6, 1962.

32. "Former Hungarian Finance Minister to Speak," *Bison,* Nov. 5, 1954, 1.

33. Ibid.

34. Gottfried and Fleming, *Conservative Movement,* 22. For an interesting discussion of the influence of the political science department at the University of Chicago during the 1920s and 1930s, see Richard Jensen, "History and the Political Scientist," in *Politics and the Social Sciences,* ed. Seymour Martin Lipset (New York: Oxford Univ. Press, 1969), 1–28.

35. Milton Friedman, cited in program for dedication of George S. Benson Auditorium, Harding College, 1980, NEP Files; Gottfried and Fleming, *Conservative Movement,* 22.

36. Jennie Schoolfield, "Dr. Melchior Palyi to Speak at Freedom Forum," *Bison,* Dec. 12, 1953, 1.

37. In general, this group comprises a "Who's Who" of what Ribuffo has categorized as the Old Christian Right. Most were leading spokesmen for the

organizations which John Saloma, in *Ominous Politics,* has labeled the "conservative labyrinth."

38. Cited in various editions of *Bison.*
39. "Dr. Fred Schwarz to Speak at Harding," *Bison,* Feb. 27, 1954, 1. See Clyde Wilcox, "Popular Backing for the Old Christian Right: Explaining Support for the Christian Anti-Communist Crusade," *Journal of Social History* 21 (Fall 1987): 117–32
40. While no similar treatment has examined the popularity of Benson's anti-communism, in all probability the variables discovered by Wilcox for Schwarz's group are applicable to Benson's followers; Benson helped Schwarz's group in its early years. Wilcox concludes that the "Christian Anti-Communist Crusade, then, arose from the same traditions and impulses as the Christian Right of the 1920s, and was supported by the same basic constituency which supports the New Christian Right in the 1980s." Wilcox, "Popular Backing," 129.
41. "Are You Bored By Freedom?" *Bison,* Oct. 20, 1951.
42. George S. Benson, *Expanding American Markets,* vi.
43. Ibid., v.
44. Ibid.
45. Harold V. Knight, "Whooping It Up for Adam Smith," *Nation* 175 (Aug. 2, 1952): 87–89.
46. Ibid. As further evidence that NEP was an effective agent against "internationalism," Benson was asked to join with similar groups who were also opposing the spread of communism in America. In 1954, Benson joined the policy committee of "For America," a group dedicated to "enlightened nationalism." It was the brainchild of *Chicago Tribune* publisher, Col. Robert R. McCormick, and Sears and Roebuck's Chairman Gen. Robert E. Wood. "'For America' Founded by McCormick," *New York Times,* Nov. 14, 1954, 42:1.
47. "Adventures in Economics" (Pamphlet, Searcy, Ark.: NEP, n.d.), 1.
48. Sutherland came to the Harding campus to investigate at first hand the program with which he was getting involved. "Hollywood Producer of Harding Movie Speaks to Students," *Bison,* Oct. 31, 1946.
49. Cited in Altman, "Contributions," 72. In the 1980s, the NEP put these ten films on videocassette and sold hundreds of copies to various organizations. "Interview with Robert H. Rowland, Director, NEP," interview by L. Edward Hicks, Oklahoma City, Okla., Mar. 14, 1990. In Hicks, "A Case Study of Conservative Political Education: George S. Benson and the National Education Program," (Ph.D. diss., Memphis State Univ., Memphis, Tenn., 1990), Appendix D: 319-91.
50. Cited in W. R. Wilkerson, "Trade Views," *Hollywood Reporter,* Feb. 23, 1951.
51. "Learning Economics With No Pain," *Business Week,* Dec. 16, 1950, 42.

52. *Your Grass Roots Report,* no. 6, edited by George S. Benson.
53. Ibid., June 1951.
54. Cited in Altman, "Contributions," 77.
55. *Your Grass Roots Report,* June 1951.
56. Altman, "Contributions," 66.
57. *Your Grass Roots Report,* Jan. 1952. In 1990, over 23,000 copies of the newsletter still were being sent out. Hicks, "Interview with Robert Rowland."
58. *Your Grass Roots Report,* June 1951.
59. Ibid., Jan. 1952.
60. Cited in Altman, "Contributions," 76–77.
61. Most of these tapes are now in the collection of L. Edward Hicks.
62. "Benson Announces American Studies Program at Harding," *New York Times,* Oct. 12, 1952, IV 9:2.
63. "Leaders of Tomorrow Trained," *Bison,* Oct. 11, 1952, 1. Ganus replaced Benson as president of Harding College in 1965; he gradually withdrew from NEP activities.
64. "Harding's High School Seminars on Americanisms Gaining Popularity; Record Number Attend Last Summer," *Bison,* Jan. 9, 1964, 5.
65. Altman, "Contributions," 76.
66. Hicks, "Interview with Robert Rowland," 353.
67. Ibid., 356.
68. Ibid.

4. Burdens of Responsibility

1. Note Goldwater's acceptance speech at the Republican National Convention and his June 18, 1964 speech on civil rights, cited in Clifton M. White, *Suite 3505: The Story of the Draft Goldwater Movement* (New Rochelle, N.Y.: Arlington House, 1967), app.
2. Karl A. Lamb and Paul A. Smith, *Campaign Decision-Making: The Presidential Election of 1964* (Belmont, Calif.: Wadsworth, 1968), 51.
3. Ibid., 52.
4. Richard Hofstadter, *The Paranoid Style in American Politics and Other Essays* (New York: Vintage Books, 1967), 93.
5. Lamb and Smith, *Campaign Decision-Making,* 49.
6. Benson had rejected an offer by President Eisenhower to head the Bureau of Indian Affairs, and in 1962 he seriously considered running for the Senate against Arkansas Sen. J. William Fulbright. According to Benson, he turned down both offers, not because he lacked partisan political support but because he considered his primary responsibility to be Christian education, not politics. Gene Foreman, "Forum Turns Guns on Fulbright: Benson Suggested as Replacement," *Arkansas Gazette,* Apr. 19, 1962.

7. Benson had replied, when asked to join with another conservative group, "Our organization could not join in any political group regardless of the fact that it would be non-partisan. In order to continue with the work we are doing we must carefully avoid political activity with any partisan implications." Letter from George S. Benson, July 29, 1958, cited in Garner, "George S. Benson," 82.

8. Lamb and Smith, *Campaign Decision-Making,* 49.

9. Barry Goldwater, *The Conscience of a Conservative* (Shepardsville, Ky.: Victor Publishing, 1960), 16.

10. Bill Curry, "Benson Speaks at Little Rock," *Bison,* Mar. 13, 1950.

11. Goldwater, *Conscience of a Conservative,* 86.

12. Quoted from a Benson speech to the American Legion convention in Corinth, Miss. "Benson Urges Watchful Attitude in Legion Address," *Bison,* Nov. 21, 1946. Benson, before 20,000 people in Madison Square Garden in New York, earlier had advocated a return to God as a cure for communism. "Dr. Benson Gives Cure for Communism," *Bison,* Jan. 15, 1946.

13. Lamb and Smith, *Campaign Decision-Making,* 49.

14. For a popular book of conservative campaign rhetoric, see Phyllis Schlafly, *A Choice Not an Echo* (Alton, Ill.: Pere Marquette Press, 1964). Through the years, Benson and Phyllis Schlafly worked closely together on many issues, from the "Stop ERA" campaign to a 1985 radio program against child abuse. George Benson to Phyllis Schlafly, Apr. 23, 1985, NEP Files.

15. Lamb and Smith, *Campaign Decision-Making,* 54. Certainly neither Lamb nor Smith anticipated that the realization of their prediction would be the landslide 1980 election of Goldwater's conservative descendent, Ronald Reagan.

16. "Goldwater's acceptance speech was intended to be a 'reasoned and eloquent conservative statement' that would set the stage for the political debate of the campaign"; instead it further alienated him from the more moderate members of both political parties. Ibid., 82. Goldwater's speech was authored by well-known conservative intellectual and political science professor at Claremont Men's College, Harry V. Jaffa, formerly of the University of Chicago, who had been trained by Leo Strauss, mentioned earlier. White, *Suite 3505,* 407.

17. See White's explanation of the defeat, in *Suite 3505,* epilogue, 409–23.

18. Arnold Forster and Benjamin R. Epstein, *Danger on the Right: The Attitudes, Personnel and Influence of the Radical Right and the Extreme Conservatives* (New York: Random House, 1964), 87.

19. Philip Horton, "Revivalism on the Far Right," *Reporter Magazine* 25 (July 20, 1961): 26.

20. George S. Benson, "Current American Economic Issues," keynote address, 25th Anniversary Convention, National Association of Real Estate Boards, cited in *NAREB News* 28, no. 45, Nov. 6, 1961.

21. Glenn Fowler, *New York Times,* Nov. 20, 1961, 31:2.
22. Cabell Phillips, "Wide Anti-Red Drive," *New York Times,* May 18, 1961, 26:1
23. "Harding to Appear on TV," *Bison,* Jan. 11, 1962, 1.
24. Cited in a NEP circular advertising "Make Mine Freedom" and "Going Places," n.d., available in NEP files.
25. Thomas F. Brady, *New York Times,* Mar. 17, 1951, 1:2.
26. Ibid.
27. Ibid.
28. Ibid.
29. A. H. Weiler, "Fresh Laid Plans," *New York Times,* Mar. 19, 1951, 17:1.
30. Ibid.
31. Cabell Phillips, "Wide Anti-Red Drive," *New York Times,* May 18, 1951, 1:2. For a parallel reading of this economic theory from the New Religious Right perspective, see Fields, "Understanding Activist Fundamentalism," 177. Fields cites Jerry Falwell's claim that the "invisible hand of the marketplace is at the end of God's arm. The role of government is to insure that the market/God is free to stimulate or reward ambition with profit and discourage lassitude with poverty. Individuals pursuing their own self-interest, tempered by religious faith and ethics, will produce the common good. 'Big Government' only obstructs the market and makes the poor dependent on welfare."
32. A. H. Weiler, "Fresh Laid Plans," *New York Times,* Mar. 19, 1951, 17:1.
33. Stevens, *Before Any Were Willing,* 239.
34. "Anti-Communist Rally at the Garden," *New York Times,* Jan. 11, 1946, 16.
35. George S. Benson, "If I Were a Communist," *Reader's Digest,* Sept. 1946, 116.
36. "Anti-Communist Rally at the Garden," *New York Times,* Jan. 11, 1946, 16. It also should be remembered that Benson's newspaper columns ran in several hundred union and industrial publications.
37. "Right to Work Drive Backed By Educator," *Oklahoma City Oklahoman,* Jan. 20, 1962.
38. "Harding 'Red' Film Distorted, Educators Say," *Arkansas Gazette,* Feb. 25, 1961, 3A.
39. Fred J. Cook, "The Ultras," *Nation* 194 (June 30, 1962): 590. In this article, Cook presented a somewhat different picture of the first meeting of Benson and General Motors head Alfred P. Sloan. According to Cook, after hearing one of Benson's "patriotic, fundamentalist, anti-labor orations," there was "almost immediately, a fine meeting of the minds. Sloan decided to bankroll Dr. Benson to insure the perpetuation of his good deeds, and in 1949 he made a gift of $300,000 to Harding College." According to Benson, the Sloan Foundation gave less than $10,000 directly to either Harding College or NEP. All of that $300,000 was paid to John

Sutherland Productions, Inc., to produce the cartoon film series. George S. Benson to Turner Catledge, managing editor, *New York Times,* Oct. 1, 1964, NEP Files.

40. John L. Fletcher, "George S. Benson—His Fight: Free Enterprise," *Arkansas Gazette,* Dec. 14, 1952.

41. It also might be pointed out that the majority of criticism aimed at NEP's apparent anti-labor stance occurred during the election campaign of 1964, in which the right to work and other union issues were definitely parts of campaign rhetoric.

42. "Industry Termed Backbone of U.S.," *Dayton (Ohio) Journal Herald,* Feb. 12, 1963.

43. F. J. Cook, "Foundations as a Tax Dodge," *Nation* 196 (Apr. 20, 1963): 323.

44. Ibid.

45. M. H. Phillips, "Old Fashioned 'Receet,' New Sound Film Strip." From *NEP Newsletter,* cited in *Seminole (Okla.) Producer,* May 8, 1960.

46. "The Far Right," *Newsweek,* May 1, 1961, 40.

47. Ibid.

48. Murray Illson, "Norman Thomas Hits Birch Group," *New York Times,* Apr. 20, 1961, 19:1.

49. "The Far Right," *Newsweek,* May 1, 1961, 42.

50. Cited in "Benson Hits Anti-Red Film Critic," *Arkansas Gazette,* Feb. 25, 1961, B1:1.

51. The film script itself had been prepared by Glenn A. "Bud" Green, NEP vice-president who later headed the National Right-to-Work Committee. Green claimed to have spent almost three years researching the script material and admitted that, "There are always a few people wherever it has been shown who think it is too alarming." Ibid.

52. "Thomas is Disputed Over Film on Reds," *New York Times,* May 10, 1961, 38:4.

53. "New Anti-Red Film," *New York Times,* July 14, 1961, 2:5.

54. Quoted from typed transcripts of the film, "The Truth About Communism," NEP Files.

55. As was to be expected after Reagan's 1980 election, copies of these films were in great demand, especially in Europe, where NEP entered into an agreement with a West German company to market these films. However, NEP never realized any profits from these sales. Hicks, "George S. Benson: Missionary Pioneer."

56. Murray Illson, "Norman Thomas Hits Birch Group," *New York Times,* Apr. 20, 1961, 19:1.

57. For a fuller explanation, see Forster and Epstein, *Danger on the Right,* 3–10. The Christian Anti-Communist Crusade of Dr. Frederick Schwarz in Calif.; the Christian Crusade of Dr. Billy James Hargis in Tulsa, Okla.; the

Twentieth-Century Reformation Hour of Rev. Carl McIntire in Philadelphia; and Robert Welch's John Birch Society were the leading ultraconservative organizations in the nation. All were associated in some way with NEP, and all, to some degree, supported Barry Goldwater in the 1964 election.

58. Cabell Phillips, "Wide Anti-Red Drive Directed From Small Town in Arkansas," *New York Times,* May 18, 1961, 26.

59. Horton, "Revivalism on the Far Right," 25–29.

60. "Revivalism on the Far Right," *Arkansas Gazette,* July 14, 1961, B1:1.

61. "Academic Capital of Ultraconservatism," *Newsweek,* Dec. 4, 1961, 20.

62. "The Ultras," *Time,* Dec. 8, 1961, 22–24.

63. Donald Janson, "Right-Wingers Invade Classroom," *Dayton (Ohio) Daily News,* Jan. 31, 1962.

64. Kenneth Eskey, "Radical Right Called Threat to Freedom By Visiting Professor," *Pittsburgh Press,* Jan. 31, 1962. Amid this ardent denunciation of NEP, Westin stated rather sheepishly that he was "glad to see the upsurge of conservatism on college campuses because it shows students are thinking about free enterprise." Ibid.

65. "Project Alert," *Arkansas Gazette,* Mar. 22, 1963. Eventually, several school districts, including the Memphis city schools, bowed to the growing criticism linking NEP with extremism and banned all the NEP films. "Shelby Schools Cease Banning Harding Films," *Arkansas Gazette,* Mar. 19, 1964.

66. Giles M. Fowler, "A Label, 'Ultra-Rightist,' Puts the Spotlight on a Small College Down in Arkansas," *Kansas City Star,* Feb. 4, 1962, 1–2.

67. "Kennedy Closing the 'Kennedy Gap,'" *Newsweek,* Nov. 27, 1961, 16. Benson had been especially critical of Kennedy's foreign policy, esp. his handling of the "Bay of Pigs" landing. Earlier Benson had spread the story, supposedly obtained from Rep. Wilbur Mills, that "U.S. participation in the ill-fated Cuban invasion was called off at the last moment because Khrushchev telephoned Kennedy just hours before and threatened to invade Turkey if the U.S. helped fight Castro." "Who's Really Bluffing Who?" editorial, *Edmond (Okla.) Sun,* Nov. 14, 1961, 4.

68. Richard Dudman, *Men of the Far Right* (New York: Pyramid Books, 1962), i.

69. Benson himself credited renewed interest in NEP to this phenomenon. Donald Janson, "The NEP," *New York Times,* Jan. 29, 1962, 22:4. Norman Thomas labeled NEP a "front for the John Birch Society." Murray Illson, "Norman Thomas Hits Birch Group," *New York Times,* Apr. 20, 1961.

70. Robert Welch, *The Blue Book of the John Birch Society* (Boston: Western Islands Publishers, 1959), xiv.

71. *Time* estimated Birch Society strength at 50,000. "The Ultras," *Time,* Dec. 8, 1961, 23.

72. Forster and Epstein, *Danger on the Right,* xvi. The other three highly critical accounts of NEP were in Dudman, *Men of the Far Right*; Ralph E.

Ellsworth and Sarah M. Harris, *The American Right Wing* (Washington D.C.: Public Affairs Press, 1962); and Donald Janson and Bernard Eismann, *The Far Right* (New York: McGraw-Hill, 1963).

73. Ellsworth and Harris, *American Right Wing,* 2.

74. "Project Alert," *Los Angeles Times,* Dec. 15, 1961, pt. 3:2.

75. Royce Lynn Money, "Church-State Relations in the Churches of Christ Since 1945: A Study in Religion and Politics" (Ph.D. diss., Baylor Univ., Waco, Tex., 1975), 107.

76. Giles M. Fowler, "A Label, 'Ultra-Rightest,' Puts the Spotlight on a Small College Down in Arkansas," *Kansas City Star,* Feb. 4, 1962, 1–2D.

77. White, *Suite 3505,* epilogue.

78. *North Central Association Report,* North Central Association of Colleges and Secondary Schools. Issued to Harding College, Searcy, Ark., 1948, in NEP files.

79. Qtd. in George S. Benson to Rep. William E. Dannemeyer of Calif. (Dec. 4, 1985; typescript in NEP Files), thanking the latter for sending Benson a copy of a book critical of Washington's involvement in public education.

80. "Harding Accredited by North Central," *Bison,* Mar. 29, 1954.

81. Cited in James L. Atteberry, "The Story of Harding College: Spring 1969" (Searcy, Ark.: privately printed by the author, 1969), 3–4. This is an explanation of Atteberry's actions during the controversy over his dismissal.

82. "Whether the accusations were true or not, Harding College definitely had an image as a factory for right-wing propaganda. Harding's image was inevitably inherited by the Churches of Christ in the eyes of those who were right-wing critics." Money, "Church-State Relations," 98.

83. Wallace Alexander, "How Free is the *Bison?*" *Bison,* Nov. 14, 1956, 2.

84. Forster and Epstein, *Danger on The Right;* Bales, *Americanism Under Fire.*

85. J. D. Bales, "Letter to the *Bison* Editor," *Bison,* May 3, 1968.

86. Dennie Hall, "Segregation: A Personal Problem," *Bison,* Oct. 26, 1955.

87. "Harding to Admit 3 Negroes," *Arkansas Gazette,* Sept. 10, 1963.

88. Jimmy Arnold, "Now Is the Time to Stand," *Bison,* Sept. 26, 1963. Benson spent over 30 years and much of his own money to help establish and operate the Namwianga Christian School in Zambia, to educate blacks for positions of authority in that African country.

89. Randy Parks, "Letter to the Editor," *Bison,* Apr. 30, 1955.

90. Alan Hughes, "Letter to the Editor," *Bison,* May 13, 1955.

91. Jennie Schoolfield, "We Must Think for Ourselves," *Bison,* Apr. 10, 1954.

92. "Editorial," *Bison,* May 7, 1955.

93. Dennis Cox, "Editorial," *Bison,* Apr. 26, 1961.

94. Suellen Tullis, "Government Peace Corps Program Front for Communist Penetration," *Bison,* Nov. 30, 1961.

95. According to Anderson, NEP could best serve the school by moving to

another location like "Kensett or Little Rock or Berlin or some place outside the city limits." Joel Anderson, "Editorial," *Bison,* Nov. 30, 1961.

96. Virginia Leatherwood, "Interview Enlightens Students as to Current Public
    Opinions," *Bison,* Feb. 8, 1962.

97. Jay Lancello, "Political Factions Sometimes Confuse Students, Need for
    Evaluation Cited," *Bison,* Dec. 11, 1962.

98. Joel Anderson, "Editorial," *Bison,* Apr. 12, 1962.

99. Joel Anderson, "Christian College, Politics, and Academic Freedom,"
    Mission 5 (Oct. 1971): 116–17.

100. Doug Smith, "George Benson," *Arkansas Gazette,* Oct. 18, 1964.

101. Qtd. in Altman, "Contributions," 79.

102. Jay Lancello, "Political Factions Sometimes Confuse Students," *Bison,* Dec.
     11, 1962.

103. James L. Atteberry, *The Story of Harding College* (Searcy, Ark: Harding Col-
     lege, 1966), 34.

104. Cited in Atteberry, "Story of Harding College: Spring 1969," 3.

105. Ibid.

106. Ibid., 50. According to Atteberry, his faculty opposition was headed by
     J. D. Bales, the leading NEP advocate on the campus. Cited in Atteberry,
     "Story of Harding College: Spring 1969," 65.

107. Cited in Money, "Church-State Relations," supp., passim. Interestingly,
     Frank Rhodes later resigned from Harding in bitterness, apparently due to
     a disagreement with Benson and Bales.

108. David Lipscomb, *Civil Government, Its Origin, Mission, and Destiny and
     the Christian's Relation To It* (Nashville, Tenn.: Gospel Advocate Co.,
     1889), 42–43.

109. Ibid.

110. See Money, "Church-State Relations," supp., esp. interviews with Athens
     Clay Pullias, president of David Lipscomb College; and with Robert E.
     Hooper, chairman of the history department at David Lipscomb Univer-
     sity. Money interviewed thirty influential leaders of the Churches of Christ.

111. Money, "Church-State Relations," 108. Most Churches of Christ leaders in-
     terviewed by Money expressed feelings similar to those of Reuel
     Lemmons about the role of NEP in Christian education. See interviews in
     Money, "Church-State Relations," supp.

112. Cited from NEP financial records, Mar. 1990, located at American Citizen-
     ship Center (ACC) Files, Oklahoma Christian Univ., Oklahoma City, Okla.

113. "Benson Honored by Freedom Foundation," *Bison,* Dec. 3, 1949.

114. Cited in Hicks, "George S. Benson: Missionary Pioneer."

115. "Dr. Benson Given Arkansas Award at APEC Banquet," *Bison,* Apr. 10,
     1954, 1.

5. The National Education Program and the Rise of the New Religious Right

1. "Opposition to ERA, homosexual rights, and abortion was part of what the New Right regarded as a crusade to save the American family." Gottfried and Fleming, *Conservative Movement*, 86.

2. The Christian Right, led by Jerry Falwell, Ed McAteer, James Robison, and Pat Robertson, "contributed more than religious fervor and moral commitment: by the 1980s Christian broadcasting was reaching millions of television viewers and radio listeners, who responded to this appeal for moral revival and patriotic dedication." Ibid., 78.

3. Kevin Phillips, *Post-Conservative America,* 47.

4. Pollster Lou Harris attributed Reagan's victory partly to the vote of "awakened Evangelicals," who by then were hardly strangers to American politics. "Much of the support of William Jennings Bryan's populist crusade had been drawn from the Evangelical churches, and the 1950s and 1960s were treated to anti-Communist political sermons by the Reverend Carl McIntire and even Billy Graham." Above all other issues, the primary catalyst for evangelical political activism of the 1970s was the *Roe v. Wade* decision on abortion in 1973. Gottfried and Fleming, *Conservative Movement,* 82–83.

5. Corwin E. Smidt, "The Mobilization of Evangelical Voters in 1980: An Initial Test of Several Hypotheses," *Southeastern Political Review* 16, no. 2 (Fall 1988): 20.

6. James L. Guth, "The Politics of the Christian Right," in *Interest Group Politics,* ed. Allan. J. Cigler and Burkett A. Loomis (Washington, D. C.: Congressional Quarterly Press, 1983), 62. See also Bruce, *Rise and Fall,* 15–24; and Guth, "Politics of Religion in America."

7. Most observers use Jerry Falwell's classification of important issues of the New Religious Right. "He called for an end to abortion for any reason, defeat of the Equal Rights Amendment, resistance to women's liberation, a stronger stand against world Communism, and rejection of secular humanism accompanied by restoration of prayer in public schools." Lee Sigelman, Clyde Wilcox, and Emmett H. Buell, Jr., "An Unchanging Minority: Popular Support for the Moral Majority, 1980 and 1984," *Social Science Quarterly* 68 (Dec. 1987): 876.

8. Mel Hailey, "The Political and Social Attitudes of Church of Christ Ministers," in *Research in the Social Scientific Study of Religion,* edited by Monty L. Lynn and David O. Moberg (Greenwich, Conn.: JAI Press, 1991), 3:233.

9. See Lee Benson, *The Concept of Jacksonian Democracy: New York as a Test Case* (Princeton, N.J.: Princeton Univ. Press, 1961); Ronald P. Formisano, *The Birth of Mass Political Parties: Michigan, 1827–1861*

(Princeton, N.J.: Princeton Univ. Press, 1971); Ronald P. Formisano, *The Transformation of Political Culture* (New York: Oxford Univ. Press, 1983); John L. Hammond, *The Politics of Benevolence: Revival Religion and American Voting Behavior* (Norwood, N.J.: Ablex Publishing, 1979); Richard J. Jensen, *Grass Roots Politics: Parties, Issues, and Voters, 1854–1983* (Westport, Conn.: Greenwood Press, 1983); Richard J. Jensen, *The Winning of the Midwest: Social and Political Conflict, 1888–1896* (Chicago: Univ. of Chicago Press, 1971); Paul Kleppner, *The Cross of Culture: A Social Analysis of Midwestern Politics, 1850–1900* (New York: Free Press, 1970); Paul Kleppner, *The Third Electoral System, 1853–1892: Parties, Voters and Political Culture* (Chapel Hill: Univ. of North Carolina Press, 1979); Paul Kleppner, *Who Voted? The Dynamics of Electoral Turnout, 1870–1980* (New York: Praeger, 1982).

10. The research of Clyde Wilcox, a noted analyst of recent election trends, indicates that "within a fairly homogeneous population, religious variables play a major role in explaining support for a political organization." Wilcox, "Evangelicals and the Moral Majority," 410.

11. Kleppner, *Cross of Culture,* 7.

12. Wald, *Religion and Politics,* 182.

13. Kleppner, *Third Electoral System,* 15.

14. Ibid., 10.

15. Kleppner, *Cross of Culture,* 19.

16. Beard denied that "all history can or must be explained in economic terms, or any other terms." Charles Beard, *An Economic Interpretation of the Constitution of the United States* (New York: Macmillan, 1913, rpt. New York: Free Press, 1986), xlviii. Ultimately, Beard dismissed noneconomic issues as "incidental and uninfluential." Lee Benson, *Turner and Beard: American Historical Writing Reconsidered* (New York: Free Press, 1960), 105–6. Turner and Beard buttressed their forceful arguments with such excellent research that there was little significant challenge to their economic interpretations of history until after World War II.

17. Jensen, *Winning of the Midwest,* xi. In Jensen's opinion, "Economic or class antagonisms (which some historians have insisted upon as the real issues) existed, too, but seem to have been of lesser importance." Ibid.

18. Robert P. Swierenga, "Ethnoreligious Political Behavior in the Mid-Nineteenth Century: Voting, Values, and Cultures," in *Religion and American Politics: From the Colonial Period to the 1980s,* ed. Mark A. Knoll (New York: Oxford Univ. Press, 1990), 146.

19. Kleppner, *Third Electoral System,* 184.

20. Formisano, *Birth of Mass Political Parties,* 137. "This ever-expanding web of benevolent enterprises provided the revivalists with their organizational base for the extermination of sin. They also became involved in pressure-group politics." Kleppner, *Third Electoral System,* 64.

21. Wald, *Religion and Politics,* 63.
22. Ibid., 266.
23. "Voting is more than simply the modal political act performed by the American public. It is the mechanism that most citizens believe to be the only one available to them for influencing what the government does." Kleppner, *Who Voted?,* 5.
24. Ibid., 6. Even though the ethnoreligious thesis of voting behavior is presently the reigning interpretation, this approach's methodology and conclusions need clarification. In particular, critics have questioned classifying individual voter responses by ethnoreligious group. Properly identifying the religious preference of the voter is a fundamental problem, and it is equally important to measure the extent to which religiosity interacts with socioeconomic and other factors to determine voting behavior. Unfortunately, researchers still rely far too much on generalization. Census reports and voting records are too incomplete to allow more than estimations of the meaning of voting results. Presently, studies discussed here are of relatively small population groups. No one has yet attempted to analyze elections on the national level, and until this is done successfully, the paradigm remains an extrapolation of the results of isolated incidents in American political history.

     Another major criticism of the ethnocultural thesis is that it fails to consider the unchurched voting population or those who do not fall easily into a major religious category; the paradigm must be regarded as a tentative framework. A third major criticism casts doubt on the ability of a one-dimensional, "either-or" scale adequately to portray complex relationships among race, ethnicity, economics, denominational differences, and religious world view.

     Despite its limitations, the ethnocultural interpretation highlights religious values as interesting and important elements of American culture that may have fueled the nation's political accomplishments. Ironically, ethnoreligious interpretation resurrects an interesting theory jettisoned by earlier American political historians. Emile Durkheim, Max Weber, and Karl Marx identified the basic elements of modernization and class-conflict theories of social change. On the basis of these theories, many historians predicted the rapid decline of religion "as a significant force in advanced societies," and, accordingly, "the decline of religious controversies in politics." Contrary to prevailing modernization theories which downplay the influence of religious ideology on American culture, Wald argues that religiosity will increasingly influence American political behavior. Wald, *Religion and Politics,* 3. For a detailed explanation of this idea in recent political history, see Robert Wuthnow, "The Political Rebirth of American Evangelicals," in *The New Christian Right,* ed. Robert C. Liebman and Robert Wuthnow (New York: Aldine, 1983), 167–85.

25. Jensen, *Winning of the Midwest,* xv.
26. Wald, *Religion and Politics,* 190.
27. Ibid., 199.
28. Ibid., 279.
29. Kevin Phillips, *Post-Conservative America,* 190.
30. According to Alan Crawford, Paul Gottfried and Thomas Fleming, Kevin Phillips, and Kenneth Wald, the two most important and influential groups within the New Religious Right were the Moral Majority of Jerry Falwell and the Religious Roundtable of Ed McAteer. Alan Crawford, *Thunder on the Right: The "New Right" and the Politics of Resentment* (New York: Pantheon, 1980), 162; Gottfried and Fleming, *Conservative Movement,* 83; Kevin Phillips, *Post-Conservative America,* 48; and Kenneth Wald, *Religion and Politics,* 209.
31. Money severely criticized Benson and NEP for using religious nationalism for financial gain for the institution. Money concluded that, "without the overwhelming financial success of this vested interest one is caused to wonder if the Americanism emphasis would have been as strong and as sustained as it has been." Money, "Church-State Relations," 189. Although Money does not appear to share David Lipscomb's basic philosophy on this subject, discussed earlier, Money indicated very strongly his belief that the religious nationalism practiced at Harding College "has caused serious damage to the Churches of Christ both from within its fellowship and beyond." Ibid., 187.
32. Money defines nationalism as "rooted in the principle of ultimate loyalty to one's nation in an effort to preserve a certain way of life through patriotic emphases. Religious nationalism weds the goals of the nation to the goals of religion, thus sanctifying national political and economic interests." Ibid., 182.
33. Wood paraphrased Martin E. Marty, who earlier had declared, "Both of Eisenhower's presidential campaigns were 'crusades for moral and spiritual values.' Throughout his presidency, Eisenhower affirmed that 'America is the mightiest power which God has yet seen fit to put upon his footstool.' Or again, 'America is great because she is good.' Both statements have come to be viewed as part of the American national faith." Martin Marty, *The New Shape of Religion,* (New York: Harper and Brothers, 1959), 83. James E. Wood, Jr., "The Problem of Nationalism in Church-State Relations," *Journal of Church and State* 10 (Spring 1968): 262. For a thorough discussion of the role of "civil religion" in American politics during this period, consult Richard V. Pierard and Robert D. Linder, *Civil Religion and the Presidency* (Grand Rapids, Mich.: Zondervan Publishing House, 1988), 184–205.
34. Frank S. Mead, *Handbook of Denominations in the United States* (Nashville, Tenn.: Abingdon Press, 1970), 85.

35. H. Richard Niebuhr, *The Social Sources of Denominationalism,* 5th ed. (New York: Meridian Books, 1960), 16.

36. Money, "Church-State Relations," 184.

37. Money cites other historians who have studied similarly fragmented denominations and have concluded that, "when a study is made of independent, fragmented religious groups, it is justifiable to assume that the views of the leaders reflect the views of the general membership." Ibid., 12. Money mentions John Lee Eighmy, *Churches in Cultural Captivity* (Knoxville: Univ. of Tennessee Press, 1972), and Harrell, *Social Sources of Division.*

38. Money, "Church-State Relations," 11–12.

39. Ibid., 9–10.

40. The growth of religious nationalism, anticommunism, and conservative activism among members of the Churches of Christ in the 1950s and 1960s can be attributed to a "triumvirate somewhat similar to the trinity of the Godhead, in that the three are one when viewed from certain perspectives. The three are Harding College, George Stuart Benson, and the National Education Program." Ibid., 89–90.

41. Ibid., 40.

42. George S. Benson, "Moral Indignation," (Searcy, Ark.: NEP, n.d.). Benson indicated elsewhere that there were "approximately 125 million people who ought to be voting in the elections in America on the personalities and issues of government, and actively fulfilling the civic duties of a free people." George S. Benson, "A Powerless Public Opinion," *NEP Newsletter,* Jan. 1971, 1.

43. Money, "Church-State Relations," 268.

44. This is obvious from figures which indicate that Churches of Christ support for George Wallace in the 1968 presidential election was well below the national total of 13.5%, and that a large number of independents voted for Nixon. Ibid., 375.

45. Ibid., 137. "Even the traditionally Democratic South is steadily losing ground to the Republicans." Ibid.

46. Ibid., supp., 491.

47. Ibid., 186.

48. Ibid., v.

49. Hailey, "Political and Social Attitudes of Church of Christ Ministers," 231.

50. Ibid., 232.

51. Ibid., 234.

52. Rowland has been in a rather unique position as director of the American Citizenship Program. Although he had worked closely with Benson since 1972 and even worked directly under him from 1982 to 1985, the two differed significantly on many issues concerning the program. Nevertheless, Rowland gave Benson tremendous credit for helping to mobilize conser-

vative opinion within the Churches of Christ. Hicks, "Interview with Robert Rowland."

53. Rowland said he "was a Democrat early on. I guess from parents who were Democrats. We were Okies who went west with the 'Grapes of Wrath' in 1937. We were migrant farm laborers although we finally settled in the central valley of California. The concept in those days was that Republicans were the owners and Democrats were the workers and the Democrats got the short end of the stick." Ibid., 8–9.

54. Ibid., 10. Rowland felt that Benson's monthly newsletter had as much to do with his own political conversion to the conservative philosophy as any single element with which he came in contact. Ibid., 7.

55. Ibid., 24.

56. Ibid. Another interesting example of the influence of Benson's Americanism programs on those who later became crusaders for conservative causes is Gary North's Institute for Christian Economics. North, who also is on the board of the Conservative Caucus, was one of the originators of an unusual economic perspective known as theonomy, or Christian reconstructionism. According to this outlook, the Bible contains a "blueprint for the right ordering of society," including its proper political and economic organization. Theonomists like North are "providing extremists in the New Right with a clearly defined agenda that is antihumanist, antisecularist, and antisocialist." John Richard Neuhaus, "Why Wait for the Kingdom? The Theonomist Temptation," *First Things: A Monthly Journal of Religion and Public Life* 3 (May 1990):13–21. Although highly critical of Benson's program because it failed "to create an explicitly Bible-based Christian political or economic philosophy" and thus failed to go far enough to the right, economically and politically, North has admitted that he was influenced positively by Benson's program. According to North, he attended his first Freedom Forum at Pepperdine College in 1959 and, although he was unimpressed by much of the program, the "NEP pamphlets were more important in my life: Mayer's piece on the prison camp collaborators in the Korean War (I vaguely recall seeing the NEP movie), Fred Schwarz's essay on Communism, and John Noble's pamphlet on his Russian prison camp experiences all influenced me, although I had first heard Schwarz in 1956, years earlier." Gary North to L. Edward Hicks, June 8, 1990. Typescript in personal collection of L. Edward Hicks.

57. "They came on the college campuses and preached and breathed those fundamentals that Dr. Benson preached." Hicks, "Interview with Robert Rowland," 18. When asked if he felt that the dissemination of Benson's philosophy to the students on campus and their going on to other educational pursuits and then returning to teach had been instrumental in making the program bigger or spreading the philosophy, Rowland agreed very strongly. Ibid.

58. Ibid., 55. In evaluating the success of the Americanism program, Rowland said, "This is the only way I know to determine the good we do, is through stories like that." Rowland continued with this explanation: "And it's quite often that I run into somebody in some office, some bank, some meeting or I speak for some program, and some person in their twenties or thirties will come to me and they'll say, 'Mr. Rowland, it's good to hear you again.' Or 'It's good to see you. I attended a seminar at the University of Tulsa, (or Phillips University, or Oklahoma Christian College, or wherever else), and that was a great week, one of the greatest in my life because I really learned to appreciate my country for the first time and understand my freedoms.' So those are the rewards I get when I run into people like that." Ibid.

59. James J. Kilpatrick, "Why Students Are Hostile to Free Enterprise," *Nation's Business* 63, no. 7 (July 1975).

60. Hicks, "Interview with Robert Rowland," 68–69.

61. Ibid.

62. Wald, *Religion and Politics,* 116.

63. "A distinctive feature of the contemporary American Right is its emphasis on progress: moving beyond the past toward a future of unlimited material opportunity and social improvement." Gottfried and Fleming, *Conservative Movement,* vii.

64. Ibid., 78.

65. Wald, *Religion and Politics,* 190.

66. Crawford, *Thunder on the Right,* chap. 5. Interestingly, the textbook controversy in Kanawa County, W.Va., centered on the wife of a Church of Christ minister who won election to the school board and secured a ban on sex education and a policy condemning the infusion of "secular humanist" ideology in district textbooks. Bruce, *Rise and Fall,* 108.

67. Wald, *Religion and Politics,* 188.

68. Ibid.

69. Ibid., 189. Kevin Phillips, along with many other observers of the conservative resurgence, assigns tremendous importance to these three figures as "key leaders of the New Right" and architects of the coalition of conservative political activism and the New Religious Right. Kevin Phillips, *Post-Conservative America,* 14.

70. "Interview with Ed McAteer, President of the Religious Roundtable," interview by L. Edward Hicks, Apr. 25, 1990. In Hicks, "A Case Study of Conservative Political Education," Appendix E: 392–457. The majority of background material on the Religious Roundtable is taken from this interview. Other sources will be cited when appropriate.

71. Kershner has been branded an "extreme Conservative" whose newspaper, *Christian Economics,* is sent free to 200,000 Protestant ministers and laymen. In addition, he wrote a weekly column for 225 daily newspapers

while producing his radio program, "Howard Kershner's Commentary on the News." Forster and Epstein, *Danger on the Right,* 267.

72. Edwards, "Paul Weyrich, Conscience of the New Right," 2; also cited in Kevin Phillips, *Post-Conservative America,* 190. As mentioned above, the name "Moral Majority" is almost synonymous with the Religious Right.

73. Hicks, "Interview with Ed McAteer," 6.

74. The Religious Roundtable has been categorized as a nonpartisan program and, by the IRS, as a 501C3 educational foundation. It is therefore tax-exempt. Ibid., 14.

75. Ibid., 6.

76. Ibid., 13. "In one sense, the formation of the Moral Majority Inc. or Religious Roundtable was merely the linking together at the federal level of a series of small movements and organizations which had been campaigning on particular elements of what became the New Christian Right platform. In this sense, the 'newness' of the New Christian Right lay in new organizational forms and a change of gear." Bruce, *Rise and Fall,* 64.

77. Hicks, "Interview with Ed McAteer," 50.

78. Ibid., 40.

79. Wald, *Religion and Politics,* 193–94.

80. See Kevin Phillips, *Post-Conservative America,* 49. Phillips cites the Harris poll released on November 4, 1980. Subsequent evidence modifies these claims somewhat and suggests that "political scientists Seymour Martin Lipset and Earl Raab are probably correct: evangelical voters may have switched from Carter to Reagan in large numbers, but they did so for the same economic and foreign policy reasons that led equally large (or perhaps larger) numbers to switch." Guth, "Politics of the Christian Right," in Cigler and Loomis, eds., *Interest Group Politics,* 74.

81. Hicks, "Interview with Ed McAteer," 55.

82. Wald, *Religion and Politics,* 202.

6. The Impact of the National Education Program on the New Right

1. Ronald Reagan, "Tribute to George Benson on his 80th Birthday," Sept. 26, 1978. Transcript of audiotape, NEP Files.

2. An increase in small donations to the NEP resulted from the distribution of the newsletter, but, more importantly, "whatever its value as a method of fund-raising, direct mail is a good method of consciousness-raising for those people sympathetic enough to read it." Bruce, *Rise and Fall,* 62.

3. Gene Fretz, "Harding Observes an Anniversary and a Way of Life," *Arkansas Gazette,* May 30, 1954.

4. Garner, "George S. Benson," 139. Even in 1990, NEP's mailing list included over 23,000 names, and more than 5,000 people still contributed to

the program in 1990. Cited from NEP financial records, Free Enterprise Center, Oklahoma Christian College, Oklahoma City, Okla.

5. Kevin Phillips, *Post-Conservative America,* 98.

6. NEP's influence on populist activism was not limited to economic issues. The NEP was a leading voice in the "Stop the ERA" movement led by Phyllis Schlafly, and on various issues associated with propagation of "secular humanist" philosophy in public schools. Bruce, *Rise and Fall,* 93, claims that stopping ratification of the ERA was the "clearest and most dramatic success" of the New Christian Right because it had seemed well on its way to passage until groups like the NEP began campaigning against it.

   The former head of NEP's women's activities, Marilyn Kreitling, left NEP in 1980 to join Phyllis Schlafly's effort to block ratification of the ERA. Kreitling earlier had been involved in a controversy with the Little Rock school superintendent over "secular humanist" education in Little Rock public schools. *Arkansas Gazette,* Feb. 21, 1980, 7A.

7. Hofstadter, *American Political Tradition,* 18–44.

8. Kevin Phillips, *Post-Conservative America,* 34: "I grant that one-paragraph descriptions of this sort inevitably generalize too much. As capsules go, however, this one is hardly unfair. Not a few of those involved have said much the same thing in doleful retrospect."

9. Qtd. in Fred J. Cook, "The Ultras," *Nation,* 565.

10. Stanley I. Kutler, Editor's Forward to Heale, *American Anticommunism,* ix.

11. Heale, *American Anticommunism,* xii.

12. "The old Christian right was concerned with the threat from 'world communism.' In the 1940s and 1950s many fundamentalists were active supporters of anti-Communist movements. Some, like Billy James Hargis and Carl McIntire, foreshadowed such New Christian Right evangelists as Jerry Falwell by using their fundamentalist radio ministries to promote anti-Communist organizations." Bruce, *Rise and Fall,* 33.

13. Kevin Phillips, *Post-Conservative America,* 176.

14. Oddly enough, Ronald Reagan first became involved in the anti-Communist argument when he, as president of the Hollywood Screen Actors Guild, failed to support several of his fellow actors against the accusations of the McCarthy committee and even testified before Congress concerning Hollywood's loyalty to basic American principles. Schieffer and Gates, *Acting President,* 172.

15. Cited in White, *Suite 3505,* 443. President Johnson's campaign strategy openly played on the public's faulty perception, with TV advertisements such as the "A Bomb" ad, which strongly hinted that Goldwater might irresponsibly initiate a global nuclear conflict.

16. Heale, *American Anticommunism,* 171.

17. Ibid., 199.

18. Carey McWilliams, *Southern California Country* (New York: Duell, Sloan and Pierce, 1946).
19. Cited in Kevin Phillips, *Post-Conservative America,* 12.
20. Ibid., 18–30.
21. Ibid., 167.
22. Ibid., 8.
23. Leopold Tyrmand, "The Conservative Ideas in Reagan's Victory," *Wall Street Journal,* Jan. 20, 1981, esp. note 1. Reagan did attribute much of his speech material to George Benson.
24. Ibid. It should be remembered that George Benson most assuredly was one of those conservative publicists who contributed to Reagan's under-standing of conservative ideology. Reagan and Benson, since the early 1960s, had been working together on different projects to expand conser-vative influence among the voting populous.
25. *Human Events,* Apr. 4, 1981, 7.
26. Gottfried and Fleming, *Conservative Movement,* 22.
27. Ibid.
28. Kevin Phillips, *Post-Conservative America,* 47; Gottfried and Fleming, *Conservative Movement,* 77–79.
29. Howard Phillips, telephone conversation with L. Edward Hicks, May 10, 1990; transcript in personal collection of L. Edward Hicks. Howard Phillips, letter to L. Edward Hicks, May 7, 1990. Transcript in personal collection of L. Edward Hicks. Another conservative Republican who was greatly influenced by Benson was John A. Stormer, who led the Missouri delegation to the 1964 Republican National Convention in San Francisco. Stormer, author of *None Dare Call It Treason* (Florisant, Mo.: Liberty Bell Press, 1964), a popular conservative diatribe which during the 1964 elec-tion supported Goldwater's ideology, stated that Benson had played a "major part in my own awakening and political transformation." According to Stormer, the sale of 7 million copies of his book was "largely the work of those great numbers of people awakened and trained during the previ-ous four or five years by Dr. Benson and others." John A. Stormer to L. Edward Hicks, June 6, 1990, in personal collection of L. Edward Hicks.
30. Kevin Phillips, *Post-Conservative America,* 108.
31. Ibid., 132.
32. Cited in ibid., 50.
33. "A distinctive feature of the contemporary American Right is its emphasis on progress: moving beyond the past toward a future of unlimited mate-rial opportunity and social improvement," without increased government direction. Gottfried and Fleming, *Conservative Movement,* vii.
34. Kevin Phillips, *Post-Conservative America,* 33.
35. Unfortunately, once in power, the conservatives have fared no better in reversing the tendency to increase the size of government. Not only did

the "liberal" President Johnson balance the budget, but "all the spending of the 39 presidents hardly mattered until Ronald Reagan took office. The nation's total debt accumulated over 200 years almost tripled in eight—from just under $1 trillion to $2.8 trillion—thanks to the man who was the most conservative president and the politician who made chopping government spending a centerpiece of his rhetoric. Remarkably, even President Reagan is being exceeded by his understudy, George Bush, who so far is in a class by himself. His first, and perhaps only, four years will add at least another $1.2 trillion." Brian Kelly, *Adventures in Porkland* (New York: Random House, 1992), cited in Brian Kelly, "Adventures in Porkland," *Montgomery (Ala.) Advertiser,* Oct. 27, 1992.

36. Kevin Phillips, *Post-Conservative America,* 50

37. Ibid., 133.

38. Max Weber, *The Protestant Ethic and the Spirit of Capitalism* (London: G. Allen and Unwin, 1930), and R. H. Tawney, *Religion and the Rise of Capitalism* (Gloucester, Mass.: Peter Smith, 1962). George Gilder, a popular Reaganite author, in 1981 proclaimed the interrelationship of capitalism and faith; and Michael Novak, a scholar in residence at the American Enterprise Institute, called for a move to define "a theology of the corporation" because "the corporation mirrors God's presence also in its liberty, by which I mean independence from the state." Cited in Kevin Phillips, *Post-Conservative America,* 12–13.

39. Palmer and Sawhill, *Reagan Experiment,* 3.

40. Ibid., 4.

41. Kevin Phillips, *Post-Conservative America,* 50–51.

42. Another organization for economic education that was greatly influenced by NEP is the Foundation for Economic Education, Irvington-on-Hudson, N.Y. Leonard E. Read, founder of the organization, often spoke on the Freedom Forums, and eventually Read hired as his assistants several from colleges supported by the Churches of Christ, including Bruce M. Evans, the current director. See Evans, telephone conversation with L. Edward Hicks, Aug. 6, 1990; notes in personal collection of L. Edward Hicks.

43. Although Benson's primary contribution to the Religious Right was providing the economic component of its profamily agenda, Benson and NEP also supported the other elements of the profamily program. Throughout the years, Benson argued against value relativism and "secular humanist" philosophy, and his organization was adamantly opposed to banning prayer in public schools. Cited in support of prayer in public schools, in George S. Benson to Arkansas Sen. Dale Bumpers, Aug. 6, 1985, NEP Files, Special Collections, Library, Harding Univ.

44. Bruce, *Rise and Fall,* 82.

Bibliography

Monographs and Dissertations

Ahlstrom, Sydney E. *A Religious History of the American People.* 2 vols. Garden City, N.Y.: Image Books, 1975.

Altman, Ted Max. "The Contributions of George S. Benson to Christian Education." Ph.D. diss., North Texas State Univ., Denton, Tex., 1971.

Atteberry, James L. *The Story of Harding College.* Searcy, Ark.: Harding College, 1966.

———. "The Story of Harding College: Spring 1969." Searcy, Ark.: privately printed by the author, 1969. A copy is available in the library of Harding College, Searcy, Ark.

Bales, James D. *Americanism Under Fire.* Searcy, Ark.: Bales Bookstore, 1965.

———. *Communism: Its Faith and Fallacies.* Grand Rapids, Mich.: Baker Book House, 1962.

Beard, Charles. *An Economic Interpretation of the Constitution of the United States.* New York: Macmillan, 1913; rpt. New York: Free Press, 1986.

Belknap, Michael. *Cold War Political Justice: The Smith Act, the Communist Party, and American Civil Liberties.* Westport, Conn.: Greenwood, 1977.

Benson, George S. *Missionary Experiences.* Edited by Phil Watson. Delight, Ark.: Gospel Light Publishing, 1987.

Benson, Lee. *The Concept of Jacksonian Democracy: New York as a Test Case.* Princeton, N.J.: Princeton Univ. Press, 1961.

———. *Turner and Beard: American Historical Writing Reconsidered.* New York: Free Press, 1960.

Bloom, Alan. *The Closing of the American Mind.* New York: Simon and Schuster, 1987.

Bozeman, Theodore Dwight. *Protestants in an Age of Science: The Baconian Ideal and Antebellum American Religious Thought.* Chapel Hill: Univ. of North Carolina Press, 1977.

Bradley, Gerald V. *Church-State Relationships in America*. Westport, Conn.: Greenwood Press, 1987.

Braeman, John; Bremner, Robert H.; and Brody, David, eds. *The New Deal: The National Level*. Columbus: Ohio State Univ. Press, 1975.

Brennan, Mary C. "Conservatism in the Sixties: The Development of the American Political Right, 1960–1968." Ph.D. diss., Miami Univ., Miami, Ohio, 1988.

Bromley, D., and Shupe, A., eds. *New Christian Politics*. Macon, Ga.: Mercer Univ. Press, 1984.

Bruce, Steve. *The Rise and Fall of the New Christian Right*. Oxford, England: Clarendon Press, 1988.

Buckley, William F. *Did You Ever See a Dream Walking? American Conservative Thought in the Twentieth Century*. New York: Bobbs-Merrill, 1970.

_____. *The Committee and Its Critics*. New York: G. P. Putnam's Sons, 1962.

_____. *Up From Liberalism*. New York: Stein and Day, 1984.

Burns, James MacGregor. *Roosevelt: The Lion and the Fox*. New York: Harcourt, Brace and World, 1956.

_____. *The Deadlock of Democracy: Four-Party Politics in America*. Englewood Cliffs, N.J.: Prentice-Hall, 1964.

Ch'i, Hsi-sheng. *Warlord Politics in China, 1916–1928*. Stanford, Calif.: Stanford Univ. Press, 1976.

Chamberlain, John. *The Enterprising Americans: A Business History of the United States*. New York: Harper and Row, 1963.

_____. *The Roots of Capitalism*. New York: D. Van Nostrand, 1965.

Clubb, O. Edmund. *Twentieth-Century China*. 2d ed. New York: Columbia Univ. Press, 1972.

Collins, Robert M. *The Business Response to Keynes, 1929–1964*. New York: Columbia Univ. Press, 1981.

Conkin, Paul K. *The New Deal*. New York: Thomas Y. Crowell, 1967.

Conspiracy Against Freedom: A Documentation of One Campaign of the Anti-Defamation League Against Freedom of Speech and Thought in America. Washington, D.C.: Liberty Lobby, 1986.

Cook, Fred J. *Barry Goldwater: Extremist of the Right*. New York: Grove Press, 1964.

_____. *The FBI Nobody Knows*. New York: Pyramid Books, 1964.

Cox, Edward Franklin. *State and National Voting in Federal Elections, 1910–1972*. Harden, Conn.: Archon Books, 1972.

Crawford, Alan. *Thunder on the Right: The "New Right" and the Politics of Resentment*. New York: Pantheon, 1980.

Crozier, Brian, and Chou, Eric. *The Man Who Lost China: The First Full Biography of Chiang Kai-shek*. New York: Charles Scribner's Sons, 1976.

Cummings, Milton C. *The National Election of 1964*. Washington D.C.: Brookings Institute, 1966.

Curti, Merle. *The Growth of American Thought*. New York: Harper Brothers, 1951.

Dillard, Dudley. *The Economics of John Maynard Keynes*. Englewood Cliffs, N.J.: Prentice-Hall, 1948.

Dudman, Richard. *Men of the Far Right*. New York: Pyramid Books, 1962.

Dunn, Charles W., ed. *American Political Theology: Historical Perspectives and Theoretical Analysis*. New York: Praeger, 1984.

Eighmy, Richard Lee. *Churches in Cultural Captivity*. Knoxville: Univ. of Tennessee Press, 1972.

Ellsworth, Ralph E., and Harris, Sarah M. *The American Right Wing*. Washington, D.C.: Public Affairs Press, 1962.

Faber, Harold, ed. *The New York Times Election Handbook: 1964*. New York: McGraw-Hill, 1964.

Formisano, Ronald P. *The Birth of Mass Political Parties: Michigan, 1827–1861*. Princeton, N.J.: Princeton Univ. Press, 1971.

_____. *The Transformation of Political Culture*. New York: Oxford Univ. Press, 1983.

Forster, Arnold, and Epstein, Benjamin R. *Dangers on the Right: The Attitudes, Personnel and Influence of the Radical Right and the Extreme Conservatives*. New York: Random House, 1964.

Fraser, Steve, and Gerstle, Gary, eds. *The Rise and Fall of the New Deal Order, 1930–1980*. Princeton, N.J.: Princeton Univ. Press, 1989.

Friedman, Milton. *Capitalism and Freedom*. Chicago: Univ. of Chicago Press, 1982.

Garner, Donald P. "George S. Benson: Conservative, Anti-Communist, Pro-American Speaker." Ph.D. diss., Wayne State Univ., Detroit, Mich., 1963.

Goldwater, Barry. *The Conscience of a Conservative*. Shepardsville, Ky.: Victor Publishing, 1960.

Goldwin, Robert A., ed. *Left, Right, and Center: Essays on Liberalism and Conservatism in the United States*. Chicago: Rand McNally, 1965.

Gottfried, Paul, and Fleming, Thomas. *The Conservative Movement*. Boston: Twayne, 1988.

Grantham, Dewey W. *The Life and Death of the Solid South*. Lexington: Univ. Press of Kentucky, 1988.

Gusfeld, Joseph. *Symbolic Crusade: Status Politics and the American Temperance Movement*. Urbana: Univ. of Illinois Press, 1963.

Guth, James L. "The Politics of the Christian Right." In *Interest Group Politics*, edited by Allan J. Cigler and Burkett A. Loomis, 60–83. Washington, D.C.: Congressional Quarterly Press, 1983.

Guttman, Allen. *The Conservative Tradition in America*. New York: Oxford Univ. Press, 1967.

Hailey, Mel. "The Political and Social Attitudes of Church of Christ Ministers." In *Research in the Social Scientific Study of Religion*, vol. 3., edited by Monty L. Lynn and David O. Moberg, 201–36. Greenwich, Conn.: JAI Press, 1991.

Hammond, John L. *The Politics of Benevolence: Revival Religion and American Voting Behavior*. Norwood, N.J.: Ablex Publishing, 1979.

Harrell, David Edwin. *Quest for a Christian America: The Disciples of Christ and American Society to 1866*. St. Louis, Mo.: Bethany Press, 1966.

_____. *The Social Sources of Division in the Disciples of Christ, 1865–1900: A Social History of the Disciples of Christ*. Atlanta, Ga.: Publishing Systems, 1973.

Hayes, Carlton J. H. *Nationalism: A Religion*. New York: Macmillan, 1960.

Heale, M. J. *American Anticommunism: Combating the Enemy Within, 1830–1970*. Baltimore, Md.: Johns Hopkins Univ. Press, 1990.

Heinsohn, A. G., ed. *Anthology of Conservative Writing in the United States, 1932–1960*. Chicago: Henry Regnery, 1962.

Hess, Karl. *In a Cause That Will Triumph: The Goldwater Campaign and the Future of Conservatism*. New York: Doubleday, 1964.

Hicks, L. Edward. "A Case Study of Conservative Political Education: Dr. George S. Benson and the National Education Program." Ph.D. diss., Memphis State University, Memphis, Tenn., 1990.

_____. "George S. Benson: Missionary Pioneer in China and the Philippines: 1925–1936." Interviews with George S. Benson, Apr. 17, 1987. Memphis, Tenn.: Oral History Research Office, Memphis State Univ., and Mississippi Valley Historical Collection, Brister Library, 1990.

Himmelstein, Jerome L. *To the Right: The Transformation of American Conservatism*. Berkeley: Univ. of California Press, 1990.

Hofstadter, Richard. *American Political Tradition and the Men Who Made It*. New York: Vintage Books, 1948.

_____. *The Paranoid Style in American Politics and Other Essays*. New York: Vintage Books, 1967.

Huntington, Samuel P. *American Politics: The Promise of Disharmony*. Cambridge, Mass.: Belknap Press of Harvard Univ. Press, 1981.

Industry and the American Economy. New York: National Association of Manufacturers, 1962.

Janson, Donald, and Eisman, Bernard. *The Far Right*. New York: McGraw-Hill, 1963.

Jeansonne, Glen. *Gerald L. K. Smith: Minister of Hate*. New Haven, Conn.: Yale Univ. Press, 1988.

Jelen, Ted G., ed. *Religion and Political Behavior in the United States*. New York: Praeger, 1989.

Jensen, Richard J. *Grass Roots Politics: Parties, Issues, and Voters, 1854–1983*. Westport, Conn.: Greenwood Press, 1983.

_____. "History and the Political Scientist." In *Politics and the Social Sciences*, edited by Seymour Martin Lipset, 1–28. New York: Oxford Univ. Press, 1969.

_____. *The Winning of the Midwest: Social and Political Conflict, 1888–1896*. Chicago: Univ. of Chicago Press, 1971.

Jorstad, Erling. *The New Christian Right, 1981–1988: Prospects for the Post-Reagan Decade*. Lewiston, Maine: Edwin Mellon Press, 1987.

Kelly, Brian. *Adventures in Porkland*. New York: Random House, 1992.

Kessel, John H. *The Goldwater Coalition: Republican Strategies in 1964*. New York: Bobbs-Merrill, 1968.

Keynes, John Maynard. *The General Theory of Employment, Interest, and Money*. New York: Harcourt, Brace and World, 1936.

Kirk, Russell. *A Program for Conservatives*. Chicago: Henry Regnery, 1954.

_____. *The Conservative Mind*. Chicago: Henry Regnery, 1948.

Kleppner, Paul. *The Cross of Culture: A Social Analysis of Midwestern Politics, 1850–1900*. New York: Free Press, 1970.

_____. *The Third Electoral System, 1853–1892: Parties, Voters and Political Culture*. Chapel Hill: Univ. of North Carolina Press, 1979.

_____. *Who Voted? The Dynamics of Electoral Turnout, 1870–1980*. New York: Praeger, 1982.

Kurtz, Paul, ed. *Humanist Manifestos One & Two*. Buffalo, N.Y.: Prometheus, 1973.

Lamb, Karl A., and Smith, Paul A. *Campaign Decision-Making: The Presidential Election of 1964*. Belmont, Calif.: Wadsworth, 1968.

Lane, Mark. *Rush to Judgement*. New York: Holt, Rinehart and Winston, 1966.

Latourette, Kenneth Scott. *A History of Christian Missions in China*. New York: Russell and Russell, 1929.

Lea, James F. *Contemporary Southern Politics*. Baton Rouge: Louisiana State Univ. Press, 1988.

Lekachman, Robert. *The Age of Keynes*. New York: Random House, 1966.

Leuchtenburg, William E. *Franklin D. Roosevelt and the New Deal*. New York: Harper Torchbooks, 1963.

Liebman, R. C., and Wuthnow, Robert, eds. *The New Christian Right*. Chicago: Aldine Press, 1983.

Lipscomb, David. *Civil Government, Its Origin, Mission, and Destiny and the Christian's Relation To It*. Nashville, Tenn.: Gospel Advocate Co., 1889.

Lipset, Seymour. M., and Raab, E. *The Politics of Unreason: Right Wing Extremism in America, 1790–1977*. Chicago: Univ. of Chicago Press, 1978.

Lokos, Lionel. *Hysteria 1964: The Fear Campaign Against Barry Goldwater*. New Rochelle, N.Y.: Arlington House, 1967.

Lora, Ronald. *Conservative Minds in America*. Chicago: Rand McNally, 1971.

Marsden, George M. *Fundamentalism and American Culture: The Shaping of Twentieth-Century Evangelicalism: 1870–1925*. New York: Oxford Univ. Press, 1980.

Marty, Martin E. *The New Shape of American Religion*. New York: Harper and Brothers, 1954.

McDowell, Edwin. *Barry Goldwater: Portrait of an Arizonan*. Chicago: Henry Regnery, 1964.

McGovern, William Montgomery, and Collier, David S. *Radicals and Conservatives*. Chicago: Henry Regnery, 1957.

McLoughlin, William G. *Revivals, Awakenings, and Reforms*. Chicago: Univ. of Chicago Press, 1978.

McWilliams, Carey. *Southern California Country*. New York: Duell, Sloan and Pierce, 1946.

Mead, Frank S. *Handbook of Denominations in the United States*. Nashville, Tenn.: Abingdon Press, 1970.

Meyer, E. H. *The Instructed Conscience: The Shaping of the American National Ethic*. Philadelphia: Univ. of Pennsylvania Press, 1972.

Meyer, Frank S. "Conservatism." In *Left, Right, and Center: Essays on Liberalism and Conservatism in the United States,* edited by Robert A. Goldwin, 5–45. Chicago: Rand McNally, 1965.

Michael, Franz. "State and Society in Nineteenth-Century China." In *Modern China,* edited by Albert Feuerwerker, 57–69. Englewood Cliffs, N.J.: Prentice-Hall, 1964.

Millikan, Robert A. *The Autobiography of Robert A. Millikan*. New York: Prentice-Hall, 1950.

Money, Royce. "Church-State Relations in the Churches of Christ Since 1945: A Study in Religion and Politics." Ph.D. diss., Baylor Univ., Waco, Tex., 1975.

Morone, James A. *The Democratic Wish: Popular Participation and the Limits of American Government*. New York: Basic Books, 1990.

Nash, George H. *The Conservative Intellectual Movement in America Since 1945*. New York: Basic Books, 1976.

Neill, Stephen. *A History of Christian Missions*. New York: Penguin Books, 1986.

Neuhaus, John Richard. *The Naked Public Square*. Grand Rapids, Mich.: Eerdman's Publishers, 1982.

Niebuhr, H. Richard. *The Social Sources of Denominationalism*. 5th ed. New York: Meridian Books, 1960.

Noble, John. *I Found God in Soviet Russia*. New York: St. Martins Press, 1959.

Noll, Mark A. *One Nation Under God: Christian Faith and Political Action in America*. San Francisco: Harper and Row, 1988.

North, Robert C. *Moscow and Chinese Communists*. Stanford, Calif.: Stanford Univ. Press, 1963.

Novak, Robert D. *The Agony of the GOP: 1964*. New York: Macmillan, 1965.

Ogden, Daniel M., Jr., and Peterson, Arthur L. *Electing the President, 1964*. San Francisco: Chandler Publishing, 1964.

Overstreet, Harry, and Overstreet, Bonaro. *The Strange Tactics of Extremism*. New York: Norton, 1964.

Palmer, John L., and Sawhill, Isabel V. *The Reagan Experiment: An Examination of Economic and Social Policies Under the Reagan Administration*. Washington, D.C.: Urban Institute Press, 1982.

Palumbo, Dennis. *Statistics in Political and Behavioral Science*. New York: Meredith, 1959.

Philbrick, Herbert A. *I Led Three Lives*. New York: Grosset and Dunlop, 1952.

Phillips, Kevin P. *Mediacracy: American Parties and Politics in the Communication Age.* Garden City, N.Y.: Doubleday, 1975.

_____. *Post-Conservative America: People, Politics, and Ideology in a Time of Crisis.* New York: Random House, 1982.

_____. *The Emerging Republican Majority.* New Rochelle, N.Y.: Arlington House, 1969.

_____. *The Politics of Rich and Poor: The American Electorate in the Reagan Aftermath.* New York: Random House, 1990.

Pierard, Richard V. *The Unequal Yoke: Evangelical Christianity and Political Conservatism.* Philadelphia: J. B. Lippincott, 1970.

Pierard, Richard V., and Linder, Robert D. *Civil Religion and the Presidency.* Grand Rapids, Mich.: Zondervan Publishing House, 1988.

Politics in America, 1945–1964: The Politics and Issues of the Postwar Years. Washington D.C.: Congressional Quarterly Service, 1965.

Pollock, John. *A Foreign Devil in China: The Story of Dr. L. Nelson Bell.* Minneapolis, Minn.: World Wide Publications, 1971.

Read, Leonard E. *To Free or Freeze.* New York: Foundation for Economic Education, 1972.

Ribuffo, Leo P. *The Old Christian Right: The Protestant Far Right from the Great Depression to the Cold War.* Philadelphia, Pa.: Temple Univ. Press, 1983.

Rorty, James, and Moshe Decter. *McCarthy and the Communists.* Westport, Conn.: Greenwood Press, 1972.

Rossiter, Clinton. *Conservatism in America: The Thankless Persuasion.* New York: Alfred A. Knopf, 1966.

Rowland, Robert H. *Economic Truths and Myths.* Oklahoma City: American Citizenship Center, Oklahoma Christian Univ., 1977.

Salmond, John A. "Aubrey Williams: A Typical New Dealer?" In *The New Deal: The National Level,* edited by John Braeman, Robert H. Bremner, and David Brody, 218–45. Columbus: Ohio State Univ. Press, 1975.

Saloma, John S., III. *Ominous Politics: The New Conservative Labyrinth.* New York: Hill and Wang, 1984.

Schieffer, Bob, and Gates, Gary Paul. *The Acting President.* New York: E. P. Dutton, 1989.

Schlafly, Phyllis. *A Choice Not An Echo.* Alton, Ill.: Pere Marquette Press, 1964.

Schoenberger, Robert A. *The American Right Wing: Readings in Political Behavior.* New York: Holt, Rinehart and Winston, 1969.

Schrecker, Ellen W. *No Ivory Tower: McCarthyism and the Universities.* New York: Oxford Univ. Press, 1986.

Shadegg, Stephen. *Barry Goldwater: Freedom Is His Flight Plan.* New York: Fleet Publishing, 1962.

Simon, William E. *A Time For Action.* New York: Berkley Books, 1980.

Sobran, Joseph. *Single Issues: Essays on the Crucial Social Questions.* New York: Human Life Press, 1983.

Spain, August O., et al. *The 1964 Presidential Election in the Southwest*. Dallas, Tex.: Arnold Foundation Monographs, 1966.

Stevens, John C. *Before Any Were Willing: The Story of George S. Benson*. Searcy, Ark.: Harding Univ. Press, 1991.

Stormer, John A. *None Dare Call It Treason*. Florissant, Mo.: Liberty Bell Press, 1964.

Strauss, Leo. *The Rebirth of Classical Political Rationalism*. Edited by Thomas Pangle. Chicago: Univ. of Chicago Press, 1989.

Suall, Irwin. *The American Ultras*. New York: New America Publishers, 1962.

Swierenga, Robert P. "Ethnoreligious Political Behavior in the Mid-Nineteenth Century: Voting, Values, and Cultures." In *Religion and American Politics: From the Colonial Period to the 1980s*, edited by Mark A. Knoll, 146–63. New York: Oxford Univ. Press, 1990.

Tawney, P. H. *Religion and the Rise of Capitalism*. Gloucester, Mass.: Peter Smith, 1962.

Thayer, George. *The Farther Shore of Politics: The American Political Fringe Today*. New York: Simon and Schuster, 1967.

The 1964 Elections: A Summary Report with Supporting Tables. Washington D.C.: Republican National Committee, 1965.

Unger, Irwin, and Unger, Debi. *Turning Point: 1968*. New York: Scribner's, 1988.

Viereck, Peter. *Conservatism Revisited: The Revolt Against Revolt, 1815–1949*. New York: Charles Scribner's Sons, 1949.

Viguerie, Richard A. *The New Right: We're Ready to Lead*. Washington, D.C.: Viguerie Co., 1981.

Wald, Kenneth D. *Religion and Politics in the United States*. New York: St. Martin's Press, 1987.

Weber, Max. *The Protestant Ethic and the Spirit of Capitalism*. London: G. Allen and Unwin, 1930.

Welch, Robert. *The Blue Book of the John Birch Society*. Boston: Western Islands Publishers, 1959.

West, Earl Irvin. *The Search for the Ancient Order*. 4 vols. Reprint, Nashville, Tenn.: Gospel Advocate Co., 1990.

White, Clifton F. *Suite 3505: The Story of the Draft Goldwater Movement*. New Rochelle, N.Y.: Arlington House, 1967.

Whitfield, Stephen J. *The Culture of the Cold War*. Baltimore, Md.: Johns Hopkins Univ. Press, 1991.

Wilbur, C. Martin. *Sun Yat-Sen: Frustrated Patriot*. New York: Columbia Univ. Press, 1976.

Wills, Garry. *Under God: Religion and American Politics*. New York: Simon and Schuster, 1990.

Wolfinger, Raymond, et al. "America's Radical Right: Politics and Ideology." In *The American Right Wing*, edited by R. Schoenberger, 9–47. New York: Holt, Rinehart and Winston, 1969.

Wright, Mary C. "Modern China in Transition." In *Modern China,* edited by Albert Feuerwerker, 5–15. Englewood Cliffs, N.J.: Prentice-Hall, 1964.

Wuthnow, Robert. "The Political Rebirth of American Evangelicals." In *The New Christian Right,* edited by Robert C. Liebman and Robert Wuthnow, 167–85. New York: Aldine, 1983.

Ziegelmueller, George W. "A Study of the Speaking of Conservatives in Opposition to the New Deal." Ph.D. diss., Northwestern Univ., Evanston, Ill., 1962.

Journals and Periodicals

Allen, C. Leonard. "Baconianism and the Bible in the Disciples of Christ: James S. Lamar and *The Organon of Scripture*." *Church History* 55 (1986): 65–80.

Anderson, Joel E. "Christian College, Politics and Academic Freedom." *Mission* 5 (Oct. 1971): 113–21.

Atteberry, James L. "The Freedom of Scholarship." *Mission* 2 (Oct. 1969): 104–9.

Bales, James D. "Is This Political Preaching?" *Firm Foundation* 79 (Oct. 1962): 646.

_____. "Leave Communism to the Government?" *Firm Foundation* 79 (Aug. 7, 1972): 504.

_____. "Searchers and Defenders." *Mission* 3 (Apr. 1970): 297–304.

Beatty, Kathleen Murphy, and Oliver, Walter B. "Fundamentalists, Evangelicals, and Politics." *American Politics Quarterly* 16, no. 1 (1988): 43–59.

Beck, Don. "Thunder on the Right?" *Firm Foundation* 79 (Aug. 7, 1962): 503.

Benson, George S. "Arkansas Should Get Along by Itself." *Congressional Digest* 25 (Feb. 1946): 45–47.

_____. "Emergency Message to the American People." *Omaha* (Nebr.) *Morning World Herald,* Oct. 27, 1941.

_____. "Federal Aid To Education." *Congressional Digest* 28 (Nov. 1949): 285–89.

_____. "Federal Aid To Education." *Vital Speeches of the Day* 15 (Jan. 15, 1949): 207–10.

_____. "If I Were a Communist." *Reader's Digest.* Sept. 1946.

_____. "Should the Public School System Be Subsidized by Federal Funds?" *Congressional Digest* 25 (Jan. 1946): 47.

_____. "Should Uncle Sam Help Our Schools?" *Scholastic* 51 (Nov. 10, 1947): 16–20.

Brodsky, David M.; Hood, Ralph W., Jr.; Morris, Ronald J.; and Swansbrough, Robert H. "Religion and Partisan Change." *Southern Political Review* 17, no. 2 (Fall 1989): 33–55.

Brookes, Warren T. "Phillips's Populist Greed." *Memphis* (Tenn.) *Commercial Appeal,* Aug. 6, 1990.

Brown, Peter. "'White Flight' Strikes at Former Stronghold of Democratic Party." *Memphis* (Tenn.) *Commercial Appeal,* May 22, 1990.

Brumit, Bill. "Our Christian Colleges: A Critique and a Proposal." Pts. 1 and 2. *Mission* 4 (July–Aug. 1972): 11–45.

Burch, Walter E., and Haymes, Don. "The Conscience of a Congressman." *Mission* 5 (Dec. 1971): 179–87.

Carpenter, Arthur E. "Social Origins of Anticommunism: The Information Council of the Americas." *Louisiana History* 30 (Spring 1989): 117–43.

Cassels, Louis. "The Rightist Crisis." *Look Magazine,* Apr. 24, 1962.

"Church and Nationalism." Editorial comment. *Firm Foundation* 81 (Nov. 17, 1964): 730.

Cook, Fred J. "Foundations as a Tax Dodge." *Nation* 196 (Apr. 1963): 323–25.

_____. "The Ultras." *Nation* 194 (June 30, 1962): 565–99.

Dunphy, James. "A Religion for a New Age." *Humanist* 43 (Jan.–Feb. 1983): 26.

Dye, Ross W. "National Righteousness." *Firm Foundation* 8 (June 13, 1967): 374–81.

"Editorial Comments." *Mission* 3 (Apr. 1970): 312–13.

Edwards, Lee. "Paul Weyrich, Conscience of the New Right." *Conservative Digest,* July 1981.

Fields, Echo E. "Understanding Activist Fundamentalism: Capitalist Crisis and the 'Colonization of the Lifeworld.'" *Sociological Analysis* 52, no. 2 (Summer 1991): 175–90.

Fletcher, John L. "George S. Benson—His Fight: Free Enterprise." *Arkansas Gazette,* Dec. 14, 1952.

Fowler, Giles M. "A Label, 'Ultra-Rightist,' Puts the Spotlight on a Small College Down in Arkansas." *Kansas City (Mo.) Star,* Feb. 4, 1962.

Fretz, Gene. "Harding Observes an Anniversary and a Way of Life." *Arkansas Gazette,* May 30, 1954.

"George S. Benson Announces Retirement From Harding," *Firm Foundation* 82, no. 20 (May 18, 1965): 320.

Guth, James L., and Green, John C. "Politics in a New Key: Religiosity and Participation Among Political Activists." *Western Political Quarterly* 43, no. 1 (Mar. 1990): 151–79.

Guth, James L.; Jelen, Ted G.; Kellstedt, Lyman A.; Smidt, Corwin E.; and Wald, Kenneth D. "The Politics of Religion in America." *American Politics Quarterly* 16, no. 3 (1988): 357–97.

Hanna, Phil S. "Man from Arkansas Stirs Congressional Committee by Plea for Economy Now." *Chicago Journal of Commerce,* May 19, 1941.

Harding College Bison. Searcy, Ark. Oct. 13, 1936–Apr. 18, 1969.

Hoover, Arlie. "The Gospel of Nationalism: A German Example." *Firm Foundation* 81 (Nov. 17, 1964): 736–40.

Horton, Phillip. "Revivalism on the Far Right." *Reporter Magazine* 25 (July 20, 1961): 25–29.

Hughes, Frank. "$75,000 Debt Just a Memory for College: President Leads It to Fame." *Chicago Daily Tribune,* Jan. 22, 1948.

_____. "College Is a Champion in U.S. Way: 25 Million Get Its Message." *Chicago Daily Tribune,* Jan. 19, 1948.

_____. "How College Finds Pro-U.S. Instructors: Looks For Truth, Christian Ideals." *Chicago Daily Tribune,* Jan. 21, 1948.

_____. "Work, Profit! It's Credo of This College: Students Live the American Way." *Chicago Daily Tribune,* Jan. 20, 1948.

Hughes, Richard T. "The Apocalyptic Origins of Churches of Christ and the Triumph of Modernism." *Religion and American Culture* 2 (Summer 1992): 181–201.

_____. "The New Shape of American Civil Religion." *Mission* 6 (Mar. 1973): 269–72.

Illson, Murray. "Norman Thomas Hits Birch Group." *New York Times,* Apr. 20, 1961.

Jelen, Ted G. "Politicized Group Identification: The Case of Fundamentalism." *Western Political Quarterly* 44, no. 1 (Mar. 1991): 209–19.

Jenkins, J. Craig. "Resource Mobilization and the Study of Social Movements." *Annual Review of Sociology* 9 (1983): 527–53.

Kilpatrick, James J. "Why Students Are Hostile to Free Enterprise." *Nation's Business* 63, no. 7 (July 1975).

Knight, Harold V. "Whooping It Up for Adam Smith." *Nation* 175 (Aug. 1952): 87–89.

"Learning Economics With No Pain." *Business Week,* Dec. 16, 1950.

Leff, Mark H. "The Politics of Sacrifice on the American Home Front in World War II." *Journal of American History* 77 (Mar. 1991): 1296–1318.

Lewis, Annie May Alston. *Harding University Bulletin,* Apr. 1990, 6.

Lynch, Dudley. "Harding and the Atteberry Case." *Christian Chronicle* 26 (June 9, 1969): 1–2.

_____. "The Politics of Harding College." *Mission* 3 (Apr. 1970): 305–11.

Mason, Perry. "This Nation Under God." *Firm Foundation* 88 (July 6, 1971): 424.

McCarthy, John, and Zald, Mayer. "Resource Mobilization and Social Movements: A Partial Theory." *American Journal of Sociology* 82, no. 6 (May 1977): 1212–41.

Morgan, Thomas B. "The Fight Against Prejudice." *Look Magazine,* June 4, 1963, 68.

National Education Association. *Proceedings of the NEA Meeting.* July 6, 1934, vol. 72.

Neuhaus, John Richard. "Why Wait for the Kingdom? The Theonomist Temptation." *First Things: A Monthly Journal of Religion and Public Life* (May 1990): 13–21.

Olbricht, Thomas H. "The Rationalism of the Restoration." *Restoration Quarterly* 11 (1968): 79.

"Organizations—The Ultras." *Time* (Dec. 8, 1961): 22–24.

Packard, Vance. "Public Relations: Good or Bad." *Atlantic* 201, no. 5 (May 1958): 53–57.

Parks, Norman. "Heroin for Our Colleges." *Mission* 6 (Feb. 1973): 227.

"Patriots vs. Nationalists: A Matter of Growth." Editorial comment. *Christian Chronicle* 27 (June 15, 1970): 2.

Philbrick, Herbert A. "Americanism Way Detected in Fight on Communism." *New York Herald Tribune,* Mar. 24, 1956.

Phillips, Cabell. "Wide Anti-Red Drive Directed From Small Town in Arkansas." *New York Times,* May 18, 1961.

Raines, Howell. "Reagan Backs Evangelicals in Their Political Activities." *New York Times,* Aug. 23, 1980, B9.

Rainey, Gene E. "Moralizing, Politics and the 1972 Election." *Mission* 6 (Oct. 1972): 99–104.

Rose, Phillip S. "Arkansas Crusader." *Saturday Evening Post* 216 (June 3, 1944): 19, 83–86.

Rusher, William A. "GOP Must Stop Efforts to Bash Reagan Era." *Memphis* (Tenn.) *Commercial Appeal,* June 27, 1990.

Searcy (Ark.) *Daily Citizen.* June 12, 1941–Apr. 18, 1962.

Sigelman, Lee; Wilcox, Clyde; and Buell, Emmett H., Jr. "An Unchanging Minority: Popular Support for the Moral Majority, 1980 and 1984." *Social Science Quarterly* 68 (Dec. 1987): 876–84.

Smidt, Corwin E. "The Mobilization of Evangelical Voters in 1980: An Initial Test of Several Hypotheses." *Southern Political Review* 16, no. 2 (Fall 1988).

Smith, Doug. "George Benson." *Arkansas Gazette,* Oct. 18, 1964.

Spiegel, Irving. "Aid to Right Wing Laid to Big Firms: Anti-Defamation Unit Holds They Donate Major Part of $14 Million Fund," *New York Times* (Sept. 20, 1964) 1:2.

Stevens, John C. "The Case for Christian Education." *Mission* 5 (Oct. 1971): 105–10.

Stewart, Leland. "Is America God's Chosen Nation?" *Firm Foundation* 82 (Dec. 23, 1969): 804–15.

Suall, Irwin. *New America,* May 5, 1961.

_____. *New America,* Nov. 24, 1961.

"The Secular State." Editorial comment. *Journal of Church and State.* 7 (Spring 1965): 169–78.

"The Ultras." *Time,* Dec. 8, 1961.

Thomas, Norman. *New America,* June 16, 1961.

_____. *New America,* Mar. 24, 1961.

_____. "The Far Right." *Newsweek,* May 1, 1961.

"Through the Looking Glass: A Critical Overview of Oliver Stone's *JFK.*" *Cineaste* 18, no. 1 (1992): 8–35.

"Thunder on the Far Right." *Newsweek,* Dec. 4, 1961.

Trimble, Mike. "Searcy: A Portrait of an Arkansas Town." *Arkansas Times,* Little Rock, Ark. (July 1986): 64.

Tyrmand, Leopold. "The Conservative Ideas in Reagan's Victory." *Wall Street Journal,* Jan. 20, 1981.

Vital Speeches of the Day, New York, City News Publishing Co., (May 1941), 7:194–97.

Wald, Kenneth D., and Lupfer, Michael B.. "'Human Nature' in Mass Political Thought." *Social Science Quarterly* 68 (Mar. 1987): 19–33.

Wilcox, Clyde. "America's Radical Right Revisited: A Comparison of the Activists in the Christian Right in Two Decades." *Sociological Analysis* 48 (1987): 46–57.

_____. "Evangelicals and Fundamentalists in the New Christian Right: Religious Differences in the Ohio Moral Majority." *Journal for the Scientific Study of Religion* 25, no. 3 (1986): 355–63.

_____. "Evangelicals and the Moral Majority." *Journal for the Scientific Study of Religion* 28, no. 4 (1989): 400–14.

_____. "Popular Backing for the Old Christian Right: Explaining Support for the Christian Anti-Communism Crusade." *Journal of Social History* 21 (Fall 1987): 117–32.

_____. "Popular Support for the Moral Majority in 1980: A Second Look." *Social Science Quarterly* 68 (Mar. 1987): 157–69.

_____. "Popular Support for the New Christian Right." *Social Science Journal* 26:1 (1989): 55–63.

_____. "The Christian Right in Twentieth-Century America: Continuity and Change." *Review of Politics* 50, no. 4 (Fall 1988): 659–81.

Wilkerson, W. R. "Trade Views." *Hollywood Reporter,* Feb. 23, 1951.

Williams, Fay. "Hard Headed Realist." *Arkansas Democrat,* July 22, 1951.

Wilson, L. R. "The Church and Politics." *Gospel Advocate* 102 (June 30, 1960): 407–9.

Wimbish, Cled. "The Gospel of Nationalism, A Warning to Us." *Firm Foundation* 80 (Feb. 2, 1963): 69–70.

Wood, James E., Jr. "The Problem of Nationalism in Church-State Relationships." *Journal of Church and State* 10 (Spring 1968): 249–64.

Young, M. Norvel. "Just Catch the Plane in Dallas or Nashville." *Firm Foundation* 77, no. 11(Mar. 15, 1960): 166.

Government Documents

Benson, George S. "Statement Before the Ways and Means Committee by Dr. George S. Benson, President of Harding College, Searcy, Ark., May 15, 1941." In U.S., Congress, *Congressional Record,* 77th Cong., 1st. sess., 1941, 87, appendix, pt. 2: A2326–28. Washington, D.C.: U.S. Government Printing Office, 1941.

Communist Infiltration of Hollywood Motion Picture Industry. Pt. 1. U.S. Government Printing Office, 1947.

Communist Infiltration of Hollywood Motion Picture Industry. Pt. 2. U.S. Government Printing Office, 1951.

United States, Congress. *Congressional Record.* 77th Cong., 1st sess., 1941, 87, appendix, pt. 10: A1185–2384. Washington, D.C.: U.S. Government Printing Office, 1941.

United States, Congress, House of Representatives, Committee on Un-American Activities. *Facts on Communism.* Vol. 1: *The Communist Ideology.* 86th Cong., 1st sess. Washington, D.C.: U.S. Government Printing Office, 1959.

_____. *Facts on Communism.* Vol. 2: *The Soviet Union, From Lenin to Khrushchev.* 86th Cong., 2d sess. Washington, D.C.: U.S. Government Printing Office, 1960.

United States, Congress, House of Representatives, Committee on Ways and Means. *Revenue Revision of 1941: Hearings Before the Committee on Ways and Means on the Revenue Revision of 1941.* 77th Cong., 1st sess., 1941. Washington, D.C.: U.S. Government Printing Office, 1941.

United States, Congress, Senate, Committee on Education and Labor. *Hearings on Senate Bill 2295, A Bill to Provide for the Termination of the Civilian Conservation Corps and the National Youth Administration.* 77th Cong., 2d sess., Mar. 23–Apr. 17, 1942. Washington, D.C.: U.S. Government Printing Office, 1941.

United States, Congress, Senate, Committee on the Judiciary, Subcommittee to Investigate the Administration of the Internal Security Act and Other Internal Security Laws of the United States. *The Communist Party of the United States of America–What It Is , How It Works: A Handbook For Americans.* Washington D.C.: U.S. Government Printing Office, 1956.

Primary Sources in NEP Files and Private Collections

"Adventures in Economics." Pamphlet. Searcy, Ark.: NEP, n.d.

Bales, James D. "Atteberry and Harding College." 1969. Pamphlet in files of Graduate School of Religion, Harding College, Searcy, Ark.

Benson, George S. "A Powerless Public Opinion." *National Education Program Newsletter,* Jan. 1971.

_____. "Crises in Christian Education During the Past Fifty Years." Unpublished article, n.d. NEP Files, Oklahoma Christian University, Oklahoma City, Okla., 1986.

_____. "Federal Aid to Education." Pamphlet. Searcy, Ark.: National Education Program, n.d.

_____. "Moral Indignation." Pamphlet. Searcy, Ark.: National Education Program, n.d.

_____, ed. *Can Private Enterprise Survive in America? Freedom Forum XXVI Lectures.* Searcy, Ark.: National Education Program, 1965.

_____, ed. "Church of Christ Mission Work: Hong Kong, South China." Report no. 11. 1926.

_____, ed. *Expanding American Markets: Freedom Forum XXV Lectures.* Searcy, Ark.: National Education Program, 1964.

_____, ed. *Oriental* (Canton) *Christian.* Vols. 1–7 (1930–36). Special Collections, Library, Harding Univ.

_____, to Bud Green, June 11, 1971. Typescript in NEP Files, Special Collections, Library, Harding Univ.

_____, to Dr. James D. Key, Nov. 20, 1986. Typescript in NEP Files, Special Collections, Library, Harding Univ.

_____, to J. D. Bales, Sept. 1, 1986. Typescript, Special Collections, Library, Harding Univ.

_____, to Rep. William E. Dannemeyer, Dec. 4, 1985. Typescript, NEP Files, Special Collections, Library, Harding Univ.

_____, to Sen. Dale Bumpers, Aug. 6, 1985. Typescript, NEP Files, Special Collections, Library, Harding Univ.

_____, to Supporting Congregations in Okla. and Ark, 1926–30. Letters from Hong Kong, China. Special Collections, Library, Harding Univ.

_____, to Ted Altman, June 23, 1970. Typescript in personal collection of Ted Altman, Harding Univ.

_____, to Ted Altman, Sept. 23, 1970. Typescript in personal collection of Ted Altman, Harding Univ.

Evans, Bruce M., telephone conversation with L. Edward Hicks. Aug. 6, 1990. Notes in personal collection of L. Edward Hicks.

Ganus, Clifton. "Memo to the Harding Faculty." July 1969. Typescript in files of Harding University Graduate School of Religion, Memphis, Tenn.

Hicks, L. Edward. "Interview with Dr. Billy Ray Cox, Former Vice-President of Harding College." Jan. 22, 1989. Notes in collection of L. Edward Hicks.

_____. "Interview with Ed McAteer, President of the Religious Roundtable." Apr. 25, 1990. In Hicks, "A Case Study of Conservative Political Education," Appendix B: 392–457.

_____. "Interview with Robert H. Rowland, Director, National Education Program." Oklahoma City, Okla., Mar. 14, 1990. In Hicks, "A Case Study of Conservative Political Education," Appendix D: 319–91.

"Interview with George S. Benson." Interview by Oral History Office, Harding Univ., 1985. Transcript at Oral History Office, Harding Univ.

North, Gary, to L. Edward Hicks, June 1990. Typescript in personal collection of L. Edward Hicks.

Origin and Purpose of the National Education Program, Searcy, Ark., NEP Pamphlet, n.d.

Phillips, Howard, telephone conversation with L. Edward Hicks, May 10, 1990. Notes in personal collection of L. Edward Hicks.

Phillips, Howard, to L. Edward Hicks, May 7, 1990. Typescript of letter in personal collection of L. Edward Hicks.

Reagan, Ronald. "Tribute to George Benson on his 80th Birthday." Sept. 26, 1978. Transcript of audiotape, NEP Files, Special Collections, Library, Harding Univ.

Stormer, John A., to L. Edward Hicks, June 6, 1990. Typescript in the author's personal files.

Your Grass Roots Report. June 1951–Jan. 1952. Pamphlets. NEP Files, Special Collections, Library, Harding Univ.

Index